the Good Old Fashioned Cookbook

the Good Old Fashioned Cookbook

Consulting Cookery Editor – Valerie van der Kaay
Dip. H. Sc.
University of Otago New Zealand.

LANSDOWNE
Sydney · Auckland · London

Melting Moments, Passionfruit Crunchies (see p. 139), Chocolate Snowballs (see p. 138)

Published by Lansdowne, Sydney
a division of RPLA Pty Limited
176 South Creek Road, Dee Why West, NSW, Australia 2099
First published 1981
Reprinted 1985
© Wellington Newspapers Ltd
Produced in Australia by the Publisher
Typeset in New Zealand by Auckland Typographical Services Ltd
Printed in Hong Kong by South China Printing Co

National Library of Australia Cataloguing-in-Publication Data
Stephens, Clare,
    The good old fashioned cookbook.
    Index
    ISBN 0 7018 1475 6
    1. Cookery. I. Title.
641.5

CONTENTS

Introduction

"THE GOOD OLD-FASHIONED COOKBOOK" is a refreshing celebration of whole-some, simple cooking.

Tried and proven by generations of family cooks, these favourite, home-grown recipes offer a wealth of imaginative suggestions for the experienced as well as the more reluctant cook.

Most of the dishes can be easily prepared without tears or expense and for those who have time, there are the more unusual delights.

But whether preparing for a daily meal or for a special occasion, imagination and care are important. A plain fish pie, for example, is instantly transformed with sliced tomatoes and a sprig of parsley. A meal must be not only nourishing but look good too!

Many of the recipes include suggested garnishes but the imaginative cook will have no difficulty in turning even the most routine meals into delicious treats.

Soups

Stock, whether it be meat, vegetable or fish, forms the basis of all soups, and it is here that the thrifty housekeeper uses up odd scraps of meat, bones, bacon, vegetable and the water in which they were cooked. Once simmered and strained, the stock is cooled and all trace of fat removed; it is then ready to be made into your favourite recipe or tried out in one on the following pages.

Wherever possible, use vegetable liquor, not water; it contains more nutriment and much more flavour. Bones are used to provide flavour and also gelatin. Meat gives flavour to soup, but most of its food value remains in the meat fibre; therefore it should be used in pies and patties. Many like a little chopped meat in the soup itself.

If a brown stock is desired, some of the meat may be browned in a little fat before adding the water. Always add cold water to bones and raw meat; hot water will seal in the flavour and juices.

Generally speaking, clear soups or consommes are served as a first course at dinner while cream soups, thickened soups, purees and broths form the main dish on a luncheon menu.

Asparagus Soup

500g asparagus
30g butter
30g flour
2.5*l* stock

Cut the heads from the asparagus, boil in a little salted water and set aside. Put the stalks into boiling water for 3 minutes and drain. Melt the butter in a saucepan, stir in the flour, add the blanched asparagus stalks and stir for 5 minutes. Pour in the stock and simmer until the asparagus is tender. Sieve, return to the saucepan and boil for 20 minutes. Pour into a hot tureen over the asparagus tops. Serves 4.

Beef Tea

1kg beef, chopped finely
2.5*l* cold water
salt
pepper
1 teaspoon Marmite
1 onion, diced
1 carrot, diced
1 parsnip, diced
1 teaspoon mixed spice
small bunch mixed herbs

Break the meat bone and remove the marrow. Cover with cold water and add seasoning. Stand for 30 minutes, then bring slowly to the boil but do not skim until it has been cooking for some time. Add the vegetables, spices and herbs tied in muslin. Simmer until vegetables are cooked, then remove. Simmer for 3 to 4 hours then strain. Serves 4–6.

Bone Stock

1.5kg beef bones
1 teaspoon salt
2.5*l* cold water
1 tablespoon grated carrot
1 tablespoon chopped parsley
pinch dried herbs
6 peppercorns
2 cloves

Break up the bones as small as possible, put in a pot with the salt and cold water and leave for 30 minutes. Bring to the boil, skim thoroughly and add the remaining ingredients. Boil gently for 4 hours, strain and remove fat when cold.

Cauliflower Soup

1 cauliflower
1 tablespoon butter
1 onion, sliced
1 stalk celery, sliced
pinch grated nutmeg
3 cups stock, or water
1 tablespoon flour
1 cup milk
salt
pepper
1 tablespoon cream, or top milk (optional)

Steam or boil the cauliflower in a little water until partially cooked. Put aside the best part and chop the remainder.

Melt the butter in a saucepan and cook the onion, celery and chopped cauliflower for 10 minutes. Add the nutmeg, cover with the stock and boil until the vegetables are soft. Pass all through a sieve, working through as much of the vegetables as possible. Return to the saucepan and thicken with the flour mixed to a smooth paste with a little cold milk. Season to taste and add the sprigs of cooked cauliflower. Cream or top milk improves the flavour. Serves 4-6.

Cheese and Pumpkin Soup

500g pumpkin
1 medium onion
1 tablespoon butter
pepper
salt
1l milk
1 teaspoon sugar
2 tablespoons grated cheese

Peel and wash the pumpkin. Chop up both pumpkin and onion and cook in a little water until soft enough to mash. Add the butter and season to taste. Heat the milk in a separate saucepan, adding the sugar (which prevents the milk from sticking) and when almost boiling, stir into the mashed pumpkin. Reheat and just before serving add the cheese. Serve with cheese biscuits. Serves 4-6.

Chicken Broth

1 chicken
1 carrot, chopped finely
1 small onion, chopped finely
1 turnip, chopped finely
2 tablespoons rice
salt, to taste
pepper, to taste
pinch nutmeg
few sprigs parsley, chopped

Bring the chicken slowly to the boil in salted water, skim well and simmer gently for 1½ hours. Add the vegetables and rice and simmer for 30 minutes. Remove the chicken carefully, season with salt, pepper and nutmeg, and garnish with strips of chicken meat and parsley. Serves 4-6.

Cream of Spinach Soup

30g dripping
1 onion, peeled and chopped
500g spinach, chopped
2 cups water
½ level teaspoon sugar
salt, to taste
pepper, to taste
1 cup milk
2 level tablespoons flour

Melt the dripping in a saucepan and steam the onion without browning for 10 minutes. Add the

spinach and cook for another 10 minutes, shaking frequently to prevent burning. Add the water and cook until the vegetables are soft. Sieve the soup, working the vegetables through with the back of a wooden spoon. Return to the saucepan and add the salt, pepper, sugar and milk. Thicken with the flour mixed to a paste with a little milk. Stir until the soup boils and thickens slightly. Serves 4.

Cream of Tomato Soup

1 x 400g tin tomatoes
1 onion
1 bay leaf
2 cloves
¼ teaspoon soda
½ teaspoon sugar
2 tablespoons butter
2 tablespoons flour
1l milk, boiled
salt, to taste
pinch paprika

Put the tomatoes, onion, bay leaf and cloves in a saucepan. Cook for 10 minutes, strain, then add the soda and sugar. Melt the butter, stir in the flour, cook for 2 minutes, then add the hot milk and season with salt and paprika. Mix with the tomato and serve at once. Do not boil after mixing. Serves 4-6.

Delicious Apple Soup

1½ teaspoons tapioca
2½ cups boiling water
2½ cups stewed apple
salt, to taste
pinch cinnamon

Cook the tapioca in boiling water, then mix with the apple. Simmer for 20 minutes, then flavour with salt and cinnamon. Serves 4.

Fish Head Soup

1kg snapper
2 onions, finely chopped
2 tablespoons rice
salt
pepper
½ cup milk
1 tablespoon finely-chopped parsley

Cut the head from the snapper and remove the eyes. Cover with water, boil for 45 minutes then remove and add the onion, rice, salt pepper, milk and parsley. Boil for 20 minutes then serve. Serves 4.

Fruit Soup

750g cooking apples
125g plums
125g grapes
sugar to taste
lemon juice
cream, whipped

Peel, core and slice apples. Put all fruit together in a saucepan with half a cup of water, sprinkle with sugar and stew gently.
Add lemon juice, chill and serve with whipped cream. A quicker method would be to cook fruit without peeling and pass it through a sieve. Serves 4.

Green Soup

500g fresh pea pods
5 cups water
1 mutton shank
1 onion
1 carrot
salt and pepper
cornflour

Wash empty pods and put in pan of water with the mutton shank, onion and carrot, and simmer for 1 hour. Lift out shank and pass soup through a strainer. Season with salt and pepper, and thicken with cornflour. The shank may be used for meat patties or shepherd's pie. Serves 4.

Kidney Soup

1 ox kidney
flour
dripping
3.5l stock, made with bones, carrots, a small
    piece of turnip, 2 onions
salt and pepper
1 tablespoon cornflour

Soak kidney in cold salted water, remove fat, cut into small pieces and flour well. Put it into a pan with the melted dripping, stirring until well browned. Then add stock and simmer for three hours. Skim off fat and thicken with the cornflour. Serves 6.

Lettuce Soup

30g butter
1 level teaspoon sugar
a little vinegar or lemon juice
1 lettuce, shredded
1 stick of celery or 1 carrot, chopped
1 onion, chopped
1 level tablespoon flour
1 egg, beaten
salt and pepper
croutons

Melt butter, add sugar and vinegar. Add vegetables, and cook over gentle heat, stirring frequently until vegetables are tender. Stir in flour and add one cup of water.
Bring to boiling point, then pass through sieve. Pour soup on to the beaten egg and return to saucepan. Stir until the egg is cooked, but do not boil. Season carefully. Serve with croutons. Serves 6.

Meat and Vegetable Soup

shin of beef
1 tablespoon salt
2 parsnips, chopped
2 carrots, chopped
2 onions, chopped
2 turnips chopped
2 leeks, chopped
salt and pepper
2 eggs, beaten
flour

Place shin in a pot, cover with water, add salt and boil for 2 hours or longer. Next day, remove the fat and add the chopped vegetables. Boil for another hour. Remove meat, mince, add salt, pepper, the beaten eggs and flour, and form into balls. Add to the soup half an hour before serving. Serves 6.

Mock Chicken Broth

bone and scrap remains of roast leg of
    lamb or mutton
1 large onion, finely sliced
½ cup rice
2 rashers bacon, chopped
1 potato, diced
salt and pepper
celery salt
2 tablespoons finely chopped parsley

Put bone and scraps in a stockpot with the onion, rice, bacon and potato. Cover with cold water and simmer for 2 or 3 hours, seasoning with salt, pepper and celery salt. Any cold left-over vegetables and a little white sauce may be added half an hour before serving. Add 2 tablespoons of parsley when ready to serve. Serves 4.

Mushroom Soup (1)

1 small onion
275g cooked mushrooms
5 cups water
2½ cups milk
1 level tablespoon cornflour
salt and pepper

Cook finely chopped onion in a little water, add mushrooms, pulped (in a pulveriser if possible), and water. Bring the milk to the boil, thicken with cornflour, season, and add to hot mushroom mixture. Serves 6.

Mushroom Soup (2)

60g butter
250g mushrooms
¼ teaspoon salt
1 tablespoon flour
2½ cups milk
juice of ½ lemon

Melt butter, add washed and sliced mushrooms and salt. Simmer for 5 minutes with lid on, then add flour, mixed with a little cold milk. Mix all well, then add rest of milk. Simmer until mushrooms are quite soft. Add lemon juice and serve. Serves 4.

Mulligatawny Soup

750g lean beef
500g beef bones
5 cups cold water
salt and pepper
1 tablespoon dripping
1 onion, sliced
½ carrot, sliced
1 apple, sliced
1 tablespoon curry powder
1 tablespoon flour
stock
bunch of mixed herbs
½ lemon
ham or bacon scraps
pinch of ground ginger

Cut meat into very small pieces, put into pan with bones and cover with water. Add seasoning of pepper and salt and let stand half an hour or longer. Put on heat and bring slowly to boiling point. Melt dripping, add onion and fry until a nice brown colour. Add carrot, apple, curry powder, flour, and continue to fry a few minutes longer. Add enough stock to make a thin sauce, and then combine with stock which is cooking. Add herbs and other ingredients and continue simmering 2 hours. Strain soup through a fine sieve and rub through a few of the vegetables. Reheat and season carefully. Serve in hot boiled rice. Serves 6.

Oyster Soup

2½ cups milk
24 oysters and juice
2 tablespoons butter
salt and pepper
2 water crackers
¼ cup celery, chopped
1 hard-boiled egg, finely chopped

Boil milk and set it aside. Remove oysters from juice, bring juice to the boil and remove scum. Put oysters over heat with juice and butter and let them simmer until the edges begin to curl. Add boiled milk, bring all to boil and add salt and pepper to taste. Mix crushed biscuit and celery with finely-chopped egg, put into a tureen and pour the soup over them. Serves 6.

Pea Soup and Ham Balls

Soup
2 cups dried split peas
8 cups water
1 tin tomato juice or 3 cups strained pulp
1 cup celery, diced
1 large onion, finely chopped
1 large potato, finely diced
1 tablespoon salt
¼ teaspoon pepper

Soak the split peas in cold water for 5-6 hours or overnight, then drain and add 8 cups of water, the tomato juice, celery, onion, potato, salt and pepper. Simmer gently for 3 hours or until peas are tender.

Ham Balls:
1 cup ham, minced
1 egg, slightly beaten
1 tablespoon flour
½ teaspoon dry mustard
¼ teaspoon pepper

Combine ingredients, form into small balls and drop into hot cooked soup and simmer for 10 minutes. Serves 6.

Potato Soup

1 tablespoon dripping
4-6 medium potatoes, sliced
1 onion, chopped
1 carrot or celery, chopped
5 cups stock or water
1 tablespoon sago
salt and pepper
1 cup milk
1 teaspoon chopped mint or parsley
croutons

Melt dripping in saucepan. Add prepared vegetables, cover and cook gently until fat is absorbed. Add stock or water and cook until vegetables are tender. Work all through a strainer. Return to saucepan, add washed sago and boil until the sago is clear. Season, then add milk and parsley. Serve with croutons. Serves 6.

Pumpkin Soup

500g pumpkin, peeled and diced
1 onion, chopped finely
1 tablespoon butter
salt and pepper
2 cups milk
1 teaspoon sugar
2 tablespoons grated cheese

Boil the pumpkin in 2 cups of water until tender, then press the pumpkin with the water through a sieve to make a purée. Sauté the onion in butter, add the purée, season and add the milk and sugar. Reheat and serve sprinkled with cheese. Serves 6.

 # Scotch Broth

1kg neck of mutton
½ cup barley
4.5l water
½ small green cabbage, chopped finely
1 leek, chopped finely
½ small turnip, chopped finely
¼ cup peas
1 large carrot, grated
salt and pepper
1 teaspoon chopped parsley

Wash the mutton, wash and drain the barley. Boil the water, add the meat and cook for 5 minutes. Remove from heat and add barley, then return to heat and boil slowly for 1 hour. Add all vegetables except carrot to broth and cook for 45 minutes, then add carrot, cooking a further 15 minutes. Season and add parsley. Remove the meat which may be served hot with mashed potatoes, mashed turnips, and a little of the broth strained and thickened with flour, which has first been blended with a little cold water. Serves 6.

Spring Soup

30g butter
1 teaspoon sugar
1 teaspoon vinegar
1 carrot, chopped
2½ cups green peas
1 small head lettuce, sliced
1 small onion, chopped
1 turnip, chopped
30g flour
2 cups water
salt and pepper
a little milk or cream
1 tablespoon finely chopped mint
croutons

Melt butter in saucepan and add sugar and vinegar. Cook prepared vegetables in this until tender but do not allow to brown. Add flour, then water gradually. Stir until boiling and then work all through a sieve. Reheat and add seasoning and milk or cream. Just before serving add mint and croutons. Serves 6.

Toheroa Soup

24 toheroas
3¾ cups stock or water
1 large onion, chopped
2 tablespoons flour
½ teaspoon ground cinnamon
1¼ cups milk
2 tablespoons chopped parsley
salt
croutons

Open toheroas, free from shells, wash well and mince finely. Put into saucepan with the stock or water. Add the onion and simmer gently for 1 hour. Make thickening with the flour and cinnamon by adding a little milk. Add remainder of milk to toheroa stock and bring gently to boil. Now add thickening and stir constantly until soup has a creamy consistency. Add chopped parsley and salt to taste and serve with croutons. Serves 6.

Tomato Bouillon

6 sprigs parsley
6 sprigs mint
1 large onion, chopped
¼ cup butter
3 large, ripe tomatoes, sliced
1 clove
3 peppercorns
¾ teaspoon salt
2 stock cubes
lemon slices
1 teaspoon sugar

Chop parsley and mint. Peel and slice onion. Melt butter in a saucepan, add onion and brown lightly. Add tomatoes, clove, peppercorns and salt to the onions. Cover and simmer for 20 minutes, stirring occasionally. Dissolve the cubes in boiling water in a large saucepan. Strain the tomato mixture into the bouillon, return to heat, cover and bring to boil. Reduce heat and cook slowly for 15 minutes. Add lemon slices, parsley, mint and sugar. Serves 4.

 # Vegetable Cream Soup

1 large carrot, chopped
2 large radishes, chopped
1 turnip, chopped
2 onions, chopped
7½ cups water
1 teaspoon celery salt
½ teaspoon pepper
2 tablespoons full cream milk powder
1 teaspoon butter
1 tablespoon cornflour
½ cup cold water.

Place vegetables in a saucepan with the water, celery salt, pepper and boil for half an hour.

Remove from heat and stir the milk powder into the liquid. Add the butter and return to the heat for a few seconds to stir in the cornflour mixed with the cold water. Serves 6.

Garnishes for Soups

1. Chopped hard-boiled egg.
2. Finely-chopped parsley.
3. Coarsely-crumbed salted biscuits.
4. Chopped green onions or chives.
5. Whipped cream.
6. Macaroni or spaghetti.
7. Grated cheese.
8. Duchess potatoes.
9. Croutons.

For creamed soups, reserve some of the cooked vegetable and place on top of soup when serving. For example, a few asparagus tips or green peas.

Croutons

Croutons are small-sized dice of crisp, toasted or fried bread. They may be cooked in deep fat or browned in the oven. For oven croutons, lightly spread a slice of stale bread with dripping. Cut into tiny dice and place on clean oven tray. Bake until a pale brown. With a fork lift the croutons as they brown on to a hot dish. Croutons should be served crisp and hot.

Duchess Potatoes

Boil or steam potatoes in their skins. Remove skins and mash well. Add good dripping or butter, pepper and salt, and cream or milk to make a rather soft mixture. Beat well. Place in rough heaps on a well-greased oven tray, or pipe into rings. Bake until puffed and lightly browned.

FISH

Baking

This method is used for baking whole stuffed fish, cutlets or prepared fish pies and casseroles. Have the oven fairly hot and the fish will cook very quickly; a whole trout will bake in about ½ hour.

Boiling

Place fish in almost boiling water, add 1 teaspoon salt to every 5 cups of water. Simmer gently after boiling point is reached, and cook in as little water as possible. A little vinegar or lemon juice added to the water helps to keep white fish a good colour. As soon as the bones separate easily from the flesh it is ready.

Frying

Fish should be clean and dried. It may be coated with seasoned flour, egg and breadcrumbs, oatmeal or a prepared batter. The fat may be deep or shallow but in either case it should be smoking hot.

For deep frying the fish is usually dipped in batter but may be soaked in seasoned beaten egg. Fry on both sides, lift out, drain and stand on clean absorbent paper or stale bread slices. Don't try to deep fry too much at once. Use clean dripping, lard or cooking oil. The latter is very suitable as then the fish is not greasy and can be eaten when cold.

Grilling

Heat the grill and grease grid or rack. Small whole fish, such as sole or flounder, should be first cut across in deep gashes to allow heat to penetrate, otherwise edges will curl up and shrivel before the inside is cooked. Cutlets of groper and similiar fish can also be grilled, but should first be basted with a little melted butter or fat.

Grilled fish should be sprinkled with salt and pepper, and cooked on both sides until flesh can come away when pressed, at thickest part. Cooking time is from 5–20 minutes, according to the size and type of fish. Serve with slices of lemon and squeeze lemon juice over each portion.

Poaching

This method is used for smoked fish, cutlets or small whole fish. Heat milk, or water and milk in a shallow pan until boiling, add fish and simmer for 10–15 minutes per 500g. Serve with sauce or melted butter.

Steaming

Use a steamer or simply place fish between 2 buttered plates. Flounders are nice done this way. When fish is cooked it will readily flake from the bone.

Fish Batters

Prior to being dipped in batter, fish should be dried and lightly floured. Batters are made from flour, baking soda, milk, water and sometimes an egg. For a rich batter use more egg and less flour. Half milk and half water makes a lighter batter than milk alone and if a very light texture is desired a little baking powder may be used. If eggs are omitted the use of soda helps to give a golden colour.

The usual method is to sift the dry ingredients and drop the egg and liquid in; then beat vigorously until the mixture is light and covered with tiny bubbles and then stand aside 10-15 minutes. The consistency should be thin, i.e., one that will pour. Serve as soon as possible, as batters soon get leathery if kept waiting. The exception to this is when they are cooked in oil and will stay crisp and non-greasy.

Suggested Batter Recipes

1. **125g flour**
   ¼ teaspoon salt
   1¼ cups milk or milk and water
   1 egg

2. **1 tablespoon flour**
   1 egg
   3 tablespoons milk
   pinch of salt

3. **½-¾ cup flour**
   pinch of salt
   pinch of soda
   water to mix
   Allow to stand before using.

4. Oyster batter.
   Use the liquor from the oysters, adding extra milk if needed.

Sauces For Fish

Cucumber Sauce
2 tablespoons vinegar
½ teaspoon salt
pinch of pepper
2 cucumbers

Mix vinegar, salt and pepper and pour over peeled, sliced and drained cucumber.

Egg or Parsley Sauce
1 hard-boiled egg
2 tablespoons chopped parsley
white sauce

Add egg and parsley to sauce, stir and serve.

Lemon Sauce
1 tablespoon cornflour
1 cup water
pinch of salt
6 very thin slices of lemon
juice of 1 lemon

Mix cornflour with a little water; add remaining water, salt and lemon slices. Cook over low heat, stir until thickened, then add lemon juice.

Horseradish Sauce
1 cup heavy cream
2 tablespoons fresh grated or prepared horseradish
2 tablespoons lemon juice
⅛ teaspoon salt
¼ cup chopped parsley

Whip cream. Mix in horseradish, then lemon juice, salt and finally parsley. Chill thoroughly. For a change, you could put the whole mixture in freezing tray and freeze.

Tartare Sauce
1 cup mayonnaise
2 tablespoons chopped olives
2 tablespoons chopped sweet gherkins
1 tablespoon minced onion
1 tablespoon chopped parsley
1 tablespoon chopped green pepper
1 teaspoon tarragon
1 teaspoon lemon juice
¼ teaspoon salt
⅛ teaspoon pepper

Mix all ingredients well, chill and serve very cold.

Hollandaise Sauce
185g butter or margarine
3 egg yolks
⅓ cup white wine – sauterne, chablis or hock seasonings

Melt butter, cool and mix in egg yolks. Add wine and seasoning gradually, beating throughly. Do not heat as it will curdle.

Fish Stuffings

60-125g butter
1 tablespoon grated onion
2 cups stale breadcrumbs
1-2 tablespoons lemon juice
1 tablespoon finely chopped parsley
½ teaspoon sage (optional)
½ teaspoon salt
⅛ teaspoon pepper

Heat butter and add onion and breadcrumbs. Stir over low heat until bread is lightly browned. Add remaining ingredients. Makes enough stuffing for 1.5-2kg fish.

Variations

Bacon Fish Stuffing
Omit the butter. Dice 4-6 strips of bacon and cook until almost crisp; add breadcrumbs and use as above.

Bacon and Mushroom Fish Stuffing
To Bacon Fish Stuffing add 1½ cups sliced mushrooms. Saute mushrooms slightly with the bacon before adding breadcrumbs.

Cucumber Fish Stuffing
Omit sage, decrease bread to 1½ cups and add 1 cup chopped drained cucumber.

Baked Nahi Curry

500g fish fillet
lemon juice
flour for dredging
½ teaspoon curry powder
1 apple, sliced
2 onions, chopped
1 tablespoon flour
½ cup cream, or top milk
2 eggs, 1 hard-boiled for garnishing
salt and pepper
1 cup milk
2 tablespoons chutney
boiled rice
lemon slices, for garnish

Steep fillets in lemon juice for 10 minutes. Dredge with flour and fry lightly until golden. Place fillets in casserole and dredge with curry powder. Fry apples and onion together in a little butter and place on top of the fish. Mix 1 tablespoon flour with cream and the beaten egg, season with salt and pepper and pour over fish. Cover and bake for half an hour at 180°C. Pour over 1 cup milk and 2 tablespoons chutney, and bake a little longer. Serve in border of boiled rice, garnished with egg and lemon slices. Serves 4.

Cod and Cabbage Toss

2 cups rice, cooked
2 cups smoked cod, flaked
4 eggs, hard-boiled and sliced
1 young cabbage heart, finely shredded
1-2 cups peas, cooked
2-3 tomatoes sliced, for garnish

Spread equal portions of hot rice onto 4 plates. Add the cod, sliced eggs and half the sliced cabbage. Pour on the hot sauce. Lightly cover with remaining cabbage and peas. Decorate with tomato slices.

Sauce
2 onions, finely sliced
4 tablespoons butter
2 tablespoons curry powder
1 tablespoon brown sugar
3 slightly rounded tablespoons flour
3-4 chillies, chopped finely
pinch turmeric
2 cups milk

Brown onions in butter and add the curry powder, brown sugar, flour, chillies and turmeric. When flour is blended thoroughly, add the milk, stir and boil for 2-3 minutes. Serves 4.

Codfish Balls

2 large potatoes, cooked, drained and mashed
1 cup cod
2 tablespoons cream
1 egg
seasoned flour

Combine all ingredients, mix well, form into balls, roll in seasoned flour and deep fry until golden brown.

Continental Fish Dish

½ cup olive oil
250g onions, sliced
500g fish steaks
½ cup vinegar
½ cup tomato sauce
salt and pepper
½ cup rice

Heat oil in saucepan and fry onions until golden. Add fish, vinegar, sauce and seasoning and barely cover the mixture with water. Bring to boil and simmer for 20-25 minutes. Remove fish and cook rice in the same liquid, return fish and reheat. Strain off surplus liquid which may be used as soup. Serves 4.

Crayfish Cakes

1 cup flour
1 teaspoon baking powder
1 teaspoon salt
1-2 eggs
milk
1 cup chopped crayfish tails
1 cup potato, cooked and mashed

Mix as for fish batter, making mixture rather sticky. Add crayfish tails and potato, form into cakes and fry in fat until golden. Serves 4.

Crayfish Pie

flaky or short pastry
2 cups potatoes, cooked and mashed
1 cup crayfish, flaked
1 teaspoon butter
1 onion, grated
1 teaspoon curry powder
salt and pepper
2 eggs, beaten
½ cup cheese, grated

Line a piedish with pastry. Combine all other ingredients, mix well and pile into pastry shell. Cover with a lattice top and sprinkle with grated cheese. Bake for 10 minutes at 200°C, reduce heat to 190°C and bake a further 20 minutes. Serves 6.

Fricassee of Crayfish

60g butter
1 tablespoon flour
1 cup milk
salt
pepper
pinch of nutmeg
flesh of 1 crayfish, minced
1 teaspoon lemon juice
2 tablespoons cream

Melt butter, stir in the flour and cook lightly but do not colour. Moisten with milk gradually and season with salt, pepper and nutmeg. Mix well, add crayfish and simmer for 10 minutes, stirring well. Add lemon juice and cream, but do not boil. Serves 4.

Delicious Chowder

1 teaspoon butter
1 onion, thinly sliced
1 cup potato, diced
1 cup boiling water
1 cup hot milk
6 large arrowroot biscuits, crushed
pepper
salt
pinch cinnamon
1 x 250g tin salmon or tuna

Melt butter in saucepan, add onion and cook until transparent. Add potato and water, and simmer. When soft, add hot milk, biscuits, pepper, salt and cinnamon. Heat well, add salmon and cook until fish is absorbed into mixture. Serve at once. Serves 4.

Fish and Bananas

8 small fish fillets
salt
pepper
1 egg, beaten
breadcrumbs
butter
4 bananas
parsley

Wash and dry the fillets, season, dip in egg and coat with breadcrumbs. If possible chill for an hour. Fry until golden and crisp. Serve each fillet topped with a half banana fried in butter, and garnish with parsley and lemon slices. Serves 4.

Fish Goulash

6-8 green tomatoes, quartered
3-4 onions, quartered
4 slices lemon
1 cucumber, peeled and sliced
2 celery stalks, chopped
seasoned flour
1 tablespoon chopped parsley
500g white fish, sliced
1 large potato, sliced
2 tablespoons butter
1½ cups white sauce
24 oysters
breadcrumbs, toasted

Toss tomatoes, onions, lemon, cucumber and celery in seasoned flour and place in a casserole. Sprinkle with parsley and add fish. Cover with water, top with potato, dot with butter, cover and cook for 1½ hours at 180°C. Just before serving combine sauce and oysters and pour over fish. Sprinkle with breadcrumbs or buttered crumbs, and serve. Serves 4.
Buttered Crumbs: Butter 2 thick slices bread, sprinkle with pepper, salt and thyme and grill until crisp. Crush with rolling pin.

Fish Puffs

1 small onion
1 level tablespoon butter
1 tomato, skinned and chopped
1 clove garlic
250g cooked and flaked fish
salt
pepper
125g flour
1 level teaspoon baking powder
salt
4 potatoes, cooked and mashed
2 tablespoons milk
lemon
parsley

Cook the onion in the melted butter. Add tomatoes and garlic and cook until tomatoes are tender. Add fish and seasoning. Cool. Sift flour, baking powder and salt; add potatoes and mix to a firm dough with the milk, knead lightly and roll to 6mm thickness. Cut into 8cm squares and place a tablespoon of fish mixture in the centre of each square. Moisten the edges, fold over and press together. Deep fry until golden. Serve hot with lemon and parsley. Serves 4.

Fish and Macaroni Pie

1 cup macaroni, cooked
500g cooked and flaked fish
¾ cup butter, melted
salt
pepper
90g grated cheese
1 cup milk
½ cup breadcrumbs
butter

Drain the macaroni. Butter a casserole and put in a layer of fish, sprinkled with butter, salt, pepper and 1 tablespoon of cheese. Then add a layer of macaroni. Repeat the layering until dish is filled. Pour over milk and garnish with breadcrumbs, remaining cheese, and dot with butter. Bake for 30 minutes at 180°C. Serves 2.

Fish and Potato Pie

500g fish, cooked and flaked
60g butter
½ cup flour
1½ cups fish stock
½ cup milk
salt
pepper
parsley, chopped
4 potatoes, cooked and mashed

Put fish in a buttered casserole and pour over a butter sauce made with the butter, flour, stock, milk, salt, pepper and parsley. Pile mashed potatoes on top and bake in a moderate oven (180°C) until top is browned. Serves 4.

Fish and Tomato Pie

4 tomatoes, sliced
salt
pepper
1 tablespoon sugar
4 small fish fillets or flaked fish
2 onions, minced

Butter a piedish, line the bottom and sides with tomato slices, sprinkle with salt, pepper and sugar, and add a layer of fish and a layer of onion. Sprinkle with salt and pepper. Continue layering until dish is filled, finishing with tomato slices. Cover with another buttered piedish and bake at 180°C for half an hour. Serves 4.

Puffed Cheese Fish

6 fish fillets
salt
½ cup cooking oil
½ cup mayonnaise sauce
125g cheese, grated
1 tablespoon chopped parsley
1 tablespoon chopped gherkins
1 teaspoon lemon juice
¼ teaspoon salt
1 egg white, beaten
lemon wedges
fried mushrooms for garnish

Wash and dry fillets, sprinkle with salt and lightly brown in oil. Drain and place on a greased baking dish. Mix mayonnaise sauce with the cheese, stir in the parsley, gherkins, lemon juice, salt and egg white and pour over fish. Bake at 200°C for 12 minutes until the coating is puffed and browned. Serve with lemon wedges and mushrooms. Serves 6.

Stuffed Fish Rolls

250g fish fillet, smoked
15g butter
15g flour
⅔ cup milk
salt
pepper
2 eggs, hard-boiled
6 soft-crust bread rolls
30g butter, melted
few sprigs watercress for garnish

Wash fish, place in a covered dish with a little water and cook at 200°C until fish will flake easily. Prepare a white sauce with the butter, flour and milk. Drain liquid from fish, flake, add to white sauce and season. Cut 6 slices of egg and reserve for garnishing. Chop up remainder and add to fish and sauce. Cut the top off the rolls, scoop out the inside, brush with the melted butter. Crisp and brown rolls slightly in the oven for 5 minutes and fill with the hot fish mixture. Top with slice of egg and sprig of watercress. Serves 6.

Fish Goulash (see p. 17)

Trout Ring

1 small salmon trout
1 cup rice, cooked
½ cup breadcrumbs, crisped
½ cup onion, finely sliced
parsley, finely cut
juice ½ lemon
salt
pepper
2 eggs, beaten
white sauce
90g cooked peas
2 small carrots, sliced and cooked

Steam fish until tender. Remove from bone and flake. Mix rice with fish and add breadcrumbs, onion, parsley, lemon juice, salt and pepper to taste. Combine all with the beaten eggs. Place mixture in a buttered ring mould and bake for 40 minutes at 180°C Turn out onto a hot dish and serve with the white sauce to which the vegetables have been added. Serve with mashed potatoes. Serves 2.

Roe a la Ritz

500g fish roe
3 eggs, separated
6 tablespoons flour
1 teaspoon baking powder
salt
pepper
3 tablespoons milk
1 small onion, grated
1 bunch parsley, finely chopped
1 teaspoon lemon juice
1 teaspoon butter

Remove skin from roe and set aside. Separate egg yolks from whites and mix yolks with flour, baking powder, salt, pepper and milk until smooth paste. Add roe, onion, parsley; mix thoroughly and add lemon juice and stiffly beaten egg whites. Pour the mixture into a frying pan and cook as an omelette. Serves 4.

Baked Salmon Trout

1 trout
salt
pepper
flour
4 tomatoes, sliced
1 onion, finely sliced
2 tablespoons chopped parsley
1 egg
½ cup milk

Remove head and scales from trout; clean and rub inside and out with salt, pepper and flour. Place trout in a casserole and around it arrange the tomatoes, onions and parsley. Bake for half an hour, covered, at 180°C. Beat the egg with milk, pour into casserole and continue to bake until

custard has set, approximately 15 minutes, uncovered. Serve with baked potatoes.

Stuffed Trout

1 trout
30g butter
1 cup breadcrumbs
2 small onions, chopped
1 egg, beaten
salt
pepper
thyme
sage
60g butter
2 tablespoons hot water
parsley sauce

Prepare trout and rub all over with butter. Combine the breadcrumbs, onion, egg, salt, pepper, thyme and sage, and stuff the trout with this mixture. Place trout in casserole with the butter and water and bake for 1-1½ hours at 180°C Serve with parsley sauce. Serves 4.

Savoury Trout

2 sprigs mint
1 whole trout
4 rashers bacon
4 tomatoes, sliced
½ cup vinegar
3 dabs butter
salt
pepper

Place the mint inside the trout. Wrap with bacon and place in baking dish. Cover with tomatoes, vinegar, butter and seasoning. Bake for 1½ hours at 180°C. Serves 2.

Salmon with Asparagus Sauce

1 x 250g tin salmon
4 tablespoons butter
4 tablespoons flour
2 cups milk
salt
pepper
grated rind 1 lemon
1 egg, beaten
1½ cups breadcrumbs

Drain and flake the salmon. Melt the butter, add flour and cook for 2 minutes, then add milk, stirring until sauce boils and thickens. Add salt, pepper, lemon rind and salmon. Turn onto a dish and cool thoroughly. Form into croquettes using a little flour. Dip in egg and breadcrumbs and fry until golden. Serves 4.

Asparagus Sauce
2 small tablespoons butter
2 tablespoons flour
1 cup asparagus tips, cooked
1 cup milk
30g grated cheese

Melt butter and add flour, then asparagus liquid, and milk and stir until mixture thickens. Add cheese. Serve hot with croquettes and asparagus tips.

✳ Salmon Loaf with Lemon Butter

3 tablespoons lemon juice
¾ cup breadcrumbs
1 egg, slightly beaten
¾ cup milk
1 x 375g tin salmon, flaked
½ teaspoon salt
½ teaspoon pepper
2 tablespoons onion, finely chopped
2 tablespoons butter, melted

Combine all ingredients and pack firmly in a buttered loaf tin. Bake for 40 minutes at 180°C.

Lemon Butter
Blend together ¼ cup melted butter, 2 tablespoons chopped parsley, ¼ cup lemon juice, ½ teaspoon salt, and pour over loaf.

Creamed Salmon and Potato Casserole

1 x 375g tin salmon
2 cups potato, peeled and thinly sliced
2 tablespoons butter
1 tablespoon finely chopped onion
2 tablespoons flour
1½ cups milk
salt
pepper
1 tablespoon chopped parsley
1 tablespoon lemon juice

Remove bones from salmon and mash fish. Cook potatoes in boiling, salted water for 10 minutes and drain. Melt butter, add onion and cook 1-2 minutes without browning. Add flour and stir until smooth. Cook gently for 2 minutes, then add milk and stir until boiling. Season and add parsley and lemon juice. Arrange fish and potatoes in alternate layers in greased baking dish. Season each layer. Pour parsley sauce over top, cover and bake for 45 minutes at 180°C. Serves 4.

Salmon Mornay

2 tablespoons butter
2 celery stalks, diced
2 tablespoons flour
salt
1 teaspoon mustard
pinch cayenne
2½ cups milk
squeeze lemon juice
500g potatoes, cooked and mashed
1 x 250g tin salmon
2 eggs, hard-boiled
2 tablespoons cheese, grated
2 tablespoons dried breadcrumbs

Melt butter in a saucepan and add celery. Cook until soft but not brown. Lift out and add flour, salt, mustard and cayenne. Stir until smooth and cook for 1 minute. Add milk and bring to boil, stirring constantly until mixture thickens. Flavour with lemon juice and add liquor from salmon. Line a greased casserole with the potatoes, fold celery, egg and salmon into sauce and spread over potato. Make a border of potato around the edge and sprinkle top with breadcrumbs and cheese Bake for 20 minutes at 180°C. Serves 4.

Coconut Salmon Loaf

1 x 250g tin salmon
2 eggs
1½ cups fine breadcrumbs
½-⅔ cup desiccated coconut
1 tablespoon milk
salt
pepper
1 teaspoon vinegar

Flake salmon and blend all ingredients, adding enough milk to make a soft, but not too wet, consistency. Put into a greased baking dish and bake for 45 minutes at 180°C. Serves 4.

Holiday Quick Lunch

2 cups thick parsley sauce
1 x 250g tin salmon
185g cooked peas
breadcrumbs
1 teaspoon butter
cold rice pudding or boiled rice

Add well-drained salmon and peas to sauce. Stir in enough breadcrumbs to make a stiff consistency. Melt butter in frying pan and drop in spoonfuls of mixture. Fry on both sides until golden. Slice the rice pudding into 12mm slices, dip in beaten egg and fry on both sides until golden. Serve together with salad. Serves 4.

Mushroom and Sardine Slice

50g butter
12 mushrooms
1 tin sardines
½ teaspoon paprika
½ teaspoon nutmeg, ground
1 tablespoon lemon juice
salt
pepper
2 eggs
½ cup milk
prepared short pastry shell
lemon slices for garnish

Gently fry the washed and chopped mushrooms in the melted butter. Remove from heat and add the sardines, paprika, nutmeg, lemon juice, salt and pepper. Add the eggs and milk beaten together, mix thoroughly and pour into pastry shell. Bake until set at 180°C. Serve hot or cold with lemon slices. Serves 4.

Friday Special

3 tablespoons flour
1 tablespoon butter
oil from sardines
1¼ cup milk
1 tablespoon mustard
½ teaspoon Worcestershire sauce
salt
pepper
185g grated cheese
1 tin sardines

Make a white sauce with the flour, butter and oil, adding milk slowly then other ingredients. Stir well until cheese has melted and finally add the drained, mashed sardines. Serve on toast with raw tomatoes. Serves 4.

OYSTERS AND SHELLFISH

Baked Oyster Omelette

4 eggs
4 tablespoons milk
salt
pepper
1 teaspoon chopped parsley
24 oysters
2½ cups white sauce
30g butter

Beat the eggs, add milk, salt, pepper to taste, and the parsley. Blanch, but do not boil the oysters, remove from pan and add to the sauce, cooking slowly for 10 minutes. Melt butter in baking dish and put in half the omelette mixture. Bake in oven at 180°C until set. Put oysters on top, add rest of omelette mixture and cook until nicely brown. Serve at once. Serves 4.

Oyster Pie Deluxe

60g butter
185g flour
pinch of cayenne
pinch of salt
1 egg separated
squeeze of lemon juice
water
oyster liquor
30g butter
1 tablespoon flour
milk
1 hard-boiled egg
pepper and salt
24 oysters
parsley, for garnish

Rub butter into the flour, sifted with the cayenne and salt. Mix with egg yolk, lemon juice and enough water to make a soft dough. Knead, roll out and line a sandwich tin. Prick base and cook for approximately 20 minutes at 180°C. Make a sauce with the oyster liquor, butter and flour. Add milk if too thick. Cook for 3 minutes and mix in chopped egg white. Add pepper and salt to taste. Pour mixture into cooled shell, top with oysters and decorate with chopped yolk of hard-boiled egg. Whip the egg white left over from the pastry, add parsley and place blobs of this meringue mixture evenly around the oysters. Brown in a hot oven to warm oysters. Serves 4.

Oyster Soufflé

12 oysters
2½ cups milk
2 tablespoons butter
2 tablespoons cornflour
1 cup soft breadcrumbs
2 eggs, separated
1 tablespoon chopped parsley
salt
pepper

Cook oysters for a few minutes, then chop finely. Make a white sauce with the milk, butter and cornflour. Add oysters, breadcrumbs, beaten egg yolks, parsley and seasoning to sauce. Beat well, then fold in stiffly beaten egg whites. Pour into a greased baking dish and bake at 180°C until set and golden. Serves 4.

Oyster and Liver Loaf

250g liver
12 oysters
1 cup breadcrumbs
1 tablespoon oatmeal
1 tablespoon chopped parsley
1 onion, grated
salt
pepper
¼ cup flour
4 rashers bacon

Mince liver and oysters and add all other ingredients except bacon. Mould into a loaf and place in a greased baking dish. Lay the bacon strips on top and bake for an hour at 150°C. Serves 4.

Oyster Mushroom Pudding

250g mushrooms
15 oysters
¼ cup breadcrumbs
3 tablespoons butter
1 cup flour
½ cup shredded suet
¼ teaspoon salt
½ teaspoon baking powder
water
salt
pepper
pinch mace
1 tablespoon lemon juice

Wash and slice mushrooms and fry in a little of the butter for a few minutes. Beard the oysters and toss the breadcrumbs in the remaining melted butter. Make a pastry from the flour, suet, salt, baking powder and water, to make a firm dough. Roll out to 6mm thickness and line a pudding basin. Fill with the prepared oysters, mushrooms and crumbs. Season with salt, pepper, mace, lemon juice and cover with pastry. Tie in a cloth and steam for 1½-2 hours. Serves 4.

Oyster Pudding

4 heaped tablespoons white breadcrumbs
12 oysters, chopped
¼ teaspoon nutmeg
¼ teaspoon salt
¼ teaspoon cayenne pepper
squeeze lemon juice
2 eggs
2 tablespoons milk
2 tablespoons oyster liquor
dash of vinegar

Into a bowl put the breadcrumbs, oysters, nutmeg, salt, cayenne pepper and lemon juice. Beat the eggs with the milk and add the oyster liquor with the vinegar. Add to the bread mixture, blending well. Steam in a buttered mould for 2 hours. Use remaining oyster liquor to make a white sauce, adding a little lemon juice. Serves 4.

Oyster Rarebit

2 tablespoons butter
125g grated cheese
18 oysters
4 egg yolks, slightly beaten
1 tablespoon Worcestershire sauce
salt
pepper

Melt the butter in top of a double boiler and add cheese, stir frequently and do not allow water in the boiler to boil, as the high heat curdles the cheese. Heat the oysters gently until the edges curl; strain, keeping the liquid. When cheese is just melted, add liquid and mix well. Stir quickly into egg yolks and return to double boiler. Now add oysters, Worcestershire sauce, salt and pepper, and stir constantly until thickened. Serve in patty shells or on toast. Serves 4.

Skewered Oysters

16 oysters
butter
16 mushrooms
1½ cups fine breadcrumbs
lemon halves for garnish

Put oysters into a small pan with their juice and a little butter, and place over a low flame for a minute. In another pan saute the mushrooms in butter. Thread oysters and mushrooms alternately on small skewers, pour melted butter over, and roll in fine breadcrumbs. Heat under griller and serve garnished with lemon halves and brown bread and butter. When mushrooms are not available, combine oysters with small slices frankfurter sausage as these go well together. Serves 4.

Oyster Cocktail

12 oysters
6 tablespoons tomato sauce
2 teaspoons vinegar
pinch salt
1 teaspoon Worcestershire sauce
dash cayenne

Arrange the oysters and their liquor in cocktail glasses. Blend the remaining ingredients and pour over. Chill and serve. Serves 4.

Scalloped Mussels

24 mussels
2 tablespoons butter
2 heaped tablespoons flour
2 cups milk
salt
pepper
cayenne pepper to taste
breadcrumbs

Put mussels in a saucepan without water and heat until shells open. When cool, remove beards and put mussels in a pie dish. Combine the butter, flour and milk to make a sauce and pour over mussels. Season cover with breadcrumbs and a few dabs of butter. Bake until light brown for 10-15 minutes at 200°C. Serve hot. Serves 4.

Pancake Toheroa

Pancake
4 large potatoes, grated
salt
pepper
1 level tablespoon grated onion

Place potatoes on a well-greased frying pan. Add salt, pepper and onion. Cover and cook slowly for ½ hour or until potatoes are thoroughly grilled. Dot with butter or bacon fat and brown under grill.

Toheroas
50g toheroas
milk
1 teaspoon salt
pepper to taste
pinch mace
1 teaspoon onion juice
½ teaspoon curry powder
cornflour, for thickening

Mince toheroas and cover with milk. Add salt, pepper and mace, and simmer for a few minutes. Add onion juice, curry powder and thicken with cornflour. Cut pancake in slices and top with toheroa mixture. Serves 4.

Toheroa Chowder

2 large onions, finely chopped
1 tablespoon butter
2 tomatoes, skinned and sliced
12 toheroas, minced
1 teaspoon ground mace
salt
pepper

Fry the onions in butter until golden, then add tomatoes and fry for 10 minutes. Add toheroas, mace, pepper and salt, stirring occasionally. Fry for 20 minutes. Serve very hot on buttered toast, or fried bread. Serves 4.

Shrimp Cocktail

125g shrimps
1 lemon, sliced
tomato sauce

Arrange the shrimps in cocktail glasses. Cover with a slice of lemon and 1 tablespoon tomato sauce. Garnish with parsley and sprinkle with cayenne. Serves 4.

Lobster Cocktail

125g prepared lobster, chopped
1 cup tomato puree
1 teaspoon white wine
1 teaspoon vinegar, or 2 teaspoons
  grapefruit juice
1 teaspoon cream
dash cayenne

Put the lobster into sherbert glasses. Prepare a sauce from the puree, wine, vinegar, cream and cayenne and pour over the lobster. Chill and serve. Serves 4.

WHITEBAIT

Steamed Whitebait

whitebait
salt
pepper
butter

Place whitebait in basin, season with pepper and salt and knob of butter. Cover with greased paper and steam 15 minutes or until cooked.

Whitebait Deluxe

6 tablespoons butter, melted
3 tablespoons breadcrumbs
2 tablespoons finely chopped parsley
1 cup whitebait
salt
pepper

Into a casserole put 3 tablespoons of the melted butter and sprinkle with breadcrumbs and parsley. Add whitebait and the remaining melted butter, breadcrumbs and seasoning. Cover and bake for 20 minutes at 220°C. Serve hot. Serves 2.

Whitebait Soufflé

1 slice bread
1 cup milk
1 tablespoon butter
2 eggs, separated
1¼ cups whitebait
salt
pepper

Soak bread in milk, add butter, and beat to pulp. Then add yolks of eggs, pepper, salt and whitebait. Lastly, add stiffly-beaten whites and pour into buttered dish. Bake for 20 minutes at 190°C. Serves 4.

Whitebait Delicious

2 cups white sauce
500g fresh whitebait
125g grated cheese
½ cup chopped parsley
garlic, crushed
salt
pepper
breadcrumbs
butter

Grease pie dish well and put layer of white sauce in bottom, then whitebait, cheese, parsley and garlic. Season well with salt and pepper. Lastly, add rest of white sauce, cover with breadcrumbs and dot with small nobs butter. Bake gently for 1½ hours at 180°C. Serves 4.

Whitebait Roll

1 cup flour
1 teaspoon baking powder
1 cup potatoes, cooked and mashed
60g butter, melted
1 egg
1 cup whitebait
1 onion, finely chopped
salt
pepper

Combine flour, baking powder, potatoes, melted butter and egg to form a dough. Roll out and cover with the whitebait. Sprinkle with the onion, salt and pepper. Roll up and bake for half an hour at 180°C. Serve hot or cold. Serves 4.

Whitebait Fritters

2 eggs, well beaten
2 tablespoons milk
½ cup flour
salt
pepper
2½ cups whitebait
fat for frying

Make a batter with the eggs, milk, flour, salt and pepper. Add whitebait and drop spoonfuls into boiling fat. Fry until golden brown. Serves 4.

Whitebait Waffles

1½ cups flour
1½ teaspoons baking powder
¾ teaspoon salt
½ teaspoon pepper
1 egg
½ cup milk
½ cup water
1 tablespoon butter, melted
250g whitebait

Sift the dry ingredients. Drop the egg into the centre, add milk and water gradually and beat well. Add butter and whitebait, blending thoroughly. Cook in waffle irons and serve garnished with lemon wedges. Serves 4.

Whitebait Flan

Flan
¾ **cup flour**
pinch salt
½ **teaspoon baking powder**
45g **butter**
30g **grated cheese**
water, to mix

Mix pastry in usual way, rubbing cheese into the flour with the butter. Roll out to 6mm, line an oven dish and fill with whitebait mixture.

Whitebait Filling
3 **tablespoons milk**
30g **flour**
1 **egg yolk, beaten**
2 **tablespoons grated cheese**
1 **cup prepared whitebait**
4 **tablespoons mashed potatoes**
1 **tomato, skinned and chopped**
1 **tablespoon chopped parsley**
salt
pepper

Mix together the milk and flour and add the egg and cheese. Then add boiled whitebait, potato, tomatoes, parsley, salt and pepper to taste. Mix well and pour into pastry case. Decorate with strips of pastry and grated cheese. Bake for 25 minutes at 190°C. Serves 6.

Stewed Whitebait

30g **butter**
1 **level tablespoon flour**
1 **cup milk or cream**
1¼ **cups whitebait**
few drops lemon juice
salt
pepper

Melt butter in a pan, add the flour and then milk gradually. When thick, add whitebait and heat thoroughly. Add lemon juice, salt and pepper and serve on toast. Serves 2.

Whitebait Surprise

2 **eggs, beaten**
1 **large cup milk**
salt
pepper
500g **whitebait**

To the beaten eggs add milk, salt, pepper and whitebait. Mix well and bake at 150°C until set. Serve with salad. Serves 4.

Whitebait Tart

250g **flaky pastry**
2 **eggs**
¾ **cup milk**
salt
pepper
250g **whitebait**

Roll out pastry, line a pie dish and prick with fork to prevent rising. Beat together eggs, milk, salt, pepper and add whitebait. Pour into pastry shell and bake at 200°C until custard is set and pastry browned. Serves 6.

MEAT

Meat is one of the most common items of our everyday diet and it is important for the housewife to know how to buy and cook meat.

Good beef should be firm, bright red in colour, have the fat well distributed and the fat should be firm and yellow-tinted. Good mutton or lamb is bright pink, the fat firm and flaky and the skin comes off easily. Both veal and pork should be pink and have white fat; never buy pork with any dark spots on it.

Cook tender cuts such as loin chops or fillet steak with a quick dry heat. Grilling, frying, roasting all come under this classification. Tougher cuts like topside, blade roasts, skirt steak and neck chops require slow moist heat such as stewing, pot roasting, casserole cooking or braising.

Many factors contribute to make meat tough. An older animal will have a firmer fibre than a younger one; the part of the animal getting most exercise becomes more fibrous than one that has comparative rest (the sirloin, a tender cut, is a good example of this), and bad cooking will toughen almost any cut. The toughness of meat is due to the presence of connective tissues which may be softened by slow moist heat, by pounding and by mincing. The white substance present in mince is not necessarily fat but may be connective tissue. The flavour of meat must be sealed in; once meat starts to cook the juices begin to flow so the outside must be seared. This is done by putting the cut into a hot oven, in hot water or frying in a hot pan. Conversely, if flavour is wanted in the stock, as in soup, or stew, the meat is then put in cold water and brought slowly to the boil.

What to Serve with Different Cuts

Roast Beef : Yorkshire pudding, roast vegetables, brown gravy.
Roast Veal : Fat bacon, sausages, lemon slices, forcemeat balls. Whole sausages may be incorporated in a rolled loin.
Roast Lamb : Mint sauce, green peas, new potatoes.
Roast Mutton : Redcurrant jelly, gravy.
Roast Pork : Apple sauce, gravy, roast vegetables.
Boiled Beef : Boiled potatoes, carrots, turnips, suet dumplings.
Boiled Ham : Mustard sauce, mashed potato, peas.
Boiled Hogget : As for mutton, or bechamel sauce.
Boiled Mutton : Parsley, caper or onion sauce, boiled carrots and onions.
Baked Ham : Stick fat with cloves, glaze and roast with pineapple slices.
Cold Ham : Mixed mustard, salad.
Cold Lamb : Cold mint sauce or mint jelly.
Corned Beef : White, parsley or mustard sauce, carrots, cabbage.
Steak : Brown, tomato, bearnaise or mushroom sauce.

Gravy

Gravy is made after the meat is cooked. Remove the meat from the roasting pan and pour off most of the fat. To the remaining fat add an equal quantity of flour or cornflour and season to taste. Add boiling water or vegetable stock until gravy is of desired consistency, then cook 5 minutes to cook the flour. Strain into a gravy boat.

Brown Gravy

1 small onion, sliced
1 tablespoon dripping, melted
1 tablespoon flour
1 cup water
salt
pepper
1 teaspoon vinegar
½ teaspoon Marmite

Brown the onion in the dripping. Sprinkle in the flour and brown lightly. Gradually stir in water and season with salt, pepper, vinegar and Marmite.

Dressed Corned Beef

2kg solid brisket
1 large onion stuck with cloves
juice and rind 1 lemon
bouquet garni
½ cup brown sugar
1 teaspoon mixed spice

Wash meat under running water, cover with water in a pot and add the onion, lemon juice and rind and bouquet garni. Cook until tender. Drain and place in a baking pan, stick with a few cloves and spread the sugar and spice over the meat. Place in moderately hot oven until sugar has melted, then cool. Serves 6-8.
This corned beef is particularly nice served cold with a green salad, bananas cut lengthwise, drenched in orange or lemon juice, dipped in mayonnaise and rolled in chopped nuts.
Can also be served as a hot meal with hot spiced beetroot cooked in the water in which beef was cooked.

Corned Beef Special

2.5kg corned beef
1 tablespoon golden syrup
1 tablespoon flour
2 tablespoons bacon fat, or dripping
15 cloves
½ cup brown sugar
⅓ cup marmalade
2 teaspoons dry mustard
2 apples, cored and sliced
juice 1 lemon
juice 2 oranges

Put beef to boil in a large pot with cold water. Simmer half an hour and drain. Cover with boiling water, add syrup and simmer until tender – approximately 45 minutes per 500g. Leave to cool, then drain, smear with flour and fat and stick with cloves. Place in roasting pan and bake 15 minutes at 220°C. Mix together the sugar, marmalade and mustard, and spread over beef. Put slices around, add fruit juices and bake at 200°C, basting frequently. Serve hot, surrounded by glazed apple slices. Serves 8.

Stuffed Corned Beef and Broad Bean Pudding

2kg silverside
1 cup breadcrumbs
1 carrot, grated
1 apple, chopped
1 onion, chopped
1 tablespoon raisins
1 tablespoon vinegar
1 tablespoon brown sugar

Cut a pocket in a lean piece of silverside and fill with a stuffing made from the remaining ingredients except the vinegar and sugar. Tie in a cloth and boil in water containing the vinegar and sugar. Simmer until tender. Serves 6-8.

Broad Bean Pudding
500g broad beans
1 cup breadcrumbs
1 onion, minced
1 tablespoon melted butter
1 tablespoon chopped parsley
1 teaspoon sugar
½ teaspoon lemon juice
pinch nutmeg
salt
pepper
1 egg, beaten
2 tablespoons butter

Cook beans until soft, then mince and combine with the breadcrumbs and onion. Add the butter, parsley, sugar, lemon juice, nutmeg, salt and pepper. Bind with the egg, put in a piedish, dot with butter and bake 15 minutes at 200°C.

Mock Christmas Ham

2kg leg lamb, brined
allspice
1 large onion, stuck with 5 cloves
bacon bones, or piece pickled pork
sprig fresh thyme, or sage
few sprigs parsley
2 lemon slices
2 peppercorns
2 tablespoons vinegar
4 tablespoons melted fat, or butter
½ cup browned breadcrumbs

Rub lamb well with allspice and leave to stand half an hour. Put into a large saucepan with the onion, bacon bones, thyme, parsley, lemon slices, peppercorns and vinegar. Cover with hot water and bring to boil. Cover and simmer allowing half an hour for each 500g of meat. Cool in brine. Remove, drain, brush with melted butter and cover with breadcrumbs. Serves 6.

Pineapple Coated Ham

2kg ham
pineapple coating
10 cloves

Simmer ham in water until tender. Remove from liquid and skin. Score surface with a sharp knife and cover with pineapple coating. Stud with whole cloves. Put in a hot oven until coat is brown and glazed. Baste with pineapple syrup while cooking.

To make pineapple coating, mix 1 cup crushed pineapple and 1 cup brown sugar and cover ham. Serves 8.

Spiced Hambake

1.5kg ham, thick end of leg
750g flour
water
2 tablespoons brown sugar
10-15 cloves
gingerale, or pineapple juice

Soak ham in cold water for 2 hours, longer if ham is very salty. Dry and trim away any discoloured parts. Make a paste with flour and water to make a soft dough and roll out 6mm-12mm thick. Mould this round the ham, joining the edges with water. Bake in greased baking dish, at 180°C allowing 20 minutes for each 500g ham and 20 minutes over. Remove ham from oven and while hot remove crust and carefully strip off outside rind. Rub with brown sugar and with a sharp knife cut fat into a diamond pattern. Stud each diamond with a clove. Place on a rack in the meat tin and sprinkle with ale or juice, pouring more into the bottom of the tin. Return to a hot oven – 220°C – for about 15 minutes basting twice with the hot juice. Serve covered with crust. Serves 8.

Casseroled Ham

1½ cups milk
1 cup soft breadcrumbs
¼ cup melted butter
1½ tablespoons chopped onion
1 tablespoon chopped parsley
seasonings to taste
125g grated cheese
3 eggs, beaten
250g cooked, chopped ham
185g cooked peas

Pour scalding milk over breadcrumbs. Add butter, onion, parsley, seasonings, cheese and eggs. Put ham and peas into a buttered casserole. Pour over breadcrumbs, milk and cheese mixture and bake for 45 minutes at 180°C. Serves 4.

Spicy Ham Loaf

250g finely chopped, cooked ham
½ cup fine breadcrumbs
¼ cup finely chopped onion
2 tablespoons finely chopped green pepper
½ teaspoon dry mustard
¼ teaspoon allspice
⅛ teaspoon ground cloves
2 eggs, slightly beaten
½ cup milk

Combine meat and all dry ingredients, add eggs and milk and mix well. Pack mixture into buttered loaf tin and bake for 45 minutes, at 180°C. Turn out and serve hot. Serves 6.

Ham Savoury

4 slices cooked ham
1½ tablespoons mustard
knob of butter
250g flour
2 teaspoons baking powder
4 tablespoons butter
2 tablespoons milk

Mince ham and mix with the mustard and butter. Sift the flour with the baking powder. Rub in the butter and mix with enough milk to make a stiff dough. Roll into an oblong, 6mm thick and spread over ham mixture. Roll up, cut into 4cm pieces, flatten and cook on cold greased tray for quarter of an hour at 210°C. Serve with a cheese sauce. Serves 4.

Baked Ham Slice

1kg ham in piece
½ cup brown sugar
10 cloves
½ cup water
½ cup vinegar
2 apples, sliced

Soak the ham in cold water for 2 hours. Drain and rub with sugar. Stick with cloves and place in covered baking dish with water and vinegar. Cook for 15 minutes at 220°C, then reduce and continue cooking for 1 hour. Cover with apples sprinkled with sugar, return to oven until apples are cooked. Serve with mashed potatoes, baked apples garnished with parsley and pineapple. Serves 6.

Surprise Hamburger Roast

¼ cup milk
1 cup breadcrumbs
750g minced steak
1 egg, beaten
3 tablespoons chopped onion
1 tablespoon Worcestershire sauce
1 teaspoon prepared mustard
1½ teaspoons salt
1 teaspoon sage
2 carrots, diced
2 celery stalks, chopped
1 tablespoon chopped onion
1 small tin tomato soup
1¼ cups water

Pour milk over breadcrumbs, add meat, egg, onion, sauce and seasonings. Mix thoroughly. Place on floured wax paper, put another sheet of paper on top and roll out to a rectangular shape. Remove top paper and spread carrot, celery and onion over meat. Roll up like a jam roll, removing paper as you do so. Place in pyrex dish and pour mixed soup and water over the roll. Cover and bake 1 hour or longer at 180°-190°C. Serves 6.

Hamburger Casserole

1 cup cooked rice
3 tablespoons flour
1 teaspoon curry powder
salt
pepper
3 tablespoons butter
250g mince
1 large onion, minced
4 tomatoes, skinned and sliced
1 x 500g tin sweet corn
parsley for garnish

Butter a casserole and spread cooked rice over the bottom. Mix flour, curry, salt and pepper and sprinkle one third over the rice. Dot with 1 tablespoon of the butter and cover with mince and onion. Season with another one third of the flour mixture and dot with more butter. Add layer of tomatoes, then the remaining flour and butter. Finally cover with the corn. Bake for 1 hour at 180°C. Garnish with parsley. Serves 6.

Surprise Meat Balls

500g cooked meat, minced
25-50g butter, softened
salt
pepper
pinch cayenne pepper
1 tablespoon Worcestershire sauce
2 tablespoons tomato sauce
200g flaky or short pastry
1 egg, separated

Combine meat, butter, salt, pepper, cayenne pepper, and sauces to moisten. The mixture should be highly seasoned. Form meat into finger-thick rolls about 10cm long. Roll pastry out thinly and cut strips 10cm long. Put a meat roll on end of pastry, roll until meat is covered, then seal edge and ends with raw egg white. Put rolls on oven tray, brush with beaten egg yolk and bake for 12-15 minutes at 210°C until brown. Serves 6.

Charlbury Casserole

500g cooked meat, minced
1 cup flour
½ teaspoon salt
2½ teaspoons baking powder
50g butter
½ cup milk
dripping, or bacon fat
1 carrot, grated
2 tablespoons chopped parsley

Place well-seasoned meat in greased casserole. Sift flour, salt and baking powder, and rub in butter, then add sufficient milk to make a soft dough. Roll out thinly (6mm), then brush with fat. Sprinkle with carrot and parsley. Roll up like a swiss roll and cut in slices. Place slices overlapping on top of meat and bake for half an hour at 200°C. Serves 6.

Stuffed Cold Beef Casserole

250g peanuts, roasted and minced
2 cups breadcrumbs
salt
pepper
½ teaspoon mustard
1 tablespoon melted fat
500g cold beef, cooked and sliced
1 large apple, sliced
1 large onion, sliced
3 tomatoes, sliced

Mix dry ingredients with the fat. Place half the cold meat in a casserole, cover with stuffing and then the remaining meat. Add apple, onion and tomato, cover and bake for 20 minutes at 200°C. Serves 6.

Spring Lamb Stew

1.25kg neck and breast lamb
3 small onions, finely sliced
3 tablespoons butter
2 tablespoons flour
2½ cups beef stock
6 carrots, chopped
4 turnips, chopped
4 potatoes, chopped
500g shelled peas

Cut meat into cubes and fry with the onion in the butter until golden brown. Remove meat and blend in flour. Add stock gradually to make a smooth sauce. Replace meat, cover and simmer for 1 hour until meat is almost cooked. Add vegetables and cook for 40 minutes longer. Serves 6.

Lamb Cutlets in Mint Jelly

1kg neck of lamb
250g fresh peas
4 tomatoes, skinned and sliced
salt
pepper
1 hard-boiled egg, sliced

Cook the lamb and peas with enough water to cover, until meat is tender. Strain off stock, lift out peas and cool meat. Cut meat into cutlets, place on a glass dish to form a ring and cover each cutlet with a layer of sliced ripe tomatoes, then 1 tablespoon green peas. Season with salt and pepper. Slice 1 hard-boiled egg in the centre with a few green peas dotted between. Cover with mint jelly.

Mint Jelly
2 level tablespoons gelatine
2 cups stock
2 tablespoons vinegar
2 tablespoons finely chopped mint

Dissolve the gelatine in stock and add vinegar and mint. Mix well and pour over cutlets, covering them completely. Cool for 2 hours, when the mould will be clear and set. Serves 6.

Lamb Parmigiana

6 lamb chops
1 egg, beaten
1 cup breadcrumbs
4 tablespoons butter
4 tablespoons flour
2 cups milk
60g grated cheese

Dip chops in egg and breadcrumbs and fry until golden brown. Melt butter and blend in flour. Add milk, stir until thick, add grated cheese and blend thoroughly. Put chops in ovenproof dish and pour sauce over. Put a little strip of cheese on each chop and cook under griller until cheese melts. Serve hot with green vegetables and creamed potatoes. Serves 6.

Lamb and Corn Pie

2 slices bread
4 tablespoons butter, melted
500g cold, diced lamb or veal
1 onion, chopped
2 tomatoes, chopped
¾ cup cooked peas
¾ cup cooked corn
2 eggs
2 cups milk
salt
pepper
1 tablespoon chopped parsley

Cut bread into fingers the depth of piedish, brush with butter and arrange round side of piedish. Grease bottom of dish and put in half the meat. Chop onion and tomato and put half over the meat, together with half a cup of mixed peas and corn. Add remaining meat, onions and tomatoes. Beat eggs with milk, season, add parsley and pour over. Arrange more bread fingers diagonally over pie and brush with more melted butter. Bake for ¾-1 hour at 180°C. Arrange remaining peas and corn between bread fingers and return to oven to heat through. Serves 6.

Lamb and Pineapple Flapjacks

125g self-raising flour
½ teaspoon salt
pinch cayenne pepper
1 egg
½ cup milk
1 tablespoon butter, melted
¾ cup cold lamb, diced
2 teaspoons grated onion
6 pineapple slices
6 tomato slices
6 rashers bacon

Sift flour, salt and cayenne into a bowl. Beat egg and milk. Make a well in the centre of flour. Add liquid, stirring from centre outwards, making a smooth batter. Fold in melted butter, lamb and onion. Mix well. Fry a heaped tablespoon at a time in a small quantity of hot fat for 7 or 8 minutes, turning once during cooking. Place a slice of pineapple on top of each flapjack, then a tomato slice. Wrap each in a bacon rasher and secure with toothpick. Cook on greased tray in moderate oven until bacon is cooked. Serves 6.

Pioneer Pot Roast

2 level tablespoons dripping
boned leg of lamb, stuffed with seasoning and
   sewn up (or 1-1.5kg topside steak)
2 onions, sliced
2 potatoes, sliced
salt
pepper

Melt dripping in a large pot. Wipe meat and put into pot over gentle heat. Cover tightly and turn meat when browned on one side, then cook very gently, basting occasionally and allowing quarter of an hour for each 500g meat. In 30 minutes add onions and potatoes, lifting out meat and placing vegetables underneath and sprinkling with salt and pepper. Cover again and cook until roast is done. Lift roast and vegetables into dish; place in oven and thicken gravy, which should be rich and brown, The success of a pot roast depends on slow cooking. If there is any fear of burning place an asbestos mat or sheet of tin under pot. If lamb is used, serve with hot mint sauce. Serves 6.

Shin and Potato Pie

500g shin beef
500g potatoes, sliced
2 onions, cubed
2 carrots, cubed
2 tablespoons chopped parsley
salt
pepper
1 teaspoon brown sugar

Cut beef into cubes and lightly fry with vegetables in a little fat. Then place them in a stewpan and gently cook, with the sliced potatoes on top. Place in a piedish, keeping potatoes on top. Add a little chopped parsley and cover with a crust. Bake at 200°C. Serves 4-6.

Mutton Rice Casserole

2 cups cooked rice
500g cooked mutton
¾ teaspoon salt
2 tablespoons grated onion
2 tablespoons grated celery
1 teaspoon grated lemon rind
¼ teaspoon thyme
¼ teaspoon caraway seeds
1 clove garlic, crushed
1 teaspoon finely chopped parsley
2 teaspoons dried breadcrumbs
1 egg, slightly beaten
stock

Butter a casserole and line bottom and sides with rice. Chop meat finely and put into a saucepan. Add salt, onion, celery, lemon rind, thyme, caraway, garlic, parsley, breadcrumbs and egg. Mix well, adding stock sufficient to be absorbed during cooking. Pour mixture into rice-lined casserole. Put casserole in pan of hot water. Bake for 20-30 minutes at 200°C Serve hot with tomato sauce. Serves 6.

Colonial Minted Mutton

boned leg mutton
olive oil
salt
pepper
1 teaspoon sugar
1 cup breadcrumbs
1 small onion, grated
2 tablespoons chopped raisins
1 tablespoon chopped mint
1 teaspoon sugar
1 teaspoon mixed herbs
1 tablespoon melted butter
2 tablespoons flour
1 level tablespoon blackcurrant jam
1 level tablespoon port wine

Rub the mutton with olive oil, salt, pepper and sugar. Leave overnight, then stuff with the breadcrumbs, onion, raisins, mint, sugar, salt, pepper, herbs and butter. Fill cavity, dredge with flour and bake at 180°C. When making gravy add the jam and wine. Strain. Serve with mashed potatoes and green peas. Serves 6.

Mutton Dish

250g sausage meat
salt
pepper
1 teaspoon thyme
1 teaspoon chopped parsley
½ cup breadcrumbs
2.5kg filleted flap
2 hard-boiled eggs, sliced
2 sheep tongues
2-3 pieces ham, or bacon
loin bones
1 onion
1 carrot

Combine sausage meat, seasoning and breadcrumbs, and spread over flap. Then cover with egg slices, tongue and ham. Roll up securely and fasten in cloth. Put loin bones in cold water with onion and carrot, and when boiling, put in the meat roll. Cook slowly for 2 hours, lift out, placing very heavy weight on it. When cold remove cloth, trim ends and glaze. Serves 6.

Glaze
½ cup water
15g gelatine
1 small onion
salt
meat extract

Put all ingredients in a saucepan and simmer until it turns into a thick syrup.

Mutton Flap with Kidney Stuffing

2 mutton flaps
2 cups breadcrumbs
1 onion, minced
2 teaspoons butter
½ teaspoon sage
½ teaspoon thyme
salt
pepper
2 sheep's kidneys
½ cup fat
1 cup water

Trim mutton flaps and make a stuffing with the breadcrumbs, onion, butter, herbs and seasoning. Lay half the mixture on 1 flap. Slice and season the kidneys and lay on top of the stuffing. Cover with remaining stuffing, put other flap on top and sew together. Place on greaseproof paper, then in a baking dish with the fat and water. Cover and bake for 1½-2 hours at 180°C. Serve hot or cold. Serves 6.

Colonial Goose

shoulder mutton
1 cup breadcrumbs
1 onion, minced
1 teaspoon mixed herbs
125g minced ham (optional)
salt
pepper
flour
1 tablespoon red, or blackcurrant jelly or
  ½ glass port wine

Bone the mutton and fill the cavity with a stuffing made from the breadcrumbs, onion, herbs, ham, salt and pepper. Sprinkle joint with a little flour, bake for 1½ hours at 180°C, basting frequently and add the jelly or wine to the gravy. Serves 6.

Barbecue Roast

1 neck mutton (6 chops in 1 piece)
1 celery stalk, finely chopped
1 level tablespoon mixed mustard
1 tablespoon lemon juice or vinegar
1 onion, finely chopped
1 garlic clove, finely chopped
1 tablespoon brown sugar
1 tablespoon Worcestershire sauce
1 x 300g tin tomato soup

Place meat in a baking dish or a small casserole with a little dripping, and bake for ¾ hour at 190°C. Remove excess fat. Heat together the remaining ingredients, pour over meat and bake for ¾ hour more. Baste frequently with the sauce. Serves 6.

Pork Bones Brawn

pork bones
knuckle veal
2 cups green peas, cooked
2 hard-boiled eggs, sliced
2 tablespoons chopped parsley
salt
pepper
2 teaspoons gelatine

Boil the bones and knuckle of veal in a little water until tender. Lift out meat and place in a bowl with alternate layers of peas, egg, parsley and seasoning. Dissolve the gelatine in 1 cup of the liquid and return to bowl. Cover with a saucer and a weight on top to press. Serve with salad. Serves 6.

Pork Chops Continental

1 chop per person
1 clove garlic
salt
pepper
paprika
2 cups breadcrumbs
1 onion, chopped
1 level tablespoon caraway seed
1 egg yolk, beaten
2 tablespoons milk
50g butter
1 pineapple ring per chop
1 egg white, beaten stiffly
½ cup grated cheese

Rub each chop with the garlic and sprinkle with salt, pepper and a little paprika. Place chops in a casserole. Combine the breadcrumbs, onion, caraway seed, salt and pepper to taste and bind with the egg yolk and milk. Spread this mixture over chops and dot all over with butter. Bake for half an hour at 200°C. Place pineapple rings on the chops, pouring juice around. Combine the egg white, cheese and a dash of paprika and cover the pineapple. Bake a further half an hour at 180°C.

Savoury Chops

1 egg
3 tablespoons flour
½ teaspoon baking powder
pinch salt
pinch pepper
6 pork chops
125g grated cheese
1½ cups white sauce
1 teaspoon mixed herbs
½ cup chopped raisins
¼ cup chopped mint

Combine egg, flour, baking powder, salt and pepper. Dip chops into batter, cover with cheese and bake for 20-30 minutes at 180°C. Serve with white sauce to which has been added the herbs, raisins and mint. Serves 6.

Pork and Corn Savoury

125g fat pickled pork
2 onions, chopped
2 cups sweetcorn, cooked and drained
2 potatoes, mashed
2 tablespoons milk
salt
pepper

Dice pork and fry until some of the fat exudes. Remove meat and fry onions. Add corn potatoes, a little milk, salt and pepper to taste. Add pork pieces place in a greased casserole, dot with butter, cover and heat for 30 minutes at 180°C. Serves 4.

Pork and Almond Casserole

2 tablespoons butter
2 celery stalks, chopped
1 cup cooked macaroni
2 tablespoons flour
salt
pepper
2 teaspoons dry mustard
2 tablespoons Worcestershire sauce
4 tomatoes, sliced
125g grated cheese
2 pork fillets, minced
1 cup breadcrumbs
1 cup roasted almonds, chopped
parsley for garnish

Melt butter in large pan. Add celery, macaroni and blend in flour, salt, pepper, mustard and sauce. Add tomatoes, cheese, pork, and half the almonds. Turn into buttered baking dish, sprinkle with breadcrumbs and remainder of almonds. Bake in oven half an hour, at 200°C. Decorate with parsley and chopped almonds. Serves 4.

Pickled Pork Luncheon

6 slices cooked, pickled pork
4 tablespoons seasoned flour
1 medium tin spaghetti
1 onion, grated
1 teaspoon sugar
salt
pepper
2 large potatoes, mashed

Sprinkle pork with flour and grill until brown. Heat thoroughly the spaghetti, onion, sugar, salt and pepper. On each pork slice place mound of potato and pour over spaghetti sauce. Serves 6.

Cheese and Pumpkin Soup (see p. 9)

Pork Delight

250g dried apricots
rind of 1 lemon, grated
rind of 1 orange, grated
4 cups breadcrumbs
60g chopped walnuts
125g butter
salt
pepper
loin of pork, boned

Soak apricots overnight, chop very finely and stew with the lemon and orange rind. Stir in breadcrumbs, walnuts, butter, salt and pepper to taste. Work well together and use as stuffing for the loin of pork. Spread over thickly, roll up, and skewer well. Cook at 190°C basting frequently. Cut and use when cold. Serves 6.

Pork Supreme

3 large kumaras, or sweet potatoes, peeled,
  cooked and sliced thickly
2 apples, cored and sliced, but not peeled
3 tablespoons melted butter
salt
4 tablespoons brown sugar
6 rib pork chops

Dip kumara and apple slices into melted butter and brown slightly on both sides in a frying pan. Sprinkle kumaras with salt and dust both apples and kumaras with brown sugar and place in baking dish in the oven for 5 minutes. Place chops in a baking dish and bake at 200°C until meat is tender. Serve with the apples and kumaras. Serves 6.

Sucking Pig Supreme

1 sucking pig
2 teaspoons sage
2 large onions, chopped
lard
salt
1 apple
small potatoes

Clean the pig, stuff with the sage and onion and sew up. Draw forefeet under and tie to hind legs. Brush with lard and sprinkle with salt to make meat crisp. Put apple in the mouth and place pig in a baking pan with small potatoes. Sprinkle with flour and roast at 180°C, allowing 25 minutes per 500g weight, basting frequently. Serve with apple sauce and green peas. Serves 12.

Bacon 'Pilau'

2-3 rashers bacon, trimmed
1 onion, chopped
1½ cups chopped left-over meat, rabbit,
  chicken, pork or lambs fry
1 apple, thinly sliced
1 tomato, thinly sliced
seasoning to taste
200g short pastry
125g grated cheese

In a baking dish place the bacon rashers and onion. Add meat, apple, tomato and seasoning. Cover with pastry and sprinkle top with cheese. Bake for 30-45 minutes at 190°C. Serves 6.

Small Sausage Patties

6 pork sausages
2 level tablespoons flour
1 egg, beaten
1 tablespoon milk
1 cup browned breadcrumbs
125g grated cheese
6 slices drained pineapple
6 slices tomato

Skin sausages and shape into flat patties, flour, and shape the size of pineapple slices. Dip in beaten egg mixed with milk, drain and toss in crumbs. Fry on both sides until nicely browned, reduce heat and fry 6-8 minutes longer, turning as necessary. Sprinkle with cheese and arrange a patty on each pineapple slice and a tomato slice on top of this. Dust with salt, pepper and grated cheese, grill until tomato is heated. Serve hot, garnished with parsley. Serves 6.

Sausage Casserole

500g sausages
6 rashers bacon
2 tomatoes, sliced
2-3 carrots, diced
500g peas
1 cup beef stock or water

Prick sausages and wrap strip of bacon around each and place in ovenproof dish. Add tomatoes, carrots and peas and pour in the stock. Simmer gently for 45 minutes. Serves 6.

Corned Beef Special (see p. 30)

Sausage loaf

500g sausages
1 onion, chopped
1 small apple, chopped
pinch of sage
salt
pepper
2 cups dried breadcrumbs
1 cup milk
1 cup beef stock or hot water
2 teaspoons Vegemite
2 eggs, beaten

Boil sausages for 10 minutes, then skin and chop finely, mixing with the onion, apple and seasonings. Add breadcrumbs, milk, and stock with dissolved Vegemite. Mix well, adding eggs, and bake in a greased loaf tin for 1 hour at 180°C. Serves 6.

Devilled Sausages

750g sausages
1 teaspoon mixed mustard
2 teaspoons vinegar
2 teaspoons tomato sauce
½ teaspoon sugar
½ teaspoon salt
6 strips cheese
2 rashers bacon

Split each sausage lengthwise and open out. Mix together mustard, vinegar, tomato sauce, sugar and salt, and spread thickly over each side of split sausage, then into each slit place a strip of cheese and a piece of bacon. Put on a greased oven tray, cover with greased paper and bake for 35-45 minutes at 180°C Serves 6.

Tasty Sausages

1½ cups rice, cooked and drained
1 onion, finely chopped
4 tablespoons tomato sauce
6 sausages, skinned and chopped
1½ cups gravy
1 cup breadcrumbs
2 tablespoons butter

Combine rice, onion and tomato sauce, and line a buttered baking dish with some of this mixture. Add sausage, cover with remaining rice mixture and pour over gravy. Sprinkle with breadcrumbs and dot with butter. Bake at 180°C for 30-40 minutes. Serves 6.

Highland Sausage Patties

1 onion, minced
250g sausage meat
¾ cup rolled oats
1½ cups boiling water
½ teaspoon dried herbs
salt
pepper
1 egg, beaten

Brown onion and meat, stirring well to break up meat. Pour off fat and reserve for frying patties. Add oats, water and herbs, bring to boil, and simmer for half an hour. Cool, add salt, pepper and egg. Grease frying pan and drop large spoonfuls into pan. Cook slowly until brown on both sides. Serve with apple sauce and brown gravy. Serves 6.

Baked Steak

1kg topside steak
2 slices bacon, chopped finely
2 large bananas, sliced
salt
pepper
pinch ground nutmeg
grated rind and juice ½ lemon

Cut a pocket in the steak. Combine bacon, banana, seasonings, lemon juice, rind and parsley if desired. Place mixture in the meat pocket and skewer firmly. Place in a baking dish with a little dripping and water, and bake for 1-1½ hours at 180°C basting frequently. Serves 6.

Creamed Steak

750g lean steak
2½ cups milk
salt
pepper
2 eggs, separated
1¼ cups cream
1 large potato, cooked and mashed
1 teaspoon chopped parsley
1 teaspoon chopped mint
1 level tablespoon grated onion
1 teaspoon baking powder

Cut steak into 2.5cm cubes and place with milk and seasoning in double boiler and cook one hour, then cool a little and turn into a casserole. Beat egg yolks, add cream, and pour over the steak. Now beat egg white until stiff, then stir in potato, parsley, mint, onion and baking powder. Spread this over meat in casserole and cook for 45 minutes at 180°C. Serve with a green vegetable. Any left-over meat is delicious on toast for breakfast or luncheon. Serves 4.

Filet Mignon Mushrooms

6 slices fillet steak
1½ cups breadcrumbs
30g grated cheese
2 slices ham, cooked and chopped
1 teaspoon grated onion
2 tablespoons chopped parsley
1 egg yolk, beaten
2 tablespoons milk
6 large mushrooms
parsley for garnish

Trim steak pieces. Combine breadcrumbs, cheese, chopped ham, onion and parsley. Bind with beaten egg yolk and a little milk. Pile on to mushrooms (stems removed), brush over with butter and bake on greased tray in moderate oven until tender. Meanwhile, grill steak, place a mushroom on each piece and garnish with parsley. Serves 6.

Galantine of Veal and Ham

1.5kg fillet or breast veal, boned
750g sausage meat
salt
pepper
2 tablespoons chopped parsley
250g ham, sliced thinly
4 hard-boiled eggs, sliced

To prepare water for boiling:
veal bones and trimmings
1 carrot
1 onion, stuck with 8 cloves
1 bunch herbs (thyme, sage, parsley)

Lay veal on pastry board, inside uppermost. Make a very few light cuts across and spread with sausage meat (seasoned with salt, pepper and little chopped parsley) about 2.5cm thick. Cover with thin strips of ham, then slices of hard-boiled eggs, and then another layer of seasoned sausage meat. Roll up veal carefully, tie lightly in good shape with tapes, put into scalded pudding cloth and place in prepared boiling water. Have sufficient water just to cover galantine, and into this place bones, trimmings, carrot, onion and herbs tied in fine muslin. After boiling hard 5 minutes, place on gentle heat to simmer steadily 2 hours, then allow to cool in own liquor. When galantine is nearly cold remove from cloth and press between two dishes or boards. Refrigerate and cut in slices. Serves 6.

Savoury Steak with Corn Puffs

500g lean steak in one piece
1 cup breadcrumbs
1 teaspoon thyme
salt
pepper
1 onion, minced
1 teaspoon butter
flour
½ teaspoon sugar
1 tablespoon dripping
corn pudding batter

Spread the meat with a seasoning of breadcrumbs, thyme, salt and pepper to taste, onion and butter. Roll up, fasten with a skewer, dust with flour, pinch of salt and sugar. Place in a baking dish with the dripping and roast for 1¼ hours at 190°C. Twenty minutes before cooked, pour into the dish dessertspoonfuls of corn pudding batter. Serve with brown gravy and a green vegetable. Serves 4.

Corn Pudding Batter
1 egg
1¼ cups milk
1 cup self-raising flour
pinch salt
310g tin sweetcorn

Beat together the egg and milk and stir in the self-raising flour, salt and corn. Mix well and drop spoonfuls into the roasting dish.

Stuffed Steak with Prunes

1kg topside steak in 1 piece
125g prunes, stoned and soaked
1 cup breadcrumbs
1 teaspoon mixed herbs
1 egg, beaten
1 tablespoon butter
salt
pepper
4 rashers bacon

Cut a pocket in the steak and into this put a layer of prunes. Make a seasoning of the breadcrumbs, herbs, egg, butter, salt and pepper to taste. Mix well, place on top of the prunes and add another layer of prunes over the seasoning. Fasten the opening with skewers, place in a roasting dish with plenty of dripping, and roast for 1 hour at 180°C turning the meat several times. Place the bacon on the meat and roast for another half hour. Serves 6.

Savoury Mince Roll

750g blade steak
½ ox kidney
1 onion
salt
pepper
3 cups water
short pastry
mixed herbs

Mince meat and onion, adding salt and pepper. Place in saucepan with 3 cups water and simmer gently for 1 hour. Drain liquid from meat and set it aside for gravy. Make short pastry substituting 1 tablespoon curry powder for 1 tablespoon flour. Roll out and spread with cooked meat. Sprinkle over a few herbs and roll as for jam roll. Place in baking dish. Bake in a moderate oven for 1 hour. Serve with gravy made from liquid thickened with cornflour. A little vegetable or meat extract may be added if desired. Serves 6.

Savoury Pot Roast

1.5–2kg roast, chuck, rump or shoulder
salt
1 clove garlic
2 cups sour cream
3 tablespoons fat
2 tablespoons grated lemon rind
carrots

Rub the roast well with salt and cut garlic. Then place garlic in sour cream to flavour it. Heat fat in a heavy pan, tightly covered. Brown roast lightly in the fat, add grated lemon rind, allow to simmer few minutes before pouring sour cream over it and spooning pan gravy over meat. Cover and cook over very low heat 2 hours, basting occasionally. About 30 minutes before meat is done, add several small carrots to brown in the sauce. The garlic clove may be left in the sauce for first 30 minutes, then removed. Serve with carrots and peas. This roast is excellent for slicing cold and delicious eaten hot. Serves 6.

Tropical Loaf

3 tablespoons brown sugar
2 tablespoons lemon juice
5 large bananas
1kg steak, finely minced
½ cup breadcrumbs
½ cup milk
2 eggs, beaten

Sprinkle brown sugar and lemon juice in greased oblong baking dish. Arrange 2 bananas in a design in the bottom. Dice remaining 3 bananas and mix in with steak, crumbs, milk and eggs. Pack carefully into baking dish. Bake for 30 minutes at 200°C. Serves 6.

Prime Veal

1kg veal in a piece
125g prunes, stoned and soaked in cold water
1 teaspoon onion
salt
pepper
flour

Wipe the veal with a damp cloth and cut a pocket by inserting a knife in the thickest part. Chop the prunes roughly, combine with the onion, salt and pepper, and insert into the prepared pocket. Sew up, or skewer, and dredge with flour. Roast for 1–1½ hours at 180°C. Serves 4–6.

Veal Casserole

90g bacon fat
1 large onion, chopped
750g fillet of veal, cut into serving pieces
2 tablespoons flour
2½ cups beef stock, or water
2 large cups breadcrumbs
2 rashers bacon
1 tablespoon chopped parsley
1 teaspoon mixed herbs
seasoning

Melt 60g bacon fat and fry onion until golden. Remove from pan, and lightly sear meat. Place in casserole with onion. Thicken the fat left in the pan with flour, add stock, stirring over gentle heat. Pour over meat, cover, and cook for 20 minutes at 180°C. Melt 30g bacon fat and mix with breadcrumbs. Cut bacon rashers into small pieces and add to breadcrumbs with parsley, herbs and seasoning. Remove lid and sprinkle over meat. Return, uncovered, to oven for approximately 40 minutes. Serves 6.

Veal Pot Roast

3.5kg leg of veal
2 teaspoons dry mustard
½ teaspoon each sage and thyme
1½ tablespoons flour
1 tablespoon sugar
2 teaspoons salt
½ teaspoon pepper
fat
2 tablespoons vinegar
1 large onion, chopped
1 tablespoon chopped parsley
6 celery leaves
500g small potatoes (optional)
250g whole carrots (optional)

Roll the meat and dredge in a mixture of the mustard, herbs, flour, sugar, salt and pepper. Brown well in hot fat, then add the vinegar, onion, parsley and celery leaves. Cover tightly and simmer for 2–2½ hours until tender. In the last part of cooking, the potatoes and carrots may be added and braised with the veal. Make gravy with the juices. Serves 6.

Veal with Chestnuts and Mushrooms

1.5kg boned leg of veal
1 thick slice fat bacon
salt
pepper

Cover the meat with the bacon, or alternatively roll in butter well seasoned with salt, pepper and chopped parsley. Season the meat well and roast for 1 hour at 180°C. Serve with chestnut cream, mashed potato and greens. Serves 4.

Chestnut Cream
30g butter
2 tablespoons brandy
125g mushrooms, chopped finely
125g chestnuts, or chestnut purée
3 tablespoons cream

Cream together the butter, brandy and half the mushrooms. Scald and skin the chestnuts and simmer in milk until tender, then strain and pass through a sieve. Put in a casserole, with the butter-brandy mixture, add the cream and cover with the mushrooms. Cook for 30 minutes at 150°C. A few minutes before serving pour brandy over and light.

Savoury Veal

2 hard-boiled eggs, sliced
2 tablespoons finely chopped parsley
500g raw veal, chopped finely
250g ham, chopped finely
salt
pepper
1 teaspoon mixed herbs
2 tablespoons vegetable fat, or butter
lettuce leaves, for garnish
cress, for garnish
mustard, for garnish

Grease an ovenproof dish or a souffle tin and line the bottom with egg slices, sprinkling with 1 tablespoon of parsley. Put in a layer of veal and ham, sprinkle well with salt and pepper, parsley and herbs. Add another layer of meat and then seasoning. Continue until dish is filled. Place small pieces of fat over the surface and add enough water to cover the meat. Cover with greaseproof paper and bake for 1 hour at 190°C. Remove the paper, lay a plate over the meat with a weight on it and bake for another hour at 150°C. When cold, turn out a garnish with lettuce, mustard and cress. Serves 6.

Using Offal

Brain and Ham Pie

4 sets sheep's brains
¼ teaspoon pepper
pinch nutmeg
125g ham, chopped
1 tablespoon lemon or orange juice
1 cup breadcrumbs
butter

Skin brains and simmer gently in salted water for 15 minutes. Drain and chop, adding pepper, nutmeg, ham and juice. Mix all thoroughly and put in greased piedish, placing small pieces of orange or lemon on top. Sprinkle over breadcrumbs and dot with butter. Bake for 20 minutes at 200°C. Serve with mixed vegetables. Serves 4.

French Kidney Pudding

5-6 kidneys
1 onion, chopped
1 tomato, sliced
salt
pepper
pinch dry mustard
1 rasher bacon, sliced
1 level tablespoon melted butter
½ cup breadcrumbs

Skin kidneys and split nearly through. Slice onion and tomato and season with salt, pepper and mustard, cut bacon into strips and place a slice of bacon, onion and tomato in each kidney and dip in melted butter and sew or skewer. Sprinkle with breadcrumbs and grill in oven. Serve with potato chips and green peas. Serves 4.

Mushroom and Kidney Grill

3 kidneys
90g butter, melted
salt
pepper
6 mushrooms
3 rashers bacon

Split and skin kidneys, dip in melted butter and season to taste. Into each slit place a prepared mushroom and a piece of bacon. Grill under a low flame. Serve with fried tomatoes on toast. Serves 6.

Italian Kidneys

90g spaghetti
90g butter
1 large onion, finely chopped
1 slice bread
3-4 kidneys
salt
pepper
4 tablespoons flour
1 cup beef stock, or water

Cook spaghetti in fast-boiling salted water for 15 minutes. Melt butter in saucepan and cook finely-chopped onions until brown. Add small squares of bread, fry brown on both sides, then lift from pan. Coat kidneys with salt, pepper and flour, add to onion and cook 10 minutes. Now add 1 cup stock or water and stir until mixture thickens. Strain spaghetti, add to onion and kidney mixture and serve on hot dish surrounded with fried bread. Serves 4.

Baked Mushrooms and Kidneys

1 tablespoon butter
1 onion, chopped
3-4 sheep's kidneys, chopped
250g mushrooms, chopped
1 tablespoon Worcestershire sauce
1 teaspoon sugar
salt
pepper
1 tablespoon water
1 level tablespoon flour
1 cup breadcrumbs

Melt butter in frying pan and lightly fry onion and kidneys. Add mushrooms, sauce, sugar, salt and pepper. Thicken with the flour and water mixed together. Place in piedish, cover with crumbs and bake for 15 minutes at 200°C. Serves 6.

Spanish Kidneys

8 kidneys
flour
2 onions, finely chopped
½ cup chopped bacon
2 tablespoons butter
1 green pepper, chopped
1 cup tomato puree, or soup
1 cup hot water
salt
pepper
1 tablespoon chopped parsley

Skin and trim kidneys, cut into thin slices and dredge evenly with flour. Fry onion and bacon in butter until golden brown, then add green pepper and kidney slices. Cook 15 minutes longer, stirring constantly. Add tomato puree and hot water and season to taste. Cover pan and simmer slowly 45 minutes. Before serving, add chopped parsley. Serves 8.

Steak and Kidney Pudding

750g stewing steak
1 sheep's kidney
1 heaped tablespoon flour, seasoned
1 onion, chopped
1 tablespoon finely chopped parsley
½ cup cold water

Cut steak in strips, removing most of the fat. Wash kidneys, remove skin and cut into small pieces. Roll kidney pieces in each piece of steak and toss in flour. Put in greased basin with onion, parsley and water, and cover with pastry.

Pastry
250g flour
1 teaspoon baking powder
½ teaspoon salt
125g finely chopped suet, or lard, or margarine
cold water

Rub fat into dry ingredients and mix to a slack dough (not too moist) with the water. Roll into a round and fit on top of basin. Cover with 2 layers of greaseproof paper and steam for 2 hours. Serves 6.

Baked Lamb's Fry and Bacon

1 lamb's fry
seasoned flour
3 tablespoons soft breadcrumbs
1 onion, grated
1 tablespoon chopped parsley
salt
pepper
1 egg yolk
4 rashers bacon
1¼ cups beef stock, or water
1 tablespoon Worcestershire sauce

Skin, dry and cut the lamb's fry into 12mm thick slices. Dust with seasoned flour. Mix breadcrumbs with grated onion, parsley, salt, pepper and egg yolk. Spread this over liver slices, cover with strips of bacon and place in greased baking dish. Pour stock over and bake at 150°C until liver is tender, approximately 1 hour. Serve with brown gravy flavoured with Worcestershire sauce. Serves 4.

Mixed Lamb's Fry

750g lamb's fry
45g butter
2 onions, chopped
5 slices lean bacon
2 bananas, chopped
5 small tomatoes, chopped
salt
pepper

Cut liver into medium-sized pieces, wash under boiling water and grill under medium heat until cooked, 15-20 minutes. Melt butter in frying pan, add chopped onion, and cook without browning until tender. Then add bacon, cut-up bananas, tomatoes, pepper and salt to ingredients in frying pan, and cook slowly 5-10 minutes. Pour mixture over liver. Serves 4.

Stuffed Fry

1 lamb's fry
1 cup breadcrumbs
1 level tablespoon chopped onion
½ teaspoon thyme
½ teaspoon grated lemon rind
1 level tablespoon butter
2 tablespoons milk, or beaten egg
2 tablespoons seasoned flour
1 cup boiling water

Cut a pocket in the thickest end of the dry, skinned liver. Combine breadcrumbs, onions, thyme, lemon and fat and bind with milk or egg. Fill prepared pocket and sew up. Dust with seasoned flour. Melt fat in pan and fry liver on both sides until a light brown. Put in an ovenproof dish with 1 cup boiling water, cover and bake for 1 hour at 180°C. Serves 4.

Liver and Tomato Mince

1 onion, minced
30g butter
500g liver, skinned and minced
1 level tablespoon flour
salt
pepper
1 cup beef stock, gravy or water
3 medium tomatoes, skinned and chopped

Lightly fry the onion in the melted butter. Add liver, stirring frequently. When browned, pour off surplus fat, add flour, salt, pepper, stock and tomatoes. Simmer for half an hour. Serves 4.

Sheep's Heart Ragout

3 sheep's hearts, washed and chopped
1 kidney, washed and chopped
1 tablespoon butter, or bacon fat
1 onion, chopped
1 cup water
½ teaspoon salt
pinch pepper
1 tablespoon flour
1 tablespoon Worcestershire sauce
2 tablespoons chopped parsley

Brown the meat in the melted fat. Add onion, and when browned add water, salt and pepper, and thicken with the flour moistened with the sauce. Put in ovenproof dish and scatter with parsley. Cover and cook for an hour at 180°C, then pour over apple batter. Serves 4-6.

Apple Batter
1 cup flour
½ teaspoon baking powder
pinch salt
pinch pepper
1 egg, beaten
2 tablespoons water
1 large apple, peeled, cored and ringed

Combine flour, baking powder, salt, pepper, egg and water, and beat until smooth. Place apple rings over meat and pour over batter. Cook for half an hour uncovered.

Sweetbread Pie

500g sweetbread
250g flaky pastry
2 onions, thinly sliced
2 tomatoes, thinly sliced
4 rashers bacon
salt
pepper
2 eggs, lightly beaten
1 cup milk
2 tablespoons chopped parsley

Boil sweetbreads in water until tender. When cool, skin and chop finely. Line a piedish with flaky pastry and cover with alternate layers of thinly-sliced onion, tomatoes, sweetbreads and bacon. Sprinkle lightly with pepper and salt. Lightly beat 2 eggs, combine with 1 cup milk and pour over the ingredients, adding chopped parsley. Cover with pastry and bake at 200°C until well browned. Serves 6.

Savoury Baked Tongue

1 ox tongue
¼ cup vinegar
1 teaspoon mixed spice
1 bay leaf
4 celery stalks, minced
1 level tablespoon treacle
2 tablespoons flour
½ cup sherry
1 cup raisins
juice 1 lemon

Wash and scrape tongue. Place in saucepan, barely cover with water and add vinegar, spice, bay leaf, celery and treacle. Simmer 2-2½ hours or until tender. Lift out, skin and trim tongue. Place in a greased baking dish, dredge with flour and pour over the sherry. Simmer raisins in lemon juice and pour over tongue. Bake for half an hour at 200°C. Press overnight. Serve with Beetroot Slices. Serves 6.

Baked Tripe

4 thin slices bread, buttered
500g diced, cooked tripe
2 cups tripe liquid
salt
pepper
1 egg, beaten
butter, as required

Butter a piedish and in the bottom place a thin slice of crustless bread. Over this spread the tripe. Cover with another slice of bread, add rest of tripe and lastly cover with 2 slices of bread, buttered side up. Season tripe liquid well, add egg, and pour over dish. Leave for 1 hour and then bake for 15 minutes at 220°C. Serves 4.

Breakfast Tripe

500g tripe
frying batter
bacon fat, or dripping
4 poached eggs
salt
pepper
parsley, for garnish

Soak tripe in cold water for 1 hour. Bring to boil and pour water away. Boil in fresh water until tender. Lift out when cold and cut into rounds. Dip in thin frying batter and fry in bacon fat or dripping. Serve with poached egg on top with pepper, salt and chopped parsley. Serves 4.

Tripe Mould

500g tripe
1 large onion
1 tablespoon chopped mint
1 tablespoon chopped parsley
1 tablespoon chopped chives
1 tablespoon lemon juice
salt
pepper
2 tablespoons gelatine
1½ cups boiling water from tripe

Boil tripe with onion until tender. When cold cut into 2.5cm squares. Mix together mint, parsley, chives, lemon juice, salt and pepper. Melt gelatine in the water and then add all ingredients. Pour into a mould to set. Serve with salad and Lemon dressing. Serves 6.

Lemon dressing
1 teaspoon dry mustard
½ teaspoon salt
½ teaspoon pepper
1 teaspoon sugar
½ cup cream
½ cup lemon juice

Mix all ingredients and chill before serving.

Tripe Poultry Illusion

500g tripe
1 teaspoon mixed herbs
1 large onion, finely chopped
1 medium carrot, grated
salt
pepper
1 cup flour, seasoned
1 egg, beaten
1 cup breadcrumbs

Bring tripe quickly to the boil, drop in herbs tied in a piece of muslin, and simmer until tender. Cool, pull tripe to pieces with fork and mash well. Add onion, carrot, salt and pepper. Mix well and roll into balls. Dip in flour, egg and breadcrumbs and fry until golden. Serves 6.

Stuffed Tripe Roast

500g tripe
1½ cups breadcrumbs
½ cup chopped parsley
1 teaspoon mixed herbs
1 onion, chopped
1 tablespoon lemon juice
1 tablespoon bacon fat, or dripping, melted
salt
pepper
1 egg, beaten
4 rashers bacon

Boil tripe in the piece until tender. Cool. Mix together the breadcrumbs, parsley, herbs, onion, lemon juice, fat and seasoning to taste. Mix well with the egg. Put stuffing on the honeycomb side of the tripe, roll and fasten. Put into a greased baking dish and cover with bacon. Bake, covered, for 40 minutes at 200°C. Serve with mashed potatoes and onion sauce. Serves 6.

FORCEMEAT AND SAUCES

Forcemeats are added to meats, poultry, fish, and game to give added flavour. The basis of all stuffing is usually dry breadcrumbs, but cooked macaroni, noodles, boiled rice or oatmeal are all suitable. Many different flavours and seasonings may be used. Sage or thyme are the common ones but minced ham, bacon, sausage meat, oysters, chopped onions, chives, celery, mushrooms, minced liver, giblets and hard-boiled eggs all make interesting stuffings.

If the stuffing is for very lean meat such as topside, veal fillet or venison, include some fat, such as dripping, butter or fat bacon. Then, if the meat is fatty, e.g., pork, don't use any added fat.

Bind the dry ingredients with milk, beaten egg, white sauce or any sauce or oyster liquor. Make it stick together but don't have it too wet; the best way is to squeeze it dry in the hands. Salt, pepper and celery salt are added to all forcemeat preparations but additional spices may include caraway seeds, mustard, horseradish, ginger, cloves, nutmeg, mace, cinnamon, cayenne or curry powder.

Apple Sauce

6 apples, peeled and chopped
1 tablespoon water
1 teaspoon sugar
1 cup brown gravy

Stew the apples with the water and sugar and when soft add the gravy, mix well and serve hot.

Bechamel Sauce

2½ cups milk, or 1¼ cups milk and
  1¼ cups stock
1 blade mace
salt
pepper
2 cloves
60g butter
3 peppercorns
2 tablespoons flour
pinch nutmeg

Blend together all the ingredients in a saucepan over low heat and cook until thick. Strain and serve.

Bearnaise Sauce

½ cup vinegar
1 spring onion, chopped
60g butter
1 teaspoon flour
¼ cup milk
3 egg yolks
juice 1 lemon
1 small onion, finely chopped

Put into the top of a double boiler the vinegar, spring onion, butter, flour and milk. Cook slowly stirring continuously, until the liquid has reduced to an eighth of its original quantity. Put the egg yolks in a bowl with the lemon juice and onion, beat well and slowly add to the vinegar mixture, stirring constantly over a low heat for a few minutes. Serve with steak or vegetables.

Bread Sauce

1 cup breadcrumbs
1¼ cups milk
1 small onion, stuck with 6 cloves
salt
pepper
30g butter

Soak the breadcrumbs in the milk flavoured with the stuck onion. Simmer gently for half an hour, then remove the onion, season to taste, and beat in the butter until dissolved.

Brown Sauce

1 tablespoon dripping
1 onion, sliced finely
1 tablespoon flour
1 cup water, or vegetable stock
1 teaspoon Marmite, or tomato sauce
  (optional)

Melt the dripping in a saucepan and when smoking hot add the onion. Brown well and add the flour, browning lightly. Remove the saucepan from the heat and add the water or stock gradually mixing all the time. Stir until boiling, season and strain. Marmite, meat extract, tomato sauce or pulp may be added.

Mushroom Sauce

6 mushrooms, chopped
½ cup water, or stock
1 tablespoon Worcestershire sauce
1 level tablespoon flour
salt
pepper

Fry the mushrooms in a little fat, add the water or stock, the sauce and thicken with the flour. Season to taste.

Mustard Sauce

1 level tablespoon butter, or olive oil
1½ cups milk
2 egg yolks, well beaten
2 tablespoons flour
½ teaspoon salt
¼ teaspoon pepper
2 teaspoons mustard
juice 2 lemons
1 onion, grated

Melt the butter in a saucepan over hot water. Add the milk and the egg yolks, then stir in the flour and seasoning mixed with the lemon juice. Add the onion just before serving.

Tomato Sauce (Hot)

1 tablespoon dripping
1 onion, sliced
3-4 tomatoes, sliced
1 cup water, or vegetable stock
1 tablespoon flour
salt
pepper

Melt the dripping in a saucepan, add the onion and cook for 10 minutes without browning. Add the tomatoes and stock, cook slowly until vegetables are soft, then press through a sieve. Thicken by adding flour mixed to a paste with cold water. Stir until boiling. Season to taste.

Forcemeat (Sample Recipe)

1½ cups breadcrumbs
1 small onion, chopped
1 teaspoon chopped parsley
125g chopped ham, or bacon
1 tablespoon dripping
1 egg, or white sauce to bind
½ teaspoon grated lemon rind, or peel
salt
pepper
½ teaspoon curry powder (optional)
1 tablespoon tomato puree (optional)

Combine all the ingredients and blend thoroughly.

Forcemeat Balls

2 cups breadcrumbs
1 onion, finely chopped
1 tablespoon chopped parsley
½ teaspoon thyme
salt
pepper
1 egg, beaten

Combine all the ingredients, blend thoroughly, form spoonfuls into balls and place around the joint half an hour before serving.

White Sauce

30g butter
4 tablespoons flour
1¼ cups milk
salt
pepper
squeeze lemon juice

Melt butter in enamel or aluminium pan. Stir in flour with a wooden spoon and wait until butter and flour bubble all over. Draw pan off flame and add a little milk. Stir briskly until smooth. Add rest of milk, stirring well continuously. Return to heat and bring to the boil, still stirring constantly. Boil for 2-3 minutes and season with salt, pepper and lemon juice. This is a plain white sauce to serve with cauliflower, fish, artichokes etc.

Variations

Caper Sauce: Make a white sauce, with ½ cup milk and ½ cup boiled mutton liquor, and add 1 tablespoon of chopped capers.

Parsley Sauce: Add a tablespoon chopped parsley to the foundation white sauce.

Onion Sauce: Add 1 large onion, chopped and previously cooked until soft in boiling water with a little salt.

Cheese Sauce: Add 45g grated cheese after sauce has boiled. Season with a little cayenne pepper and salt.

Celery Sauce: Add 2 sticks celery, cooked until soft and chopped small.

POULTRY AND GAME

What to serve with Poultry and Game

Roast duck: Orange sauce, sage, chestnut or oyster stuffing, gravy made from giblets.
Roast goose: As for duck, or serve with apple sauce, baked apple rings, apple forcemeat gravy.

Roast Chicken: Sage or oyster stuffing, bread sauce, bacon or ham, gravy.
Roast turkey: Sage or oyster stuffing, cranberry sauce or japonica apple jelly, gravy made from giblets.
Steamed chicken: White or parsley sauce, bacon.
Steamed rabbit: Parsley or onion sauce, bacon.
Venison: Gravy with port wine flavouring, apple rings, bacon.

Baked Spring Chicken

2 broiling chickens
250g sausage meat
6 tablespoons melted butter
4 rashers bacon
4 large celery stalks, sliced
4 large onions, halved
4 carrots, quartered lengthwise
salt

Split chickens in two. Wash, dry well and cover inside lightly with a layer of sausage meat. Brush with melted butter and place skin side up in a covered baking dish. Put a slice of bacon on each chicken half. Wash celery, and scrape well. Cut peeled onions in half crosswise. Scrape carrots and quarter lengthwise. Brush vegetables with melted butter, place round chicken, and sprinkle salt all over. Cover and bake for 50 minutes at 180°C. Half-way through cooking time, brush chicken again with melted butter. Serve with small, new potatoes, tossed in melted butter and then finely-grated cheese. Serves 8.

Baronet's Curry

1 chicken
60g butter
1½ teaspoons curry powder
½ teaspoon salt
1½ teaspoons flour
½ cup desiccated coconut
1¼ cups milk
½ teaspoon sugar
30g blanched, ground almonds
1 tablespoon cream
juice ½ lemon

Joint chicken into serving pieces and fry lightly in hot butter. Remove and add to the pan the curry powder, salt, flour, coconut, and stir until dry but not brown. Add milk and when boiling, add sugar, almonds and chicken joints. Cook for 1½ hours, stirring occasionally, then add cream and, just before serving, the lemon juice. Serves 4.

Boiled Chicken

1 chicken
salt
1 onion
1 carrot
6 white peppercorns
1 slice turnip
2 tablespoons butter
1 teaspoon lemon juice
2 tablespoons flour
1½ cups hot chicken stock
1 large carrot, cooked
125g peas, cooked
2 egg yolks, beaten
salt
pepper
pinch paprika
1 tablespoon chopped parsley

Boil chicken in water and add a little salt, the onion, carrot, peppercorns, and turnip. When cooked remove to a hot serving dish. Boil liquor to reduce to 2½ cups. Melt the butter, add the lemon juice, stir in the flour and then slowly stir in the stock. Keep stirring until boiling. Boil 2 minutes, then add the cooked carrots, peas, egg yolks, a little salt, pepper and paprika. Stir until quite hot, pour around chicken and sprinkle with the parsley. Serves 4.

Chicken Croquettes

½ cup milk
salt
pepper
2 tablespoons chopped parsley
2 tablespoons flour
1 tablespoon butter
2 cups cooked, chopped chicken
1 egg, beaten
1 cup fine breadcrumbs
oil or lard for frying

Make a sauce with the butter, flour, milk, salt, pepper, and parsley. Stir in the cold chicken. When cold, shape into rolls, dip in egg and breadcrumbs and fry in hot lard until golden brown. Serves 4.

Chicken Ham Kedgeree

2 tablespoons shortening
2 tablespoons minced ham
1 cup cooked chicken, minced.finely
1 cup cooked rice
1 tablespoon tomato sauce
½ teaspoon mixed herbs
1 hard-boiled egg, sliced
2 tablespoons finely chopped parsley

Melt shortening in a saucepan and warm the ham. Add the chicken, rice, sauce and seasonings and cook 3 minutes longer. Serve in individual dishes garnished with egg slices and parsley. Serves 4.

Creamed Chicken Pie

1 young chicken
1 onion, peeled
4 cloves
1 blade mace
125g butter
4 tablespoons flour
1 cup cream
185g flaky pastry

Place chicken in a saucepan, cover with water, add the onion, cloves and mace, and boil without salt until tender. Remove all bones, fat and skin, cut into small pieces and place in a piedish. Melt the butter and when bubbling stir in the flour. Stir until mixture froths, then add the cream. When well blended add the chicken broth. Stir until smooth, then pour over chicken and leave until cold. Cover with pastry and bake at 210°C until pastry is browned. Serves 6.

Chicken Fricassee with Kumara Scones

2 x 1.5kg chickens
8 cups boiling water
1 onion, sliced
1½ teaspoons salt
6 tablespoons corn flour
½ cup cold water

Cook the chickens until tender in a saucepan with the water, onion and salt. Remove from broth, skin and remove bones, leaving the chickens in fairly large pieces. Thicken gravy with the flour blended to a smooth paste with the cold water. Bring to the boil and add the chicken meat. Serve with hot kumara scones. Serves 6.

Kumara Scones
1 large kumara, or sweet potato, cooked
   and mashed
⅔ cup milk
4 tablespoons melted butter
125g flour
2 teaspoons baking powder
1 tablespoon sugar
½ teaspoon salt

Mix together the kumara, milk and butter. Add the remaining ingredients to make a soft dough. Turn out on to a floured board and toss lightly until outside looks smooth. Roll out 2cm thick, cut into small scones and bake on a greased tray for approximately 15 minutes at 230°C.

Chicken Puffs

2 onions, chopped
2 rashers bacon, chopped
1 large potato, diced
1 medium tomato, chopped
1 tablespoon curry powder mixed with a little
   cold water
½ meat cube dissolved in ½ cup hot water
salt
pepper
2 cups cooked, diced chicken
250g puff pastry

Fry the onions, bacon, potato and tomato. Add the curry, meat extract, salt and pepper and fry until tender. Add the chicken and thicken if necessary. Cut pastry into rounds, place 1 tablespoon of the mixture in the centre of each, fold over and bake at 230°C until pastry is cooked. Serves 4.

Christmas Mixup

1 cup cold, minced turkey
½ cup dry breadcrumbs
¼ teaspoon pepper
¼ teaspoon dry mustard
¼ teaspoon curry powder
½ onion, grated
1 tablespoon butter, melted
parsley for garnish

Mix together the turkey, breadcrumbs, pepper, mustard, curry powder, onion and butter. Heat through, adding enough gravy to make a stiff consistency. Serve on toast. Garnish with parsley. Serves 4.

Spanish Chicken Mould

6 medium tomatoes, stewed
1 stalk celery, finely chopped
1 small onion, sliced
1 tablespoon chopped parsley
1 bay leaf
3 cloves
3 peppercorns
2 tablespoons gelatine
¼ cup cold water
1 cup cold, cooked and diced chicken or turkey
1 cup cooked and diced ham
4 hard-boiled eggs, chopped

Put tomatoes in a saucepan with the celery, onion, parsley, bay leaf, cloves and peppercorns. Cook for 20 minutes, then strain. Soften gelatine in the cold water, stir into the tomato mixture and pour into a mould which has been brushed with olive or salad oil. Chop up the poultry and ham and combine with the chopped eggs. When gelatin mixture has begun to set, add the meat and egg and leave to set. To serve turn out on to a plate lined with lettuce leaves. Serves 6.

Chicken Salad Pies

250g short pastry
90g cheese, grated
2 cups diced, cooked chicken
2 tablespoons finely chopped onion
1 stalk celery, diced
1 hard-boiled egg, finely chopped
2 tablespoons chopped pickles
½ green pepper, finely chopped
30g walnuts, chopped
1 tablespoon lemon juice
¼ teaspoon salt
½ cup mayonnaise
2 hard-boiled eggs, cut in wedges
watercress and lettuce, for garnish
olives, for garnish

Roll out pastry 6mm thick, sprinkle lightly with cheese and roll cheese into the dough. Line 4 individual tins with the dough, prick with a fork and bake blind for 15-20 minutes at 190°C. In a chilled bowl combine the chicken, onion, celery, egg, pickles, green pepper and walnuts. Sprinkle mixture with the lemon juice and salt and chill thoroughly. When ready to use, blend chilled mixture with mayonnaise. Fill pastry shells with the salad and garnish with egg wedges. Arrange shells on a platter or salad dish and alternate with sprigs of watercress and lettuce leaves. Fill lettuce leaves with mayonnaise and garnish with olive slices. Serves 4.

Perfect Fried Chicken

1 cup flour
1½ level tablespoons paprika
1½ teaspoons salt
1 steamed chicken, jointed
fat, for frying

Mix flour, paprika and salt, and rub into the surface of the chicken. Place on a rack to dry before frying. Heat fat in a heavy pan so that fat is 6mm deep. When very hot, fry the large joints and reduce heat gradually when browning starts. Do not overcrowd pan. Turn two or three times. Add 2-3 tablespoons of water when all the joints are browned, and simmer gently until chicken is tender – approximately 15-20 minutes. If a small chicken is used it may be possible to fry the joints without steaming them first. In this case, give 50-60 minutes' simmering time. Remove cover of pan for last 15 minutes' cooking time to restore crispness. The secret of the rich golden brown colour lies in the generous quantity of paprika used in the covering. Serves 4.

Creamed Chicken

3 tablespoons flour
3 tablespoons butter, melted
1½ cups milk
salt
pepper
1-2 cups cooked, cubed chicken

Add the flour to the melted butter and stir until smooth. Add milk gradually, then salt and pepper, and cook for 10 minutes stirring constantly. Stir in the chicken and heat through. Serve with rolls. If preferred as a hot dish, place the rolls in a casserole and pour the creamed chicken over them. Bake at 180°C until heated through. Serves 4.

Chicken Ham Rolls

¾ cup cooked rice
2 tablespoons chopped parsley
90g slivered toasted almonds
3 tablespoons melted butter
salt
pepper
½ teaspoon mixed herbs
6 slices cooked ham

Mix together the rice, parsley, almonds, butter and seasoning. Place some of the mixture on each slice of ham, and roll up. Place rolls on a serving plate and serve with green peas and creamed chicken. Serves 6.

Boiling Fowl Casserole

1 boiling chicken
4 rashers bacon
3 tomatoes, sliced
1 cup white stock (which has been made from skimmed liquid over which fowl has been steamed)
1 cup milk
flour, for thickening
1 tablespoon chopped parsley

Steam bird for 1½ hours. Cool, then cut into sections. In bottom of casserole lay the bacon rashers and a layer of tomato. Arrange chicken pieces on top and add the stock and the milk. Cook gently in a covered casserole until tender, about 1-1½ hours. Lift out, skim and thicken stock and add parsley. Serve with new potatoes, and green peas. Even the toughest bird will be made tender by this method. Serves 4.

Braised Fowl

4 rashers bacon
1 onion, sliced
2 carrots, quartered
1 turnip, quartered
1 boiling chicken
2 rashers bacon
4 cloves
1 tablespoon mixed herbs
2½ cups water
2 tablespoons flour

Put bacon, onion, carrot and turnip in a large saucepan. Place fowl on top with a few bacon slices on the breast. Season with cloves and herbs and add water. Cover all with greaseproof paper, keeping the lid on all the time and simmer 2-2½ hours, basting through the paper from time to time. When tender, lift fowl into a baking dish and sprinkle with flour. Pour over brown gravy and place in oven for 10 minutes. Serve with new potatoes and green peas. Serves 4.

Brown Gravy
1 small onion, sliced
1 tablespoon dripping, melted
1 tablespoon flour
1 cup water
salt
pepper
1 teaspoon vinegar
½ teaspoon Marmite

Brown the onion in the dripping. Sprinkle in the flour and brown lightly. Gradually stir in water and season with salt, pepper, vinegar and Marmite.

Three-in-One Chicken

bouquet garni
1 large, boiling chicken, washed and dried well
1 tablespoon barley per person and 1 extra for pot
1 large carrot, grated or diced
1 parsnip, or turnip, quartered
cornflour, optional

Place bouquet garni inside the chicken before sewing up. Place in a large pot with salted, tepid water, barley and vegetables and simmer for 1½-2 hours. The broth can be served, sufficiently salted and thickened, if desired, with cornflour.

Sauce for Poultry
2 tablespoons butter
2 tablespoons flour
1 cup milk
1 cup chicken stock
hard-boiled eggs, or cooked asparagus, mushrooms, gherkins or any available garnish
125g breadcrumbs

Remove bones, keep in neat portions and place in a greased casserole. Make a sauce with the butter, flour, milk and stock and pour over poultry. Decorate with garnish, sprinkle with crumbs and place in oven to heat. Serve with green peas and new potatoes.

For Savoury
Place any remains of mixture between thick buttered toast and grill few minutes. An alternative method is to mince portions of remaining fowl with grilled bacon, and place between toast, with one side spread thickly with mustard.

Giblet Pie

giblets
1 onion
2 hard-boiled eggs
185g black pudding, sliced
185g short pastry

Simmer for 1½ hours the neck, heart, wings, gizzard and liver of a chicken with the onion. Put a small cup into the centre of a piedish, pour the simmered giblets around and garnish with the egg and black pudding slices. Cover with pastry and bake until well browned. Serves 4.

Chicken Salad Pies (see p. 53)

Roast Goose with Raisin Stuffing

5-6kg young goose
baking soda
salt
pepper
poultry seasoning
cinnamon apples for garnish

Clean goose thoroughly, then wash well in water to which is added a little baking soda. Rub goose inside and out with salt and pepper mixed with the seasoning, and leave overnight. There are various kinds of fillings suitable for goose, and the old-time one of sage and onions is a good bread dressing seasoned and flavoured. The more nourishing and wholesome filling is raisin and apple stuffing. Serves 8.

Raisin and Apple Stuffing
3 cups breadcrumbs
60g currants, cleaned
90g raisins, chopped, seeded
1 tart apple, pared and chopped
60g butter, melted
salt
pepper
⅛ teaspoon paprika

Combine all the ingredients and stuff the goose. Truss for roasting, rub all over with flour and place in a pan, breast down, in a moderately hot oven – 220°C. Allow 15-25 minutes per 500g, basting occasionally with orange juice or cider, as this helps to tenderise the flesh.

Cinnamon Apples
1 cup cider
220g sugar
1 teaspoon cinnamon
4 small, tart apples, pared and cored

Bring to the boil the cider and sugar, cook for 5 minutes and add cinnamon. Pour over whole apples and bake at 180°C until tender, but not broken. Drop spoonfuls of tart jelly in the centre of each apple and arrange around goose with parsley sprigs.

Casseroled Wild Duck

1 duck
4 onions, chopped
30g butter
1 tablespoon burnt sugar
1½ cups breadcrumbs
salt
pepper
dash cayenne pepper
1 level tablespoon chopped sage
2 rashers bacon
2½ cups milk
cornflour, to thicken

Truss the duck. Fry the onion in the butter until brown, adding the sugar. When almost done add the breadcrumbs, salt, pepper and cayenne and cook a little longer, keeping the mixture dry. Add the sage. Stuff the duck. Place in a casserole with bacon on top. Pour over the milk and cook for 1½ hours or until tender. Add a little water to the milk in the casserole and thicken with cornflour for the sauce. Serves 4.

Steamed Wild Duck

1 wild duck
8 oysters
125g breadcrumbs
salt
pepper
2 tablespoons butter
2 tablespoons cream

Stuff the prepared duck with a mixture of oysters, breadcrumbs, seasoning, butter and cream. Place duck in a baking dish with a little butter, oyster liquor, salt and pepper. Cover well and stand dish in another dish of boiling water. Steam for one hour or until cooked. Serve hot with rich oyster sauce or cold with orange sauce.

Oyster Sauce
12 oysters
1¼ cups white sauce
squeeze lemon juice
salt and pepper

Heat oysters slowly in their juice, add the white sauce, lemon juice, salt and pepper to taste and pour over the duck.

Orange Sauce
1-2 large oranges
1 tablespoon chopped parsley
1 teaspoon olive oil
salt
pepper
½ teaspoon sugar

Peel the oranges and cut in thin slices, removing seeds and pith. Sprinkle with chopped parsley, add olive oil, a little pepper and salt and sugar.

Chicken Ham Kedgeree (see p. 52)

Curried Bombay Duck

1 duck
flour
salt
pepper
1 teaspoon ground ginger
3 tablespoons butter or oil
1 onion, sliced
1 tablespoon sultanas
1 apple, sliced
1 banana, sliced
2 cups water
½ clove garlic, sliced
1 tablespoon vinegar
1 level tablespoon sugar
1 tablespoon desiccated coconut
1 teaspoon curry powder

Hang duck for 1-2 days, then pluck and clean. Cut into joints, flour and season with salt, pepper and ginger. Brush each joint with melted butter and fry until golden brown. Place in a large stewing pan with the onion, sultanas, apple, banana, water, garlic, vinegar and sugar. Simmer for 2 hours. Just before serving add the coconut and curry powder and serve hot with plain boiled rice. Serves 4.

Jugged Wild Duck

1 duck, plucked and cleaned
flour
vegetable stock
1 onion, stuck with 6 cloves
125g button mushrooms, washed
½ cup port wine

Joint the duck, dust with seasoned flour and place in a pot with the stock and onion. Simmer slowly until tender. Just before serving add the mushrooms and wine. Serve surrounded with curried rice or mashed potatoes, flavoured with chopped parsley and onion. A sauce may be made by thickening the liquor in which the duck was cooked. A rabbit or hare may be cooked this way. Serves 4.

Ducks in Orange Juice

2 ducks, half roasted
salt
pepper
juice 2 large oranges
apple sauce

Carve the ducks so that meat remains attached to the bones. Dust over with fine pepper and salt and pour over the juice. Turn on to a plate and press until nearly flat. Place in a pan set on a hot stove until very hot, then turn over and let breasts cook until golden. Serve hot with apple sauce. Serves 6.

Wild Duck with Chestnut Stuffing

3 ducks
1 lemon, halved
3 cups breadcrumbs
1 teaspoon salt
½ teaspoon pepper
¼ cup hot milk
2 cups boiled chestnuts, finely chopped
1 small onion, grated
butter, for roasting

Prepare ducks, rub inside and out with lemon and fill with a stuffing made from the breadcrumbs, salt, pepper, milk, nuts and onion. Sew up and roast in butter for 1-1¼ hours at 200°C. Serves 8.

Wild Duck and Wine Sauce

2 ducks
1 orange, chopped
duck's liver and kidney, chopped
125g breadcrumbs
1 small onion, chopped finely
1 tablespoon butter
few drops red wine

Hang ducks for 2-3 days. Make a stuffing with the orange, liver, kidney, breadcrumbs and onion. Mince together, adding the butter and wine. Dress, stuff and roast the ducks. Serves 6.

Wine Sauce
2 large apples, chopped finely
1 tablespoon sugar
1 tablespoon butter
1 cup red wine

Cook the apples, sugar and butter until a pulp. Add wine, heat lightly and serve hot. The wine brings out the flavour from the duck.

Roast Duck

1 duck
2 sour apples, peeled, cored and chopped
125g breadcrumbs
1 small tin green peas
1 tablespoon butter
1 onion, finely chopped
½ tablespoon chopped mint
½ teaspoon mixed herbs
salt
pepper
dripping

Prepare duck for roasting. Make a stuffing with the apples, breadcrumbs, peas, butter, onion, mint, herbs, salt and pepper. Mix well and stuff the duck. Place in brown paper bags, put into a meat dish with some good dripping and a little water, and bake at 200°C for 2 hours or until cooked. Serves 4.

Wild Duck a la Canterbury

2 ducks, jointed
1 large onion, sliced
butter, for frying
45g flour
1½ cups chicken stock or water
1 onion, stuck with 8 cloves
bouquet garni
1½ cups port
3 turnips, chopped

Fry the duck pieces and onion in butter until golden brown. Remove meat, add flour to pan and stir until smooth. Add the stock, onion, bouquet garni and port. Return duck to pan and simmer gently for one hour. Cook the turnips in stock and when both turnips and duck are tender, remove meat and skim the fat from the gravy. Thicken if necessary and pour over the duck. Garnish with turnip pieces. Serves 6.

Casserole of Creamed Rabbit

1 rabbit
2 large potatoes, sliced
1 large onion, sliced
½ teaspoon salt
½ teaspoon pepper
½ teaspoon mixed herbs
1 x 350g tin celery soup
2½ cups milk
1 tablespoon flour
1½ tablespoons capers
2 hard-boiled eggs for garnish

Soak the rabbit for half an hour in salted, cold water. Wipe dry and joint. Place in layers in a casserole with the potatoes, onions and seasoning.

Pour the soup over, cover and bake for 2 hours at 200°C. Heat the milk and blend in flour, add to the casserole and bring to the boil. Lastly add the capers. Serve hot, garnished with egg slices. Serves 4.

Curried Rabbit

1 young rabbit, jointed
½ teaspoon ground ginger
30g flour
2 onions, chopped
2 sour apples, chopped
30g bacon fat or butter
1 teaspoon salt
1 tablespoon curry powder
1¼ cups vegetable stock
milk of ½ coconut
½ small coconut, freshly grated

Rub the rabbit with ginger and flour. Fry the onions and apples in fat until golden. Add the rabbit, seasoning and curry powder, Stir well and add the stock and coconut milk. Simmer for approximately 1½ hours. Lift out the meat, strain the sauce and bring to the boil. Add meat to reheat. Serve with grated coconut on top and arrange a border of rice around meat. Serves 6.

Rabbit in Marrow Log

1 rabbit
125g cooked ham
125g soft breadcrumbs
1 tablespoon butter
1 egg
salt
pepper
1 tablespoon chopped parsley
stock, or water
1 vegetable marrow

Boil rabbit in salted water until tender. Cut all meat from the bones and chop finely.
Chop ham and combine with rabbit meat, breadcrumbs, butter, egg, salt, pepper, parsley and sufficient stock to bind.
Wipe marrow, cut end off and score skin lightly to resemble a log. Scoop out seeds and fill with the meat mixture.
Replace end, fasten with skewers and bake in a covered, greased casserole for 35-45 minutes a180°C. Serves 6.

Fried Rabbit with Tomato Sauce

1 rabbit, jointed
1 egg, beaten
½ cup flour
salt
pepper
125g dry breadcrumbs
5 rashers bacon
500g tomatoes, halved
500g mushrooms, peeled

Bring rabbit slowly to the boil in salted water. Simmer for a few minutes, drain and cool. Brush the rabbit with egg and the seasoned flour. Brush again with egg and press on the breadcrumbs. Fry rabbit in hot fat until golden brown and tender. When cooked, arrange on a dish and keep hot. Trim rind from bacon and fry. Cook tomatoes until soft. Cook mushrooms until tender. Arrange bacon, tomatoes and mushrooms around the rabbit and keep hot while preparing the sauce. Serves 6.

Tomato Sauce
1 tablespoon butter, melted
1 onion, chopped finely
bacon rinds
500g tomatoes
2 tablespoons flour
1¼ cups vegetable stock
1 small carrot, grated
salt
pepper
1 teaspoon sugar

Fry the onion and bacon rinds in butter until onion is almost tender. Add tomatoes and cook for a few minutes. Stir in the flour and stock, stirring constantly until it boils. Add the carrot, salt and pepper and cook gently for 20 minutes. Strain, reheat and add sugar. Sauce may be prepared before hand and reheated when required.

Rabbit Casserole

1 rabbit
8 rashers bacon
1 onion, finely chopped
3 tablespoons uncooked rice
salt
pepper
250g mushrooms, or tomatoes
1 egg yolk
1 tablespoon chopped parsley

Cut rabbit into 8 serving pieces and wrap strip of bacon around each. Arrange onion and rice in a casserole and cover with water. Lay rabbit pieces on top and season to taste. Place mushrooms, or skinned tomatoes on top, cover first with buttered greaseproof paper and then the casserole lid, and cook for 1½ hours at 180°C. When cooked, lift out rabbit and vegetables and add the egg yolk and parsley to the rice. Mix well and arrange in the centre of a dish with the rabbit and vegetables served around. Serves 8.

Rabbit Scone Dumpling

1 rabbit, soaked in water for 1 hour
salt
pepper
2 rashers bacon, chopped
1 onion, grated
1 tablespoon chopped parsley
scone mixture

Joint the rabbit and cook in sufficient water to cover, adding salt and pepper when meat is tender. Remove, cool a little and remove meat from bones. Combine meat with bacon, onion and parsley. Line a pudding basin with half the scone dough, add rabbit mixture and cover with the remaining scone dough. Tie buttered greaseproof paper and cloth over the top and boil for 2 hours. Serves 6. Serve with Tomato Soup Sauce.

Tomato Soup Sauce
1 cup tomato soup
1 tablespoon sugar
1 tablespoon chopped parsley
1 onion, grated
1 tablespoon butter

Combine all ingredients in a saucepan and cook for 10-15 minutes and thin with a little rabbit stock.

Rabbit and Pineapple Canton

1 rabbit, soaked in salted water for 1 hour
2 tablespoons Worcestershire sauce
1 tablespoon sugar
½ teaspoon salt
½ teaspoon ground ginger
¼ cup cooking oil, or fat
1 teaspoon chopped garlic
1 cup pineapple syrup
1 cup water
2 tablespoons cornflour
¼ cup water
1½ cups diced pineapple

Joint and dry the rabbit. Combine the Worcestershire sauce, sugar, salt and ginger and coat the joints with this mixture. Heat oil in a heavy pan, add the garlic and rabbit and brown evenly on both sides. Place pineapple juice and water in a large saucepan, add the balance of sauce mixture, oil and garlic. Arrange meat in pan, cover and cook for 1 hour. Remove meat and keep hot. Stir in cornflour blended with water. Add pineapple, stir until mixture boils and simmer for 5 minutes. Arrange meat on a hot serving plate and pour sauce over. Serves 6.

Jugged Rabbit or Hare

1 rabbit
2 tablespoons flour
2 tablespoons butter
125g bacon
vegetable stock
bouquet garni
6 cloves
3 whole allspice
½ teaspoon pepper
little lemon peel
2 tablespoons flour
1 tablespoon butter
½ cup port

Wash rabbit and cut into neat joints. Flour and fry lightly in butter until lightly browned. Fry bacon and dice. Put rabbit in saucepan, cover with stock or boiling water, add the herbs and spices tied in a muslin cloth, the pepper and lemon peel and simmer until tender, approximately 2 hours. Remove all scum as it boils. When cooked, remove meat, strain liquor and thicken with the flour rubbed into the butter. Add the port, boil a few minutes and pour over the rabbit. Serve very hot with redcurrant jelly. Serves 6.

Deluxe Rabbit Pie

1 rabbit, soaked in cold, salted water for 1
  hour
salt
pepper
1 blade mace
2 cloves
¼-½ cup chopped bacon
2 tablespoons flour
½ tablespoon curry powder
1 onion, sliced
2 apples, sliced
1 tablespoon chopped parsley
1¼ cups vegetable stock
2 teaspoons lemon juice
1 tablespoon Worcestershire sauce
185g flaky pastry

Joint the rabbit, place in a saucepan, cover with boiling water and bring to the boil. Add the salt, spices and bacon and simmer for 1½ hours. Remove rabbit, cool, then roll in the flour with curry powder. Place in a greased casserole, cover with a layer of onion and apple. Top with bacon and parsley. Mix the stock, juice and sauce and pour over. Roll pastry 6mm thick and cover the pie. Bake for 10 minutes at 230°C, reduce heat and bake a further ¾ hour at 190°C. Serves 6.

VENISON

Venison becomes more tender if hung or put in a refrigerator a few days before use. Venison steak is very tender and may be cooked very quickly in a lightly-greased frying pan. Joints of this meat, however, tend to be dry due to the lack of fat in the muscle tissue. Therefore, when preparing a joint, cover it well with fat and baste frequently while cooking.

If it is to be stuffed, incorporate a good bit of lard or dripping in the forcemeat. Another way is to make deep cuts in the joint and pack them with bacon and apple slices. Venison is best if kept covered during cooking as this keeps in the steam.

Venison loaf

500g cooked venison, minced
1 small onion, minced
few sprigs mint, chopped finely
few sprigs parsley, chopped finely
½ cup soft breadcrumbs
2 tablespoons tomato sauce
2 teaspoons Worcestershire sauce
2 tablespoons melted butter
1 egg, beaten
4 rashers bacon

Combine the minced meat, onion, herbs, breadcrumbs, sauces, butter and egg. Turn on to a floured board and roll unto a loaf shape. Put into a greased loaf tin, cover with bacon rashers, cover and cook for 1 hour at 180°C. Raw minced venison may be used but longer cooking will be necessary. Serves 6.

Stuffed Venison

leg or shoulder venison joint
flour
salt
pepper
3 cups cold, mashed potatoes
½ cup dry oatmeal
1 small onion, finely chopped
½ teaspoon sage
1 teaspoon chopped parsley
dripping

Cut thin slices of meat and roll in flour with the salt and pepper to taste. Combine the potatoes, oatmeal, onion and herbs. Put a spoonful on each slice of meat, roll up and tie with string. Heat the dripping and when hot, fry the meat until browned, then pour off the dripping and add a little water. Simmer another hour or until tender. Serves 6.

Mock Duck (Using Venison)

6 thin slices venison steak
salad oil
dry mustard
½ cup soft breadcrumbs
1 small onion, chopped
1 tablespoon chopped parsley
1 tablespoon butter, shredded suet
salt
pepper
1 egg, beaten
6 rashers bacon
redcurrant jelly

Marinate meat in oil for 1 hour. Drain and smear with mustard. Mix breadcrumbs, onion, parsley, butter, salt and pepper, and bind with the egg. Place a spoonful of this mixture on each steak, roll up, wrap a bacon strip around each and secure with a toothpick. Put into a greased baking dish, cover with a little fat and cook for 1-1½ hours at 180°C. Serve with redcurrant jelly. Serves 6.

# EGG AND CHEESE DISHES

As eggs and cheese so often appear together in the same recipe and have similar high food values they are being classified together in this section. Both are very high in proteins and should appear in the daily diet, especially in the case of growing children.

Breakfast, luncheon and entree dishes all make use of these foods, but either or both make excellent meat substitutes and could occasionally be used in the main meal of the day.

Routine Ways of Cooking Eggs

Fluffy Omelette

4 eggs, separated
salt
pepper
4 tablespoons milk
2 teaspoons butter

Beat yolks with the salt, pepper and milk. Beat whites until stiff. Heat pan and add butter making sure all of the pan is covered. Fold the yolk mixture carefully into the whites and turn into the hot pan. Spread evenly and reduce heat. Cook until set and put under the grill to set the top. Fold over and serve. Serves 2.

Plain Omelette

4 eggs
8 teaspoons milk, or cream
60g butter
parsley for garnish

Break eggs in a basin and beat with a fork. Blend in milk or cream. Heat the butter well in a pan and pour in the eggs, stirring the eggs with a fork a few times. Move the pan continuously so the eggs do not stick, then leave for 2-3 seconds to brown. Fold over and serve. Garnish with parsley. Serves 2.

Poached

Use a deep flat pan, almost fill with water, add salt and 1 tablespoon vinegar (this keeps the white firm.) Bring to boil, remove from heat and slip eggs in from a saucer. Simmer 3 minutes, longer if egg is to be hard.

Fried Eggs

4 eggs
½ cup melted fat, or oil

Break eggs individually into a cup. Heat fat in a pan. Tilt the pan and slip each egg in one at a time. Cook for 2-3 seconds then turn quickly, remove at once and serve. Serves 4.
When cooking eggs by this method, do one at a time. To test the oil, drop in a small piece of bread and if it sizzles it is hot enough.

Hard-boiled

Boil 13-14 minutes, depending on size of egg. If egg is very large allow a further half a minute. If to be shelled and sliced dip at once in cold water.

Egg Mollet

Here the white is set and the yolk remains runny. Proceed as for soft boiling but allow 5-6 minutes, depending on size of egg.

Scrambled

125g butter
salt
pepper
4 eggs
2 tablespoons cream

Butter the frying pan with half the quantity of butter. Beat eggs with salt and pepper to taste, until blended but not frothy. Pour into pan and cook gently, stirring continuously. Now add remaining butter in pieces. When eggs start to thicken, remove from heat and continue stirring until liquid is set. Add cream and serve at once on toast. Serves 4.

Soft-boiled

Drop egg from a spoon into boiling water and boil 3 minutes. Remove and serve at once. If egg must be kept, put in a cup of hot water (not boiling).

Apple Omelette

2 apples, peeled and chopped
75g butter
2 tablespoons castor sugar
4 eggs, beaten

Fry the apple in 50g of the butter until lightly brown. Sprinkle with sugar and allow to cool. To the eggs add 1 tablespoon of sugar and mix in the cooked apples. Fry in the remaining butter as an ordinary omelette. Roll up and serve very hot, dredged with castor sugar. Serves 2.

Asparagus Eggs Au Gratin

500g asparagus, cooked
2 tablespoons butter
3 eggs
salt
pepper
½ cup grated cheese

Cut the asparagus into 3cm stalks and place in a buttered ovenproof dish. Dot with butter and bake for 3 minutes at 200°C. Break eggs into a basin and add salt and pepper to taste. Beat well and pour over the asparagus. Sprinkle with grated cheese and bake for 20 minutes at 180°C. Brown under grill. Serves 4.

Baked Egg Squares

2 tablespoons butter
3 tablespoons cornflour
½ teaspoon salt
¼ teaspoon pepper
1 cup milk
4 egg yolks, slightly beaten
4 egg whites, slightly beaten
tomato sauce

Melt butter in a saucepan, remove from heat, add cornflour, salt and pepper, and blend well. Add milk gradually and mix until smooth. Cook over medium heat, stirring constantly until thick and mixture boils. Remove from heat and pour slowly over the egg yolks, mixing well. Fold egg yolk mixture lightly into the egg whites and pour into an ungreased 20cm square pan and stand in a pan of warm water. Bake for 50 minutes at 180°C. Cut into squares and serve immediately with tomato sauce. Serves 4.

Savoury Bread and Butter Custard

1 x 310g tin creamed sweetcorn
125g cheese, grated
1 small onion, grated
4 slices stale bread, buttered
2 eggs, beaten
1¼ cups milk
pinch salt
pinch cayenne pepper

Mix together the corn, half the cheese and onion, and spread thickly on the bread. Arrange slices in an ovenproof dish and pour over the eggs and milk, well beaten with salt and pepper. Top with remainder of grated cheese and bake at 180°C until custard is set and top is golden brown. Serves 4.

Egg Nests

4 eggs, separated
4 slices hot buttered toast
salt
pepper
50g cheese, grated

Beat egg whites until stiff, and pile onto the slices of toast, making a depression in the centre with the back of a spoon. Carefully slide the egg yolks into the depressions and sprinkle with salt and pepper to taste. Sprinkle with grated cheese, making sure egg white is covered. Place under grill until egg is set and cheese melted. Serves 4.

Egg and Asparagus Pie

1½ cups thick white sauce
1 teaspoon mixed mustard
salt
pepper
2 hard-boiled eggs, sliced
60g cooked ham, chopped
1 x 340g tin asparagus
1 cooked and cooled short crust pastry shell
    flavoured with 1 tablespoon grated cheese

To the prepared white sauce stir in the mustard. Add salt and pepper to taste and the eggs, and stir into the sauce. Add ham and the strained and chopped asparagus. Keep tips for decoration. Spread mixture into the pastry shell and reheat to serve hot. Serves 4-6.

Cheese Custard

2 eggs
2½ cups milk
1½ cups soft breadcrumbs
1½ teaspoons salt
pinch pepper
125g cheese, grated
paprika

Beat together the eggs and milk and add the breadcrumbs, salt, pepper and cheese. Butter a baking dish or 6 small ones, and pour in the custard. Set in a pan of hot water and bake for 1 hour at 180°C. Sprinkle paprika on top just before serving. Serves 6.

✳ Baked Cheese Rice

3 cups cooked rice
2 tablespoons butter
185g cheese, grated
½ teaspoon salt
1 cup milk
¼ cup breadcrumbs

Line the bottom of a greased baking dish with 1 cup of rice and dot with butter. Alternate the cheese and remaining rice in layers, dotting each layer with butter. Sprinkle with salt and add milk Spread breadcrumbs on top and bake for 20 minutes at 180°C until cheese has melted and breadcrumbs browned. Serves 6.

Cauliflower Cheese Pie

1 onion, sliced
30g butter
1 cauliflower, cooked and broken into
    flowerets
2½ cups white sauce
185g cheese, grated
2 tins sardines
185g short pastry

Fry the onion in butter until golden. Remove from pan and toss the cauliflower in the fat. To the white sauce add half the cheese and the cauliflower. Spread layers of onion and sardines at the bottom of a piedish and cover with the cauliflower mixture. Sprinkle with the remaining cheese and cover with pastry. Bake for 20 minutes at 200°C. Serves 6.

Carrot Au Gratin

3-4 carrots, cooked and sliced
1 cup white sauce
salt
pepper
2 tablespoons buttered breadcrumbs
50g cheese, grated

Grease a piedish and fill with alternate layers of carrot and well-seasoned white sauce, finishing with a layer of sauce. Cover with breadcrumbs and cheese and bake at 200°C until heated through and breadcrumbs are browned. Serves 6.

Cheese and Bacon Roast

1 onion, grated
2 tablespoons butter
500g haricot beans, cooked and minced
250g cheese, grated
1 cup breadcrumbs
salt
pepper
2 tomatoes, skinned and chopped
1 cup dried breadcrumbs

Cook the onion in 1 tablespoon of butter and a little water. Combine all ingredients except 1 cup dried breadcrumbs, mix well and form into a roll. Brush with the remaining butter, melted, roll in breadcrumbs and bake at 180°C until nicely browned, basting occasionally with melted butter. Serve hot or cold with tomato sauce. Serves 6.

Cheddar Pudding

½ loaf sandwich bread
2 eggs, beaten
185g cheese, grated finely

Cut bread into 12 cubes, without crusts. Dip in the egg and roll in cheese. Place on greaseproof paper and bake at 180°C until cheese is melted. Cover with hot spanish sauce. Serves 4.

Spanish Sauce
3 tablespoons butter
4 tablespoons chopped onion
2 celery stalks, chopped finely
500g tomatoes, sliced
salt
pepper
pinch cayenne pepper

To the melted butter add the onion and celery and fry until golden brown. Add the tomatoes, salt, pepper and cayenne, and cook slowly until sauce is thick.

Oeufs à la Tripe

2–3 onions, thinly sliced
60g butter
½ tablespoon flour
1¼ cups hot milk
salt
pepper
sprig parsley
4 hard-boiled eggs

Parboil the onions in slightly salted boiling water for 8-10 minutes. Drain well and wipe with a dry cloth. Melt butter in a saucepan, and when hot put in onions and stir with a wooden spoon for 5 minutes. On no account should the onions brown, and therefore they have to be cooked on a very slow fire or, better still, use a boiling mat. Cover saucepan and let onions simmer very gently 15 minutes. Stir occasionally. Then sprinkle them with a little flour, mixing well, and add gradually hot milk, season with salt and pepper, and a sprig of parsley. Bring to the boil and simmer gently for another 10 minutes, stirring constantly. Slice eggs, put on a hot dish and remove parsley from sauce and put onions and sauce over them. Serves 4.

Eggs Mimosa

4 hard-boiled eggs
1 cup cheese sauce
salt
pepper

Halve the eggs, remove yolks and slice whites, putting them in a hot dish. Pour sauce over them, rub yolks through a sieve and sprinkle thickly over all. Season with salt and pepper to taste and serve very hot. Serves 4.

Cottage Cheese

sour milk
salt
pinch pepper
cream, or top milk

Measure the quantity of sour milk and pour into a saucepan or top of a double-boiler. Place over hot, not boiling water and keep warm until the curd separates from the whey. Pour into a clean piece of butter muslin and hang until all the whey has drained off. Turn the cheese into a bowl and for each 5 cups of sour milk used add ¼ teaspoon salt and a dash of pepper. Cream or top milk may be added to make a better spreading consistency.

Egg and Bacon Custard

4 rashers bacon
4 slices buttered bread
2 eggs
1 cup milk
salt
pepper
60g cheese, grated

Fry bacon until crisp and make into sandwiches using the bread. Place in ovenproof dish and cover with a custard made with the eggs and milk. Season to taste and bake at 180°C until custard sets. Remove, cover with cheese and grill until cheese is melted. Serves 4.

Cheese Puffit

1 level tablespoon finely chopped onion
1 cup diced ham
2 tablespoons butter
2 slices bread, cut 2cm thick
125g cheese, sliced thinly
2 eggs, separated
½ teaspoon salt
pinch cayenne pepper
1¼ cups hot milk
1 level tablespoon chopped parsley

Fry onion and ham lightly in 1 tablespoon butter, place in deep greased casserole or ovenproof dish. Break bread into small pieces and cut cheese into thin wafers. Beat yolks, add balance of melted butter, bread, cheese, salt, cayenne, hot milk and parsley. Stand 15-20 minutes.
Beat egg whites stiffly and fold into mixture, pour on ham onion mixture and bake for 45-50 minutes at 180°C. Test with clean skewer; it should come out free of mixture. Serves 6.

Fried Cheese Balls

3 medium-sized potatoes, peeled and grated
60g grated tasty cheese
1 tablespoon grated onion
1 cup flour
1 teaspoon baking powder
salt
pepper
pinch mustard
milk, as required
fat, or oil for frying

To the potatoes add the cheese, onion, flour, baking powder and seasoning. Mix well using enough milk to make a stiff batter. Drop spoonfuls into deep hot fat, fry until golden, drain and serve hot.

Eggs in Corn Sauce

1 x 310g tin sweetcorn
1 cup milk
1 teaspoon sugar
salt
pepper
1 teaspoon curry powder
1 onion, grated
1 cup left-over ham or chicken
1 tablespoon cornflour
4 hard-boiled eggs, sliced
2 tablespoons chopped parsley

Combine corn, milk, sugar, salt, pepper, curry powder, onion and meat in a medium saucepan. Heat and thicken with blended cornflour, add egg slices and parsley and serve with mashed potatoes or fingers of toast. Serves 4.

Fried Hard-boiled Eggs à l'Indienne

4 hard-boiled eggs, sliced thickly
2 tablespoons salad oil
4 tablespoons fine white breadcrumbs
1 heaped teaspoon curry powder
salt
2 tablespoons butter

Brush each egg slice with a little oil, coat with breadcrumbs to which has been added curry powder, season with salt and fry in hot butter for 10 minutes, turning frequently. Put slices on a hot dish, pouring over the remaining frying butter. Serves 4.

Imitation Omelette

4 slices stale bread
milk
salt
pepper
1 egg
bacon fat, or butter

Remove crusts from bread, crumble and cover with milk. Allow to soak a few moments and then beat with a fork, seasoning to taste. Break the egg into this mixture and beat well. Fry in very hot fat. Serves 4.

Onion Cheese

1 large onion per person
1½ cups white sauce
125g grated cheese

Boil whole onions, drain and put in a piedish. Make a plain white sauce, add cheese and pour over onions. Sprinkle more cheese on top and bake at 200°C until browned.

Macaroni Cheese

125g macaroni
3 tablespoons butter
6 tablespoons flour
1 cup milk
salt to taste
75g cheese, grated
¼ teaspoon cayenne pepper

Soak macaroni 1 hour in cold water, then boil until tender. Melt butter, dredge in flour, stir well, add milk and salt, and stir until boils. Then add macaroni and mix well. Pour some mixture into a piedish, sprinkle with a layer of grated cheese mixed with cayenne, then layer of macaroni mixture, and so on, finishing with layer of cheese. Sprinkle few bits butter over top layer. A border of pastry may be placed round edge of dish. Bake until nicely browned at 180°C. Serve hot or cold. Serves 6.

Silver Beet and Cheese

500g silverbeet stems, cooked
2½ cups thick white sauce
60g cheese, grated

Place layer of cold cooked stem of silver beet in a greased piedish. Cover with a rather thick white sauce, sprinkle with grated cheese and repeat the layers until dish is full. Have sauce for top layer. Sprinkle with cheese. Bake at 180°C until cheese browns and vegetable is heated through. Serves 4.

Mushroom Golden Omelette

500g mushrooms, washed and chopped
30g butter
salt
pepper
2½ cups milk
1 tablespoon flour, or 1 level tablespoon
   cornflour
4 eggs, separated

Place mushrooms in a saucepan with the melted butter, pepper, salt and 1¾ cups of the milk. Gently simmer until cooked, remove mushrooms, thicken the liquid with flour and keep hot. Beat egg yolks with 4 tablespoons milk, pepper and salt and add gently to stiffly-beaten egg whites. Melt 1 tablespoon butter in a frying pan. Pour in the omelette mixture and cook slowly until underneath is golden brown and top is set. Smother half the omelette with mushrooms, fold over other half, cover with hot mushroom sauce and serve with thin rashers of grilled bacon. Serves 2.

Poached Eggs à L'Italienne

60g butter
750g tomatoes, quartered
salt
pepper
1 bay leaf
bouquet garni
4 poached eggs
4 tablespoons grated cheese

Melt butter in a saucepan and when hot, add tomatoes. Season to taste, add bay leaf and bouquet garni. Cook on brisk heat at first, stirring continuously, crushing tomatoes to a pulp. Then simmer gently for 30 minutes. Put poached eggs on a hot dish and strain tomato puree over them. Sprinkle with cheese. Serves 4.

Stuffed Potato Scramble

4 large potatoes, baked whole
2 eggs
salt
pepper
2 tablespoons tomato sauce
½ teaspoon curry powder or hot sauce

Cut off both ends of potatoes and hollow out about half the potato with a spoon. Stand upright and fill with the eggs which have been lightly scrambled with the seasoning and sauces. Save the scraped out potato for thickening soup. Serves 4.

Potato Cheese Pie

750g potatoes, cooked and mashed
2 hard-boiled eggs, sliced
2 tablespoons butter
4 tablespoons self-raising flour
2½ cups milk
125g cheese, grated
½ cup browned breadcrumbs

Place potatoes and egg slices in a greased piedish. Melt butter in a saucepan, stir in flour, add milk and stir until boiling. Cook for a few minutes, add 90g of the cheese, season and pour over the potatoes. Put remaining cheese on top and sprinkle with breadcrumbs. Bake for 15 minutes at 180°C. Serves 4.

Omelette Puffs

½ cup self-raising flour
salt
pepper
2 tablespoons chopped parsley
2 eggs, separated
½ cup milk
60g chopped ham (optional)
2 tablespoons finely-grated onion
   (optional)

Sift the flour and add the seasoning and parsley. Lightly beat egg yolks with the milk and add to the dry ingredients. Add ham and onion, if used. Lastly fold in the stiffly-beaten egg whites. Drop spoonfuls in hot fat and fry until golden. Serves 4.

Welsh Rarebit

155g cheese, grated
½ teaspoon mustard
½ teaspoon salt
pinch cayenne pepper
2 teaspoons butter
¼ cup top milk
1 egg, beaten

Place cheese in top of a double-boiler. Mix together the mustard, salt and cayenne pepper and sprinkle over cheese. Add the butter and milk and stir until cheese completely dissolves. Finally add the egg and stir a moment longer. Too much cooking causes curdling. Serve at once on toast. Serves 2.

Soufflés

Sweet or savoury mixtures may be incorporated into soufflés but the basic recipe and method of preparation is the same. A white sauce is made, it is flavoured with whatever ingredient is to be added, such as cheese, minced chicken, chocolate, fruit pulp, etc., and the slightly-cooled hot sauce is poured over the beaten egg yolks. Finally, the mixture is cut and folded into the beaten egg whites.

When possible, use a special soufflé baking dish. Butter it and tie lightly-greased paper around the outside, well above the rim of the dish, as the soufflé rises. Bake in a hot oven 20-30 minutes; the centre should be set and the top brown. Remove the paper and serve immediately. To keep soufflé soft, as with vegetable and fish mixtures, stand the souffle dish in a pan of hot water and bake ½-1 hour.

Plain Soufflé

4 tablespoons butter
1 teaspoon salt
pinch pepper
3 tablespoons flour
1 cup milk
3 eggs, separated

Make a white sauce from the butter, salt, pepper and flour, adding milk gradually. Beat egg yolks and add the white sauce. Fold in the stiffly-beaten egg whites. Turn into a buttered soufflé dish. Set in a pan of hot water and bake for 1 hour at 180°C. Serve at once. Serves 4.

Variations

Cheese Soufflé
Add ½ cup strong grated cheese to white sauce mixture, stir until dissolved and make as for plain soufflé.

Meat Soufflé
Add 1 cup chopped meat, ham, fish, or any cooked meat.

Vegetable Soufflé
Add 1 cup chopped or mashed vegetable. Spinach, mushrooms, corn or mixed vegetables are all suitable.

Cabbage Patch Soufflé

125g bacon
1 cup flour
dash pepper
1 cup milk
3 eggs, separated
2 cups chopped cabbage, cooked
60g cheese, grated

Dice bacon and fry until crisp, then drain on absorbent paper. To the bacon fat (should be 3-4 tablespoons) add flour and pepper. Blend thoroughly and add milk. Bring to the boil, stirring constantly. Lightly beat yolks and add to thick sauce, beating well. To this now add the cabbage, bacon and cheese. Fold in stiffly-beaten egg whites and pour into a buttered baking dish. Stand in a pan of hot water and bake for 1 hour at 180°C. Serve at once. Serves 4-6.

Macaroni Soufflé

250g macaroni
2 eggs, separated
1 onion, grated
60g cheese, grated
1 x 300g small tin mushroom, or tomato
   soup
1¼ cups milk
salt
pepper

Cook the macaroni in salted water and strain. Add egg yolks to the macaroni, then the remaining ingredients except the egg whites. Just before putting into the oven fold in the stiffly-beaten egg whites. Bake for 15-20 minutes at 180°C. Serves 4-6.

VEGETABLE DISHES

Remember When Cooking Vegetables

1. Soaking in water removes vitamins, minerals and flavour, so prepare vegetables just prior to cooking unless they can be kept fresh and dry in a refrigerator.

2. Much of the mineral is just beneath the skin of root vegetables so if possible cook potatoes, pumpkin, carrots, etc. in their skins. Carrots should be well scrubbed, not scraped or peeled unless the skin is very rough and dirty.

3. Salted water is slightly hotter than unsalted so always put vegetables to be boiled in boiling salted water, thus saving cooking time and loss of food value through cooking. Always use iodised salt.

4. Use a tight-fitting lid, always.

5. Serve them the minute they are cooked. Keeping them hot spoils their appearance and flavour, as well as destroying valuable vitamins. This is especially true of greens and mashed potatoes.

6. Keep all vegetable water and use in soups, gravies, stews, sauces – or it may be strained, and with bouillon cube it makes a lovely drink.

7. Never add soda. If vegetables are cooked properly they will not lose their colour and soda destroys the vitamins. An exception is in making tomato soup, when a pinch of soda prevents curdling.

8. Try and have fresh vegetables. If storage is unavoidable, keep them in a cool dry place and do not wash or cut them until needed.

9. Serve one green leafy vegetable daily. In preparing cabbage, spinach, etc., use very little cooking water. Spinach has enough moisture left after washing; simply add a little butter or oil and cook with tight-fitting lid on saucepan. Cabbage should be finely shredded and put into 1.25cm salted boiling water, to which is added 1 tablespoon butter or cooking oil. Cook 2-3 minutes only; cabbage is delicious done this way.

10. Baked potatoes cook more quickly and are easier to handle if threaded on a metal skewer.

11. When cooking cauliflower whole, slice once or twice through the stem; it will then cook in the same time as the flowerettes.

Approximate Cooking Times

Peas, spinach, asparagus.................... 15-20 mins.
Potatoes, cauliflower,
green beans, young carrots .... 20-30 mins.
Turnips, young beets, parsnips, kumaras, onions,
carrots, celery .... 30-45 mins.

Asparagus Casserole

750g–1kg asparagus
60g butter
1 teaspoon mixed herbs
¼ cup vegetable stock
2 tablespoons cream
pinch nutmeg

Cut the asparagus into 4cm pieces, cook in a little salted water until half tender and strain, keeping the liquor. Heat the butter with the herbs in a casserole and gradually add the stock. Continue cooking the asparagus in this until tender. Finally add cream and nutmeg. Serves 4.

Bean and Bacon Loaf

500g haricot or lima beans
125g chopped ham or bacon
salt
pepper
1 small onion, finely chopped
1 tablespoon chopped parsley
1 cup white sauce
1 egg, beaten

Soak the beans overnight, drain and boil until soft. Mash and add the ham, salt, pepper, onion, parsley, sauce and egg, keeping 1 teaspoon of egg for glazing. Mix together, brush top with egg and bake for 1 hour at 190°C. Serves 6.

Bean Chowder

2 rashers bacon, diced
1 onion, sliced
1½ cups sliced, raw potato
2 cups milk
2 tablespoons flour
2 tablespoons melted butter
1 small tin beans, or peas
salt
pepper
1 tablespoon chopped parsley

Fry bacon and onion together and add potato and 1 cup milk. Simmer for 15 minutes. In a separate pan blend the flour into the butter and add the remaining milk and liquid from the beans. Season to taste and add parsley. Cook for 10 minutes and then add beans. Pea chowder can be made by omitting beans and parsley and substituting peas and chopped mint. Serves 4.

Savoury Green Beans

500g French, or runner beans
½ cup milk
30g butter
30g flour
1 tablespoon chopped onion
1 level teaspoon sugar
1 level teaspoon chopped parsley
salt
pepper

Prepare beans and cook in ½ cup salted water until tender. Strain, keeping the liquid. Add enough milk to make ½ cup of liquid. Melt butter, add flour and cook a few minutes. Pour in the liquid, add onion and sugar, and simmer for 5 minutes. Add beans and cook another minute. Mix in parsley, season and serve hot. Serves 4.

Bean Loaf

500g lima, or haricot beans
¼ teaspoon thyme
1 onion, stuck with 6 cloves
1 cup breadcrumbs
2 tomatoes, skinned and sliced
1 egg, beaten
1 tablespoon melted butter, or fat
salt
pepper

Soak beans in hot water overnight. Put onto the boil in fresh, cold water. Add thyme and onion, and cook gently until beans are soft. Strain, mash well, removing cloves and thyme. Add breadcrumbs, tomato and egg. Stir in the butter and season well. Pour mixture into a well-greased deep piedish, sprinkle well with breadcrumbs and bake for 30–45 minutes at 190°C. Serve with brown gravy, bacon sauce or hot tomato sauce. Serves 6.

Bean Tops

250g broad bean tops
salt
pepper
butter

The tops from broad beans make an excellent green vegetable in the early spring. Pinch off the top growth from each bean stalk. Wash well. Put into a large saucepan, pressing it down well. Enough water for the cooking will cling to the leaves after washing. Cook, stirring frequently until tender. Drain, pressing the water well out. Add a little butter, season and chop.

Cabbage Lunch

1 cabbage heart
250g sausage meat
60g chopped almonds
3 canned artichoke hearts, sliced
60g sliced olives
salt
pepper

Wash cabbage well but leave intact. Open centre and fill the hollow with alternate layers of sausage meat, almonds, artichoke, olives and seasoning. Tie up leaves around this and boil slowly 1 hour. Serve with onion sauce and plain, boiled rice. Serves 4.

Onion Sauce
1 small onion, finely chopped
1 cup milk
1 tablespoon cornflour
salt
pepper

Boil the onion in a little water until cooked. Add milk, bring to boiling point and thicken with cornflour. Season to taste and serve.

Creamed Cabbage

250g cold, cooked cabbage
1¼ cups white sauce
few drops vinegar, or lemon juice
½ cup buttered breadcrumbs
125g cheese, grated (optional)

Place layer of chopped cabbage in a greased piedish. Cover with some white sauce to which some vinegar has been added, and repeat with layers of cabbage and sauce until dish is full, finishing with a layer of sauce. Cover with breadcrumbs and cheese, (if used) and bake at 200°C until crumbs are browned. Serves 6.

Celery and Mushroom Shortcake

Pastry
250g flour
2 teaspoons baking powder
1 teaspoon salt
90g butter
½ cup milk

Sift dry ingredients, rub in butter and add milk. Do not overmix. Divide into two and pat out each to fit a sandwich tin. Grease the tins and fit in one half; brush over with melted butter and cover with second layer of pastry. With a large, floured pastry-cutter, cut a circle through the top layer, but do not remove. Brush with melted butter, and cook for 20 minutes at 200°C, until golden. When cooked remove the centre circle and add the filling.

Filling
1 head celery, diced
60g butter
1 tablespoon chopped onion
185g mushrooms, chopped
⅔ cup milk
3 tablespoons celery water
4 tablespoons flour
1 tablespoon grated cheese
salt
pepper

Cook the celery in 2½ cups salted water. In 30g of the butter fry the onions and mushrooms until tender but not brown. Make a sauce with the milk, celery water, remaining butter and the flour. Lastly add the cheese and seasoning. Stir in the drained celery, mushrooms and onion. Serves 6.

Corn Fricassee

3 onions, chopped finely
60g butter
1¼ cups milk
1 tablespoon cornflour
1 x 310g tin corn
3 hard-boiled eggs
few asparagus stalks, or any left-over
    vegetables, diced
salt
cayenne pepper

Make a sauce with the onions, butter and milk thickened with cornflour. Add the corn, eggs and asparagus stalks, season well and heat thoroughly before serving. Serves 4.

Fried Cauliflower

1 cauliflower, cooked
1 egg
2 tablespoons milk
1 cup breadcrumbs
oil for frying

Break the cold cauliflower into sprigs and dip each into the egg beaten with the milk. Roll in breadcrumbs and deep fry. Drain on absorbent paper and serve with brown gravy or tomato puree. Serves 4.

Baked Cabbage

250g cold, cooked cabbage
30g butter, or dripping
2 eggs, beaten
1 cup milk
salt
pepper

Chop cabbage and add the melted fat, egg and milk. Season well. Put into a well greased piedish and bake until set, at 180°C. Silverbeet, French beans and spinach can all be utilised in this way.

Prime Veal (see p. 42)

Fried Celery

4 celery stalks
milk
water
salt
pepper
1 egg, beaten
1 cup breadcrumbs

Cut celery into 5cm pieces. Boil in milk and water until tender. Drain celery and season, then dip each piece into beaten egg and roll in breadcrumbs. Fry in deep fat. Use milk and water in which celery was cooked for a white sauce to serve with the fritters. Serves 4.

Health Savoury

250g silverbeet stalks
2 cups sliced onion
½ cup wholemeal flour
500g tomatoes, sliced
1 teaspoon Marmite
1 cup boiling water

Place stalks in a greased casserole, then add a layer of onion, sprinkle with flour and add tomatoes. Dissolve Marmite in the boiling water and pour over. Cover casserole and cook for 1½ hours at 180°C. Serves 4.

Stuffed Cucumbers

1 large cucumber
2 pork sausages
1 onion
2 tomatoes, skinned
salt
pepper
30g butter
1 tablespoon chopped parsley

Cut cucumber into 6cm lengths, peel thinly and scoop out seeds. Skin sausages, then chop up with onion and tomatoes and mix all together with salt and pepper (pour off excess liquid). Now melt butter in ovenproof dish, then place in the pieces of stuffed cucumber and sprinkle with chopped parsley. Place lid on dish and cook half an hour in moderate oven. When cooked, put each section of stuffed cucumber on a piece of fried bread, and pour over a little of the sauce formed by liquid in dish. Serve very hot. Sliced tomatoes can be added as an accompaniment. Serves 6.

Lentil Rissoles

30g fat
1 onion, sliced
½ teaspoon curry powder
salt
pepper
1 tablespoon tomato sauce
1 cup cooked lentils
1 cup breadcrumbs and 1 egg for coating
1 egg, beaten
1 cup cooked and mashed potatoes, or rice

Fry onion in the fat until lightly browned. Add curry powder and cook a few minutes. Stir in all other ingredients except breadcrumbs and egg, and mix well. Turn on to a floured board and form into cakes. Dip into egg and breadcrumbs, and fry until golden brown. Serve with apple rings. Serves 4.

Apple Rings
2-3 apples
1 tablespoon bacon fat

Core the apples and slice into rings without removing the skin. Melt the fat and when smoking add the apple, frying carefully a few minutes. Place lentil rissoles in the centre of a hot dish and place apple rings around.

Marrow Onion Pie

1 small marrow
125g cheese, grated
1 cup breadcrumbs
salt
pepper
500g onions, peeled and sliced
2 tablespoons butter

Peel, seed and cube the marrow. Grease a piedish and lightly cover bottom with a mixture of cheese and breadcrumbs. Fill with alternate layers of marrow, onions and seasoning. Sprinkle top with cheese mixed with half its weight in crumbs. Cover with knobs of butter and bake at 180°C until marrow is cooked. Serves 4.

Stuffed Marrow

1 small marrow
2 medium potatoes, sliced
1 onion, grated
500g cold minced meat
salt
pepper
1 teaspoon tomato or Worcestershire sauce
3 tablespoons gravy made with Marmite

Scrape out marrow and line inside with raw, salted potato slices. Mix onion, mince, salt, pepper, sauce and gravy and fill marrow keeping potato lining in place. Seal marrow and bake in a baking dish with a little dripping at 180°-190°C. Serves 4.

Omelette Puffs (see p. 68)

Marrow and Mushroom Savoury

1 small marrow
60g cheese, grated
125g mushrooms, chopped and sauteed
salt
pepper
½ cup breadcrumbs
2 tablespoons butter

Peel the marrow, cut into rounds and remove seeds. Sprinkle a little cheese over marrow rounds, fill centres with mushrooms and season. Cover with breadcrumbs and a knob of butter. Bake at 200°C until marrow is cooked. Serves 4.

Mushroom Croquettes

250g mushrooms, peeled and stalked
milk
1 cup boiled rice
2 teaspoons chopped onion
2 teaspoons chopped parsley
1 tablespoon butter
1 tablespoon flour
2 eggs, beaten
salt
pepper

Stew the mushrooms for half an hour in a saucepan with enough milk and water to cover. Strain, retaining the stock, chop mushrooms coarsely and mix with rice, onion and parsley. Melt butter, stir in flour and stock, and stir until it boils. Now add mushroom mixture and 1 beaten egg, and stir over heat until well mixed. Season, turn on to a plate to cool, and shape into balls. Brush with egg, coat with breadcrumbs and fry in hot fat until golden brown. Serves 6.

Stuffed Baked Mushrooms

16 large mushrooms
1 onion, chopped
salt
½ teaspoon nutmeg
2 tablespoons cream

Remove mushroom stalks and scoop out the insides. Combine the mushroom pulp and onion and return this mixture to the cases. Sprinkle with salt and nutmeg, lay in a greased casserole, cover with cream and bake for half an hour at 180°C Serve on toast using the cream as a sauce. Serves 4.

Mushroom Deluxe

½ cup chopped onion
60g butter
250g mushrooms, sliced
salt
pepper
pinch paprika
pinch grated nutmeg
250g rice
2½ cups creamy milk
30g butter
125g grated cheese
2 tablespoons cider or white wine

Fry onion in the melted butter until golden brown. Add the mushrooms, salt, pepper, paprika and nutmeg. Cook gently a few minutes, then add rice, milk and butter, and simmer until rice is cooked. Remove from heat, stir in cheese and finally add cider. Serves 4.

Mushroom Savoury

250g mushrooms, chopped finely
2 tablespoons butter
1½ cups white sauce
3 tablespoons minced onion
1 tablespoon finely chopped parsley
3 tablespoons finely chopped celery
1½ teaspoons salt
pinch brown sugar
3 hard-boiled eggs, sliced
½ cup breadcrumbs
2 tablespoons butter

Fry mushrooms in butter for a few minutes. To the white sauce add the mushrooms, onion, parsley, celery, salt and sugar. Lastly add the egg slices and put mixture in a greased oven dish. Sprinkle with breadcrumbs, dot with butter, place in a pan of hot water and bake for 20 minutes at 200°C. Serves 4.

Mushroom Sunshades

250g mushrooms
2 cups mashed potato
1 tablespoon grated onion
1 tablespoon chopped parsley
salt
pepper
1 tablespoon butter
1 tablespoon milk
4 rashers bacon, fried
60g cheese, grated

Wash and peel the mushrooms, but do not remove the stalks. Combine the potato, onion, parsley, salt, pepper, butter and milk. Place the bacon between layers of potato in an ovenproof dish. Arrange mushrooms on top, sprinkle with cheese and grill under strong heat. Serves 4.

Hot Luncheon Mixup

4 tablespoons white rice
1 large onion, finely chopped
60g butter
1 clove garlic, chopped
salt
pinch paprika
2 medium tomatoes, sliced
1 packet mushroom soup

Wash rice well in cold water. Fry the onion in half the butter until golden brown. Remove from pan and fry the rice in the remaining butter, stirring frequently. Combine rice and onions in the pan with garlic, salt, paprika and tomatoes. Add soup made up to equal 5 cups with the addition of water or stock. Cover and simmer for 20-30 minutes, stirring frequently to prevent sticking. Add more water or stock if necessary. Serves 6.
May be varied by adding any of the following:-
Chopped mussels, oysters, chopped bacon, or 2 beaten eggs just before serving.

Nut Meat

1 cup cold, boiled brown rice
1 large onion, minced
1 cup brown breadcrumbs
1 sprig parsley
185g mixed minced nuts
½ teaspoon thyme, or sage
1-2 tomatoes, chopped finely
vegetable stock or Marmite water to mix

Combine all ingredients and mix thoroughly. For a nut roast press the mixture into a greased mould and bake for 30-40 minutes at 200°C. Serves 6. For rissoles form mixture into balls, dip in beaten egg and breadcrumbs and fry until golden brown.

Pease Pudding

1 cup split peas, soaked for 24 hours
2 cups vegetable stock, or water
1 onion, finely chopped
1 sprig mint
salt
pepper

Soak the peas in the stock, combine with other ingredients and bake in a casserole for 2 hours at 160°C until the peas are floury. Serves 4.

Savoury Roly Poly

500g wholemeal flour
250g butter
1 teaspoon baking powder
salt
pepper
2 large tomatoes, skinned and sliced
1 small onion, grated
1 teaspoon curry powder

Rub together the flour, butter, baking powder, salt and pepper. Mix with water and roll into an oblong shape. Fry the tomatoes with the onion, a little salt, and curry powder and spread on dough mixture. Roll up and place in a greased, cylindrical tin. Steam for 1½- 2 hours. Serves 4.
The filling may be varied by using cheese with tomatoes in place of onions.

Stuffed Onions

4 large tender onions
1½ cups forcemeat
salt
pepper
60-90g dripping, melted

Remove onion skin and the centre from each onion, forming a cup or case. Finely chop the removed onion and add forcemeat. Season each onion and fill with forcemeat. Bake the onions in a baking pan with the dripping, until tender and well browned. Baste frequently. Remove onions to a hot dish and serve with brown gravy. Serves 4.

Brown Gravy
dripping residue
1 teaspoon flour
1 cup cold water, or vegetable stock
salt
pepper

Pour off nearly all the dripping from the onion pan. Sprinkle with the flour and mix well. Add water and stir until boiling. Season and strain around onions.

Stuffed Peppers

4 green or red peppers
1½ cups mashed potatoes
90g cheese, grated
1 onion, grated
60g ham, or bacon, chopped
salt
pepper
½ cup breadcrumbs
2 tablespoons butter

Remove stems and seeds from peppers, drop in salted water, simmer 5 minutes, drain and fill with the mixture of potatoes, cheese, onion, ham, salt and pepper. Sprinkle with breadcrumbs and a dab of butter. Place in a greased baking dish, add 2-3 tablespoons water to dish and bake at 190°C until cooked. Serves 4.

Potato Cutlets and Sauce

1 onion, thinly sliced
2 rashers bacon, chopped
1 tablespoon fat
2 cups mashed potatoes
1 cup soft breadcrumbs
125g cheese, grated
1 tablespoon chopped parsley
salt
pepper
1 egg, beaten with a little milk
1 cup dry breadcrumbs
lemon slices ⎫
parsley ⎭ garnish

Fry the onion and bacon lightly in the fat and mix with the potatoes, breadcrumbs, cheese, parsley and season to taste. Shape into cutlets, roll in flour, and dip in egg and breadcrumbs. Fry in deep hot fat until golden brown. Garnish with lemon and parsley and serve with tomato-celery sauce. Serves 4.

Sauce
250g cooked, or tinned tomatoes
4 celery stalks, chopped finely
1 onion, chopped
salt
pepper

Mix tomatoes, celery and onion, and cook until slightly thickened. Season to taste and pour over cutlets.

Potato Wheat Germ Cakes

8 large potatoes, boiled and mashed
2 tablespoons butter
1 large onion, grated
salt
pepper
125g cheese, finely grated
2 eggs, beaten
1½ cups wheat germ
butter for frying

Combine the potatoes, butter, onion, salt, pepper and cheese. Add eggs and roll the mixture into cakes. Dip in wheat germ and fry until golden brown. If a variation is required, add 1 teaspoon anchovy paste to half of the mixture. Cut 2 apples into slices, dip in egg and wheat germ and fry until golden. Serves 6.

Scalloped Potatoes

3-4 potatoes, sliced
2 onions, sliced
salt
pepper
½ cup flour
½ cup milk
¼ cup water

Grease a piedish and fill with alternate layers of potato and onion. Sprinkle each layer with salt, pepper and flour and barely cover vegetables with milk and water, taking care there is no flour or seasoning on the top layer. Bake at 190°C until vegetables are soft. Serves 4. A little grated cheese or chopped ham or bacon may be added to each layer.

Potato Moulds

2 cups mashed potatoes
1 tablespoon flour
1 tablespoon butter, or dripping
1 egg, beaten
1 tablespoon milk
500g savoury filling

To the potatoes, add the flour, fat, egg and milk and beat well. Line well-greased individual moulds with the potato mixture, leaving space in the centre. Fill the centre with mince, forcemeat, tomato, rice or other savoury filling. Cover with more potato and bake at 200°C until sides are golden brown. Turn out and serve with brown gravy. Serves 4.

Savoury Tomatoes

3-4 firm tomatoes
salt
pepper
sugar
2-3 tablespoons mince, or forcemeat
1 cup breadcrumbs

Halve the tomatoes and scoop a little flesh from the centre of each half. Season tomato cups and add a little sugar to each. Combine the tomato pulp and mince and return to the tomato cups, piling mixture up. Cover with breadcrumbs and bake at 200°C until tomatoes are soft. Serves 4-6.

Tomato Cheese

1 onion, sliced
30g dripping
3-4 tomatoes, skinned
1 cup cooked rice, or macaroni
60g cheese, grated
salt
pepper
chopped parsley for garnish

Fry the onion in fat without browning. Add the tomatoes and cook gently until soft. Add rice, cheese and seasoning. Stir until hot and cheese has melted. Pile on hot dish and garnish with parsley. Serves 4.

Tomatoes in Marrow

½ small marrow
3-4 tomatoes
1 cup breadcrumbs
salt
pepper
1 teaspoon sugar

Cut marrow in half lengthwise without removing the skin, and scoop out the seeds. Dip tomatoes in boiling water to remove skins. Fill centre of marrow with sliced tomatoes, breadcrumbs, salt, pepper and sugar. Tie grease-proof paper over the top and place in a piedish. Bake at 200°C until vegetables are tender – approximately 30 minutes. Serve·from the half shell. Serves 4.

Tomato Scone Pie

½ cup chopped onion
2 tablespoons butter
3 tablespoons flour
1⅔ cups vegetable stock, milk or tomato
   juice
3 carrots, cooked and sliced
3 celery stalks, cooked and chopped
185g beans or peas, cooked
½ teaspoon salt
½ teaspoon Worcestershire sauce

Fry onion in butter until golden. Blend in flour, then gradually add liquid. Heat and stir until thickened. Add vegetables, salt and sauce and put into a large casserole or piedish. Arrange scones on top.

Tomato Cheese Scones
2 cups flour
2 teaspoons baking powder
1 teaspoon salt
3 tablespoons butter
125g cheese, grated
2 tablespoons chopped parsley
¾ cup tomato juice

Sift flour, baking powder and salt together. Rub in butter, add cheese and parsley and mix well. Stir in just enough tomato juice to make a soft dough. Turn on to a floured board, knead half a minute, then pat or roll 2cm thick. Cut into shapes and arrange on top of vegetables. Bake for 20 minutes at 200°C, until browned. Serves 6.

Vegetable Curry

3 large onions, diced
1 large apple, diced
1 carrot, diced
1 turnip, diced
1 parsnip, diced
2 cups vegetable stock
1 tablespoon plum jam
1 teaspoon salt
1 teaspoon curry powder
juice 1 lemon
1 tablespoon wholemeal flour
250g chopped nutmeat

Put a little oil or butter in a large saucepan. Add vegetables and fry until golden, then add stock, jam, seasoning and lemon juice. Simmer until vegetables are soft. Thicken with flour or oatmeal. Lastly add nutmeat and heat thoroughly. Serve with rice. Serves 4.

Vegetable Fritters

¾ cup cooked peas
¾ cup cooked beans
½ cup cubed carrots, cooked
2 eggs, beaten
⅕ cup milk
1⅖ cups flour
¾ teaspoon salt
2 teaspoons baking powder

Drain vegetables. To the eggs add the milk and half the sifted dry ingredients. Fold in vegetables and then the remaining dry ingredients. Cook spoonfuls in hot fat for 4 minutes. Serves 6.

Mock Whitebait Fritters

2 eggs
1 tablespoon flour
2 tablespoons milk
salt
pepper
½ teaspoon baking powder
1 large potato, coarsely grated

Make a batter with the eggs, flour and milk. Season to taste and add baking powder and potato. Fry spoonfuls in hot fat until golden. Serves 4.

SALADS

Not only are crisp cold salads just the thing for summer meals, they are one of the most health-giving items in our diet. They may be served as a complete meal, or as part of a dinner menu, when they should be small and served directly after the meat course.

When preparing salads, aim to have all utensils and ingredients chilled. Add dressings to salad greens just prior to serving as the lettuce or cabbage will wilt if left soaking. Don't always be preparing the same old salad menus. Vary them from day to day, using whatever vegetable or fruit is in season. Aim to make them as colourful and attractive as possible.

Apple Salad

2 apples, peeled and diced
4 celery stalks, diced
½ cup mayonnaise
1 tablespoon chopped nuts

Combine the apples, celery and mayonnaise and sprinkle the nuts on top. Serves 4.

Beetroot and Celery Salad

2 beetroots, cooked and cubed
3 celery stalks, chopped finely
salad dressing
parsley sprigs or lettuce leaves for garnish

Combine the beetroot, celery and dressing and decorate with parsley or lettuce. Serves 4.

Cheese Salad

2 hard-boiled eggs
1 tablespoon salad oil
1 teaspoon sugar
1 teaspoon prepared mustard
1 teaspoon salt
1 teaspoon pepper
1 tablespoon vinegar
250g dry cheese, grated
1 lettuce
1 large tomato sliced

Blend the yolk of 1 hard-boiled egg together with the oil, sugar, mustard, salt and pepper. When well blended add the vinegar gradually and finally the cheese. Arrange lettuce leaves on a serving dish and place spoonfuls of cheese mixture on each. Decorate with tomato and egg slices. Serves 4.

Chicken Salad

500g cold, diced chicken
1 cup crisp, chopped celery
1 teaspoon capers
salt
paprika
1¼ cups mayonnaise
lettuce
pimento strips, celery tips, or olives for garnish

Combine the chicken, celery, capers, salt, paprika and mayonnaise and mix lightly. Pile mixture on lettuce leaves and garnish. Serves 4.

Hot Potato Salad and Frankfurters

1 rasher bacon, chopped
½ cup sliced onion
1 teaspoon flour
⅛ teaspoon pepper
1 teaspoon salt
½ teaspoon mustard
4 potatoes peeled and diced
500g frankfurters skinned and halved lengthwise
¼ cup vinegar
¼ cup water

Saute the bacon in pressure cooker until crisp. Add onion and brown slightly. Stir in flour and seasonings. Add potatoes, frankfurters, vinegar and water. Bring up to pressure and cook for 4-6 minutes. Serves 6.

Hot Rice – Cabbage Salad

2 cups cooked rice
1 onion grated
2 hard-boiled eggs, chopped
1 teaspoon chopped parsley
1 teaspoon curry powder
90-125g ham or bacon, chopped
salt
pepper
1 young cabbage, shredded
½ cup mayonnaise

Combine the rice, onion, eggs, parsley, curry powder, ham, salt and pepper. Scatter the cabbage over rice mixture and pour over the mayonnaise.

Continental Salad

2 apples, diced
1 onion, chopped finely
2 hard-boiled eggs, chopped
1 x 300g tin green peas
¼ cup cream
½ teaspoon dry mustard
¼ cup vinegar
2 teaspoons sugar
pinch salt

Combine the apple, onion, egg and peas. Mix separately the cream, mustard, vinegar, sugar and salt. Add to apple mixture and blend well. Serve with cold meats and lettuce. Serves 4.

Crayfish Salad

1 crayfish, cooked and flaked
¼ teaspoon curry powder
1 cup cooked rice, or mashed potatoes
1 teaspoon onion juice
1 tablespoon chopped parsley
salt
pepper
lettuce leaves
½ cup cream
1 teaspoon mustard
pinch cayenne pepper
1 teaspoon sugar
2 tablespoons vinegar
½ cup grated cucumber

Mix together the crayfish, curry powder, rice, onion juice, parsley, salt and pepper. Arrange lettuce leaves in a bowl and put crayfish mixture on top. Combine the cream, mustard, cayenne, sugar, vinegar and cucumber, mix well and pour over crayfish. Serves 4.

Cucumber Nests

1 apple cucumber per person
chopped ham
grated apple
grated cheese
thick mayonnaise

Peel cucumbers leaving them whole. Cut off the bottoms to enable them to stand. Scoop out seeds, fill the centres with a mixture of ham, apple and cheese and top with a teaspoon of mayonnaise. Serve on lettuce leaves.

Fish Salad

250g cooked, flaked fish
lettuce leaves
1 cup shredded cabbage
3 celery stalks, chopped
¼ cup salad dressing
¼ cup chopped nuts
1 tablespoon chopped parsley

Place the fish on lettuce leaves. Combine the cabbage, celery and dressing and pile on top of the fish. Sprinkle with nuts and parsley. Serves 4.

Fruited Bean Salad

185g butter beans
½ lettuce, shredded
1 onion, chopped
1 cup cooked peas
½ cup diced pineapple
½ cup grated cheese

Cook the beans in a little water until tender. When cold, chop them and place in a bowl with the lettuce, onion, peas, pineapple and cheese and serve with Fruit Mayonnaise. Serves 4.

Fruit Mayonnaise
1 cup pineapple juice
grated rind and juice ½ lemon
1 egg, stiffly beaten
1 tablespoon melted butter
2 tablespoons cream, or condensed milk
pinch mustard
salt
pepper

Combine all ingredients, blend well and serve with salad and cold meats.

Macaroni Cheese Salad

250g macaroni, cooked
2 tablespoons vinegar
1 cup diced cheese
½ cup chopped green pepper
¼ cup diced celery
2 tablespoons chopped tomato
2 level tablespoons chopped onion
¾ cup salad dressing
1 green pepper, cut into rings
dill

Drain and cool the macaroni. Add vinegar, toss lightly and allow to stand for 10 minutes. Add cheese, green pepper, celery, tomato, onion and dressing. Toss and blend well. Garnish with pepper rings and dill. Serves 6.

Pineapple Salad

1 fresh pineapple, cut in rings
2 lettuces, shredded
½ cup mayonnaise
125g shelled Brazil nuts, shredded
1 bunch watercress
2 walnuts, may be pickled, shredded

Arrange the pineapple rings on lettuce bed, coat with mayonnaise and sprinkle with Brazil nuts. Decorate with watercress and walnuts. Serves 6-8.

Pork Aspic Salad

1 piece belly pork
2 sheep's tongues
pepper
1 teaspoon onion juice
1 level tablespoon gelatin

Boil the pork and tongues in water until tender. Skin tongues, slice lengthwise, place on pork and roll up. Season 2 cups of hot pork liquid with pepper, onion juice and dissolve in the gelatin. Place meat in a bowl and cover with the aspic. Press down with a plate and heavy weight, and leave to set. Serves 6.

Watercress Salad

2 cups chopped watercress
2 hard-boiled eggs, chopped
1 cup cooked peas
1 tablespoon chopped parsley
mayonnaise
sliced beetroot for garnish

Combine cress, eggs, peas, parsley, and blend in the mayonnaise. Decorate with beetroot. Serves 4.

Potato Salad

2 large potatoes, cooked and diced
4 celery stalks, chopped
1 onion, finely chopped
2 tablespoons chopped parsley
salad dressing

Combine the potato, celery, onion, parsley and dressing. Leave to stand to allow dressing to flavour potato. Sprinkle with parsley and serve. Serves 4.

Hot Potato Salad

4 potatoes, cooked in jackets
2 tablespoons chopped parsley
2 tablespoons grated onion
1 hard-boiled egg, sliced

Skin and slice the potatoes. Place neatly in a bowl with the parsley, onion and egg and pour over hot bacon dressing. Serves 4.

Hot Bacon Dressing
2½ cups milk
2 tablespoons flour
90g bacon fried and chopped
pinch mustard
salt
pepper
½ cup grated cheese
2 tablespoons breadcrumbs

Make a white sauce with the milk and flour. Add the bacon, mustard, salt and pepper. Sprinkle with cheese and breadcrumbs and brown in oven.

Sardine Salad

1 tin sardines
1 tablespoon capers
4 potatoes, cooked and diced
salad dressing
endive leaves
cooked, cold cauliflower, broken into
   flowerets

Combine the sardines, capers and potatoes. Mix gently with dressing and pile on to a bed of endive leaves. Decorate with lettuce leaves and flowerets. Serves 4.

Waldorf Salad

2 apples, diced
½ cup chopped walnuts
4 tablespoons salad dressing
lettuce leaves

Combine the apple and nuts and mix in the dressing. Arrange on lettuce leaves. Serves 4.

Salad Surprise

1 crisp lettuce, shredded
3 tomatoes, sliced
1 cup cooked green peas
1-2 oranges, segmented
few lettuce leaves
1 cup grated carrot
¼ cup chopped walnuts
salad dressing

Place alternate layers of lettuce, tomato and peas in a bowl. Arrange orange segments around the edge. Fill small lettuce leaves with the carrot and nuts and place on top of the salad. Serve with dressing. Serves 6.

Spring Salad

½ small cabbage, shredded finely
2 eating apples, diced
½ cup chopped celery
2 tablespoons sultanas
1 teaspoon lemon juice
2 tablespoons mayonnaise
salt
pepper

Combine all ingredients, season to taste and blend thoroughly. This salad is improved by refrigerating for several hours. Serves 6.

Tangy Savoury Salad

2½ cups lime jelly
¾ teaspoon salt
dash pepper
2 tablespoons vinegar
2 teaspoons grated onion
1½ cups any cooked or raw vegetables
   (carrots, peas, beans, potatoes etc).
lettuce leaves
dressing

To the still liquid jelly add the salt, pepper, vinegar and onion. When slightly thickened, fold in the vegetables. Chill in individual moulds and serve on crisp lettuce leaves, with dressing. Serves 4-6.

Watercress and Corn Salad

bunch watercress, finely chopped
1 celery stalk
1 x 310g tin sweetcorn, drained
1 cup cooked, minced ham, chicken or mutton

Combine all ingredients in a bowl and mix lightly. Serves 4.

Tuna Fish Salad

500g tuna fish, diced
1 cup finely chopped celery
2 tablespoons capers
salt
pinch paprika
1 cup mayonnaise
lettuce cups
stuffed olives, for garnish
celery tips, for garnish

Combine the fish, celery and capers, season to taste and toss all together, lightly mixing in the mayonnaise. Pile mixture on to lettuce cups, and decorate with olives and celery tips. Serves 4.

Asparagus Shape

bunch fresh asparagus
2 level tablespoons gelatin
¼ cup hot water
1¼ cups combined clear stock and asparagus
   water
½ cup mayonnaise
½ cup flaked, cooked fish or meat
½ cup chopped celery
½ cup chopped carrots
¼ cup grated cheese
lettuce, for garnish
radish, for garnish

Cook asparagus in usual way. Drain and reserve the liquor. Dissolve the gelatin in hot water and add to the stock and asparagus liquor. Cook and when about to set, stir in the mayonnaise and fold in the solid ingredients. Line a wet mould with asparagus tips placed downwards and pour in the gelatin mixture. Serve surrounded with lettuce leaves and radish roses. Serves 6.

Smoked Codfish Shape

1 tablespoon gelatin
½ cup cold water
2 egg yolks, beaten
¾ cup milk
¼ teaspoon cayenne pepper
1 teaspoon mustard prepared with 1 teaspoon
   sugar
1 tablespoon melted butter
3 tablespoons lemon juice, or vinegar
2 cups flaked, smoked cod
lettuce

Soak the gelatin in water. Mix the egg yolks, milk, cayenne pepper and mustard in the top of a double boiler. Cook until thickened, stirring constantly. Add butter, lemon juice and gelatin. When gelatin has dissolved, stir in the fish. Place in a wet ring mould. When set, unmould on to a bed of lettuce. Serves 6.

Cheese Salad Mould

1 level tablespoon gelatin
¼ cup cold water
2 cups grated, mild cheese
¾ teaspoon salt
⅛ teaspoon paprika
½ cup cream or milk
½ cup pineapple pieces
6 dates
1 orange
1 cup sliced bananas or strawberries
salad dressing mixed with 2 tablespoons of
  whipped cream

Soak gelatin in cold water for 5 minutes, then dissolve over hot water. Mash the cheese, add seasonings, cream and gelatin and turn into a wet ring mould. Chill and when set, turn on to a bed of lettuce. Fill the centre with the fruit mixed with salad dressing. Serves 4–6.

Jellied Tomatoes

4 tomatoes, sliced
salt
pepper
1 teaspoon butter or cream
2 level tablespoons gelatin
¼ cup hot water
parsley, for garnish

Cook the tomatoes until soft. Add salt, pepper and butter and while still hot press through a sieve. Dissolve the gelatin in hot water, stir into the tomato pulp and pour into wet moulds. Serve with cold meat and garnish with parsley. Serves 4.

Herring Mould

1 x 400g tin herrings in tomato sauce
1 tablespoon vinegar
1 tablespoon gelatin
3 tablespoons cold water
1 hard-boiled egg, sliced
½ cup cooked, green peas
lettuce leaves

Mash the herrings and add the vinegar. Dissolve the gelatin in water and melt over hot water. Arrange egg slices and peas at the bottom of a wet mould. Add the gelatin to the herrings, mix well and pour into mould. When set, unmould on to a bed of lettuce. Serves 4–6.

Perfection Salad

1 tablespoon gelatin
¼ cup cold water
¼ cup vinegar
1 cup boiling water
juice ½ lemon
½ teaspoon salt
¼ cup sugar
1 cup diced celery
½ cup shredded cabbage
¼ cup chopped red or green peppers
lettuce leaves
mayonnaise

Soften the gelatin in water. Mix the vinegar, boiling water, lemon juice, salt and sugar. Bring to the boil and add gelatin. Chill and when mixture begins to thicken add the vegetables. Put into individual moulds and chill. Turn out on to lettuce leaves and serve with mayonnaise. Serve 6.

Savoury Walnut Shape

1 packet lemon jelly crystals
½ cup cold water
2½ cups hot water
1½ cups peeled, diced apples
60g sugar
2 tablespoons lemon juice
1 cup diced celery
½ cup sweet pickle
½ cup chopped walnuts
lettuce leaves
mayonnaise
walnut halves for garnish

Dissolve jelly in cold water, then gradually add the hot water. Cool. Combine the apples, sugar, lemon juice, celery, pickle and walnuts. Pour over the dissolved jelly and chill. When set serve on lettuce, with mayonnaise. Serves 6.

DRESSINGS AND MAYONNAISE

Boiled Dressing

½ tablespoon salt
1 teaspoon mustard
1½ tablespoons sugar
⅛ teaspoon cayenne pepper
½ tablespoon flour
2 egg yolks
1½ tablespoons melted butter
¾ cup milk
¼ cup vinegar

Mix dry ingredients, add slightly-beaten egg yolks, butter, milk and vinegar, very slowly. Cook over boiling water until mixture thickens, strain and cool.

French Dressing

½ teaspoon salt
4 tablespoons vinegar
¼ teaspoon pepper
4 tablespoons olive oil

Mix ingredients and stir until well blended. A few drops of onion juice may be added.

Quick and Economical Dressing

2 tablespoons powdered milk
2 tablespoons sugar
½ teaspoon salt
1 tablespoon lemon juice or vinegar
fresh milk

Mix dry ingredients well, make into paste of required consistency with fresh milk and add lemon juice or vinegar drop by drop, stirring all the time as it thickens. A little more milk may be added if necessary. Condensed milk may be used instead of powdered milk and sugar.

Mayonnaise

1 teaspoon mustard
2 teaspoons icing sugar
1 teaspoon salt
pinch cayenne pepper
2 egg yolks
1½ cups olive oil
2 tablespoons vinegar
2 tablespoons lemon juice

Mix dry ingredients, add to yolks and mix thoroughly. Add a few drops of oil at a time until half a cup is used, beating with egg-beater or wooden spoon. Then add alternately a few drops vinegar and lemon juice and remainder of oil, taking care not to lose the stiff consistency. It should be a thick dressing and not added to food until just before serving. Have all ingredients and utensils thoroughly chilled and place mixing bowl in a pan of crushed ice while blending. If dressing curdles, take another egg yolk and add curdled mixture to it slowly, beating constantly. Another method of blending is to mix dry ingredients, add to yolks and mix thoroughly. Add vinegar and lemon juice slowly, beating well. Add oil slowly.

Mayonnaise (Condensed Milk)

salt
pepper
¼ teaspoon mustard
2 tablespoons condensed milk
3 tablespoons fresh milk
vinegar, to thicken

Mix salt, pepper and mustard. Add fresh and condensed milk gradually, then stir in enough vinegar to thicken slightly. This dressing thickens more on standing. If too thick add a little more fresh milk. Will keep well.

Russian Dressing

½ cup mayonnaise
¼ cup finely chopped red and green pepper
¼ teaspoon tomato sauce
1 teaspoon lemon juice

Mix all ingredients thoroughly and serve.

Thousand Island Dressing

1 cup mayonnaise
2 tablespoons chilli sauce
2 tablespoons tomato sauce
2 tablespoons chopped olives or gherkins
2 tablespoons finely chopped pimento
2 hard boiled eggs, chopped
½ cup whipped cream

Combine all ingredients except cream, which is added just before serving.

Mayonnaise of Hard Boiled Eggs

4 hard boiled eggs, chopped
1 cup mayonnaise
1 tablespoon capers
1 gherkin, chopped
1 small chilli, finely chopped
salt to taste

Combine all ingredients and blend thoroughly.

Salad Garnishes

Radish Roses
Cut the skin of the radish into 6–8 sections to within 6mm of the stem. Separate skin from the centre, place in cold water to curl.

Celery Curls
Cut the celery stick into 6cm strips. Slash from one end of the strip to within 1.5cm of the centre. Place in cold water to curl for half an hour.

Mock Carrots
Soften some creamed cheese with a little salad dressing and tint with red colouring. Mould into small carrot shapes and put a tiny piece of parsley in the top for the green leaves.

Salad Lilies
Make a smooth potato salad mixture. Take small thin slices of luncheon sausage and put 2 teaspoons of salad in each. Roll the meat around the mixture and fasten the base with a toothpick. Put a small stick of carrot in the centre of each. A spring onion may be used as a stem.

Stuffed Prunes
Fill cooked, drained prunes with finely-grated cheese. Place a caper or piece of gherkin in the centre of each.

Rainbow Rings
Over small sliced tomatoes put thin slices of hard-boiled egg, then a thin wafer of gherkin and finally a caper or piece of cherry.

DESSERTS

The main secret of pastry-making is to have everything very cold while preparing it, then to bake in a hot oven.

Short pastry should only be rolled out once, flaky pastry should be rolled very lightly and evenly, keeping the strip of pastry straight and of even thickness. Put the knobs of butter or other shortening on in even rows, for evenness is as important as lightness in pastry-making. Always use fresh dripping, butter, or suet, as the case may be. If using suet, remove skin and grate very finely. Do not use dripping that vegetables have been baked in. Do not use baking powder unless suet, butter, or dripping is half the weight of the flour, in order to obtain crispness. Suet pastry is the best for boiling, while pastry made with butter or dripping is best for baking. To glaze meat pies, use beaten yolk of egg, and for fruit pies beat white of 1 egg with 2 tablespoons sugar for 3 minutes, and brush over pie with brush.

PASTRY AND PIES

Plain Short Crust

½ teaspoon soda
½ cup iced water
125g dripping, or lard
2 cups flour
1 teaspoon cream of tartar

Dissolve the soda in water. Beat the dripping to a cream, and mix well with the flour and cream of tartar. Add water and roll out lightly. Use for fruit pies. Sufficient for 1 medium pie.

Rich Short Pastry

2 cups flour
pinch salt
1 teaspoon castor sugar
175g butter
1 egg yolk
2 teaspoons iced water

Sift flour, salt and sugar. Rub butter into flour. Mix yolk with 2 teaspoons iced water adding more water if necessary. Stir well but lightly. Sufficient for one medium pie.

Flaky Pastry

2 cups flour
pinch salt
175g butter
½ cup iced water

Sift flour and salt together and rub in 25g of butter. Stir in water gradually, roll dough lightly into long narrow strip, keeping sides straight and of even thickness. Divide butter into 3 portions, put a third in small knobs, even distances apart, over two-thirds of pastry, and fold dough into three, unbuttered end first. Press edges and centre lightly with rolling-pin and give pastry a half-turn to left. Roll out again, put a third of butter as before, and fold again. Roll, use remaining third of butter as before, and fold once again, and pastry is ready. Use for meat pies, sausage rolls or fancy pastries. Sufficient for 1 medium pie.

Puff Pastry

2 cups flour
pinch salt
250g butter
squeeze lemon juice
cold water

Sieve flour and salt, and rub in a small knob of butter. Add lemon juice and enough water to make a soft dough. Lightly knead until smooth. Make butter into an oblong shape and place on half the rolled out pastry. Fold other half over and seal edges. Leave to cool. Turn pastry so that fold is to right and repeat the rolling, folding, turning and cooling until it has been done 6 times. Cook at 220°C until lightly browned. Suitable for jam puffs, oyster patties, vanilla slices etc.

Rough Puff Pastry

150g butter
1½ cups flour
juice ½ lemon
½ teaspoon salt
cold water

Chop butter into walnut-sized pieces and mix through the flour. Make a well and pour in lemon juice and ½ teaspoon salt. Add enough cold water to mix to a soft, not wet, consistency. Roll out until about 30cm square, fold into three and again into three. Roll a little to make even and stand in a cool place for quarter of an hour. Roll out and fold as before and leave again. Repeat once more and then use. Bake at 210°C. Ideal for sausage rolls or cream horn cases.

Never-Fail Short Pastry

4 cups flour
1 level tablespoon baking powder
pinch salt
250g butter
milk, as required

Sift the flour, baking powder and salt together. Grate in the butter and mix to a soft consistency with the milk. Suitable for pie shells, sausage rolls, meat pies and tarts. Bake at 190°C.

Suet Pastry

2 cups flour
1 teaspoon baking powder
½ teaspoon salt
125g chopped suet
1¼ cups cold water

Sift flour, baking powder and salt. Stir in the suet and mix with enough cold water to make a firm dough. Roll out and use as required. Suitable for puddings.

Wholemeal Pastry

75g butter
1½ cups wholemeal flour
pinch salt
cold water

Rub butter into flour. Add salt and mix with water to a soft dough. This pastry should be slightly wetter than that made with white flour. Bake at 190°C.

Easy Way Pastry

1 teaspoon baking powder
2 cups flour
250g butter
warm water

Add baking powder to the flour and then mix in the chopped butter. Mix with warm water to make a firm dough. Leave for 1 hour. Roll 3 times and bake at 200°C.

Apple and Cheese Pie

rich short pastry
1 cup sugar
1 level tablespoon flour
¼ teaspoon nutmeg
½ teaspoon cinnamon
6 tart apples, peeled and sliced
1 tablespoon butter
50g grated cheese

Line a 23cm pieplate with half of the pastry. Combine the sugar, flour, nutmeg and cinnamon, and sprinkle a little of this mixture into the pastry shell. Fill with apples, add remaining mixture, dot with butter and sprinkle with cheese. Cover with remaining pastry and bake at 200°C for 30-45 minutes. Serves 6.

Apple Coconut Tart

rich short pastry
2 cups stewed apple, sweetened
2 tablespoons butter
½ cup sugar
1 egg, beaten
1 cup coconut

Line a pieplate with pastry, and add the apples. Cover with a topping made with the butter, sugar, egg and coconut combined. Bake for half an hour at 180°C or until pastry is cooked. Serves 6.

Blackberry and Peach Pie

1½ tablespoons tapioca
⅔ cup sugar
pinch salt
1 teaspoon orange rind
1 uncooked, 23cm, rich short pastry shell
2 cups blackberries
2 cups sliced peaches
pastry strips

Mix together the tapioca, sugar, salt and orange rind and sprinkle 2 tablespoons of this mixture in the pastry shell. Combine berries and peaches and place in shell and sprinkle with remaining tapioca mixture. Cover with pastry strips and bake for 40 minutes at 190°C. Serves 6.

Chocolate Chestnut Pie

250g chestnuts
¼ cup sugar
½ cup cocoa, or chocolate powder
milk, as required
1 egg, beaten
rich short pastry

Prick the chestnuts with a fork and simmer for half an hour in boiling water. When cool, remove shells and inner skins and mash until smooth. Stir in the sugar, cocoa and sufficient milk to make the consistency of thick cream. Add the egg and blend well. Pour into a pieplate lined with pastry and bake at 200°C until lightly browned. Serves 6.

Curd Tart

1¼ cups sour milk
1¼ cups fresh milk
short pastry
¾ cup hot, unseasoned, mashed potato
juice ½ lemon
50g butter
¼ cup castor sugar
pinch salt
2 eggs, beaten
¼ cup currants
¼ cup sultanas

Bring the sour and fresh milk to simmering point, when mixture will curdle. Turn into a cheesecloth and hang in a cool place to drain. Leave 5-6 hours or overnight. Line a pieplate with pastry and neaten the edge. Combine the potato, lemon juice, butter, sugar and salt. Stir in the curds, eggs and fruit and pour mixture into the pastry shell. Bake for 10 minutes at 200°C then for half an hour at 180°C or until top is lightly browned. Serve warm or cold. Serves 6.

Gingerale Mince Pie

175g cake crumbs
1 cup sultanas
½ cup raisins
grated rind and juice ½ orange
grated rind and juice ½ lemon
1 apple, chopped
pinch salt
½ teaspoon cinnamon
½ cup gingerale
rich short pastry

Mix together the crumbs, fruit, rind, juice, apple, salt and cinnamon. Pour over the gingerale. Roll out half of the pastry and spread with the fruit mixture. Cover with the remaining pastry and bake for 30 minutes at 190°C. While still hot, spread with a thin layer of lemon icing. Seves 6.

Ginger Date Tart

⅖ cup brown sugar
¾ cup milk
1 egg, separated
1 tablespoon butter
1½ cups chopped dates
pinch salt
1 teaspoon vanilla
200g rich short pastry
½ cup preserved ginger
¼ cup chopped walnuts

Make a 23cm pastry case, bake blind and cool. Place sugar, milk, egg yolk, butter and dates in top of double saucepan. Stir over boiling water for 10 minutes. Beat smooth. Fold in stiffly-beaten egg-white, salt and vanilla. Cool and fill pastry shell. Decorate with ginger and walnuts. Serve with whipped cream or ice-cream. Serves 6.

Grape Pie

5 cups dark grapes
¾ cup sugar
1½ tablespoons lemon juice
1 tablespoon grated orange rind
1 tablespoon rapid tapioca, or sago
rich short pastry

Skin the grapes, reserving the skins. Cook the grapes until seeds loosen then press through a sieve. Mix together the pulp, skins, sugar, lemon juice, rind and tapioca and leave to stand for 5 minutes. Line a 23cm pieplate with pastry and fill with grape mixture. Cut pastry strips to form a lattice top and bake for 10 minutes at 200°C, then at 180°C for 20 minutes. Serve cold with whipped cream. Serves 6.

Green Tomato and Ginger Pie

1½ cups flour
1 teaspoon baking powder
pinch salt
2 tablespoons butter
1 egg, beaten
cold water, to bind
½ cup stale cake crumbs
2 tablespoons golden syrup
2-3 tablespoons sliced preserved ginger
1 teaspoon grated lemon rind
2 green tomatoes, finely sliced
1 quince, thinly sliced
sugar

Make a short crust with the flour, baking powder, salt, butter, egg and water. Roll out half this mixture and partly bake in a greased sandwich tin. Then sprinkle with cake crumbs and over this put the syrup, ginger, rind, tomatoes and quince. Sprinkle with sugar, cover with remaining pastry and bake for 45 minutes at 190°C. Serves 6.

Mint Tart

1½ cup currants
½ cup sugar
cornflour, for thickening
¼ cup chopped mint
rich short pastry

Put the currants and sugar in a saucepan with water barely covering the fruit. Cook until soft and thicken with cornflour.
Add the mint to the fruit and pour mixture into a pieplate lined with pastry.
Bake for 30-40 minutes at 180°C.
Serve 4.

Novel Tart

short pastry
2 beetroot, cooked, skinned
3 cooking apples, sliced
½ cup of golden syrup

Line a medium piedish with pastry, retaining a portion for a cover. Slice the beetroot thinly. Dip both beet and apples slices in syrup and place in alternate layers on top of pastry. Cover with a pastry crust and bake at 200°C until pastry is cooked, then reduce heat and cook until apples are soft – approximately 10-15 minutes. Serves 6.

Persimmon Pie

1 tablespoon lemon juice
1 cup persimmon pulp
1 cup sweetened, whipped cream
1 cold, baked, rich short pastry shell
walnut halves, for decoration

Stir the lemon juice into the pulp and fold in the cream.
Pile into pastry shell. Chill and decorate with walnuts. Serves 6.

Pumpkin Pie

1 teaspoon cinnamon
1 teaspoon ginger
pinch ground cloves
pinch nutmeg
pinch salt
¼ cup hot water
2 eggs, beaten
¾ cup brown sugar
1½ cups pumpkin, cooked, drained and
  mashed
1 cup fresh milk
1 x 23cm unbaked, rich short pastry shell

Stir spices and salt into the hot water and combine with other ingredients. Blend well but do not beat. Pour into the pastry shell and bake for 1 hour at 180°C. Serves 6.

Nutty Fruit Pie

1 cup flour
1½ teaspoons baking powder
100g butter
pinch salt
3 tablespoons peanut butter
cold water, to mix

Make pastry with the flour, baking powder, butter, salt, peanut butter and water. Roll out and line a pieplate.

Filling
1 cup chopped raisins
1 cup chopped dates
1 cup crushed pineapple
1 level tablespoon sugar
pastry strips

Combine the raisins, dates, pineapple and sugar, and put into the pastry shell. Place pastry strips over the top to form a lattice, and bake for 25 minutes at 180°C.

Topping
½ cup sugar
½ cup water
1 tablespoon gelatine
1 teaspoon lemon juice
¼ cup chopped walnuts

Place the sugar, water and gelatine in a saucepan and boil for 10 minutes. Allow to cool. Add the lemon juice and beat until white and thick. Spread over pie and sprinkle with walnuts. Serve with cream or ice-cream. Serves 6.

Strawberry Chiffon Pie

1 chip (punnet) strawberries
½ cup sugar
1 tablespoon gelatine
¾ cup cold water
3 eggs, separated
½ cup sugar
1 tablespoon lemon juice
1 cooked, 23cm, rich short pastry shell
½ cup cream, whipped

Cut half the strawberries into small pieces and cover with first quantity of sugar. Soften the gelatine in water. Combine egg yolks with second quantity of sugar and lemon juice, and cook in the top of a double boiler until thick. Add gelatine and stir until dissolved. Remove from heat, fold in strawberries and set aside to cool. Carefully fold in the stiffly beaten egg whites and pile into the pastry shell. Garnish with remaining strawberries and cream. Serves 6.

Strawberry Chiffon Pie

Passionfruit Flan

2 tablespoons butter
2 tablespoons sugar
1 egg, beaten
6 tablespoons flour, sieved
1 teaspoon baking powder
milk, as required
½ cup brown sugar
1 cup milk
2 tablespoons flour
2 egg yolks
1 tablespoon butter
pulp of 3 passionfruit
2 egg whites, whisked stiffly
6 tablespoons castor sugar

Cream the butter and sugar. Add the egg, flour and baking powder. Make a soft dough with a little milk. Press into a round sandwich tin and bake until brown at 190°C.
In a saucepan put the brown sugar, milk, flour and egg yolks. Stir well and cook on low heat until thick. Add a little butter and pulp from 2 of the passionfruit, and pour into the baked pastry shell. To the whisked egg whites, add the sugar and whisk again. Fold in the remaining fruit pulp and spread over the filling. Brown at 150°C, cool, and cut with a wet knife. Serves 6.

Rhubarb Pie

200g rich short pastry
6-7 rhubarb stalks
2 tablespoons cornflour
1 cup sugar

Line a 20cm pieplate with half the pastry. Cut the rhubarb into 1.2cm lengths and remove strings and soak in boiling water for 1 hour. Drain well then flour with cornflour until well covered and put into pastry shell. Spinkle with sugar and cover with remaining pastry. Bake at 190°C until pastry is cooked, approximately 40 minutes. Dust with icing sugar and serve hot or cold. Serves 6.

Walnut Tart _Pecan?_

125g butter
1 cup sugar
1 egg, beaten
1 teaspoon almond essence
1 cup flour
1 teaspoon baking powder
2 tablespoons jam
½ cup walnut halves

Cream the butter and sugar. Add the egg and essence. Sift in flour and baking powder and knead to a dough. Press half the mixture into an ungreased tin. Spread with jam, then cover with remaining dough.
Cover with walnut halves and bake at 180°C for 30-40 minutes. Serves 4-6.

Meringue Pies

Any plain or short crust may be used in making meringue pies but flaky or puff pastry is unsuitable. Line a shallow pieplate with the crust, trim edges, prick the surface well with a fork and bake in a hot oven until brown. The filling is added next and the meringue piled on top. Return to the oven to brown and set the meringue, which should be firm but not crisp and hard as when making meringues or a pavlova. For an attractive topping the meringue may be put through a forcing bag.
Eat the pie as soons as it has cooled. The filling and pastry may be made the day before and the meringue prepared shortly before the meal.

To make meringue

2 egg whites, stiffly beaten
¼ cup sugar

To the beaten egg whites add the sugar and beat until mixture will stand in peaks. Pile on top of a pie filling and bake at 180°C until lightly browned, approximately 15 minutes.

Butterscotch Pie

1 cup milk
1 cup dark brown sugar
1 tablespoon butter
2 egg yolks, beaten
1 cooked, rich sweet short pastry shell
meringue mixture

Mix together the milk, sugar, butter and egg yolks, and cook over boiling water, stirring constantly until the mixture thickens. Pour into the pastry shell and top with meringue. Bake for 10 minutes at 180°C. Serves 6.

Caramel Pie

1 cup brown sugar
3 tablespoons butter
1 cup hot water
3 tablespoons cornflour
1 teaspoon vanilla essence
2 egg yolks, beaten
1 baked, rich short pastry shell
meringue mixture

Heat together the sugar and butter. Add the hot water. Mix the cornflour with the essence and egg yolks and to this add the hot mixture. Pour into shell and top with meringue. Bake for 10 minutes at 180°C until meringue is set and lightly browned. Serves 6.

Tomato Scone Pie (see p. 79)

Cream Pie

½ cup sugar
⅕ cup cornflour
pinch salt
2 cups milk
1 tablespoon butter
½ teaspoon vanilla essence
2 egg yolks, beaten
1 baked, rich short pastry shell
meringue mixture

Combine the sugar, cornflour, salt and milk. Cook in a double boiler stirring until the mixture thickens. Cook another 5 minutes and add the butter and essence. Pour this mixture into the beaten egg yolks then pour into the prepared shell and top with meringue. Bake for 10 minutes at 180°C until meringue is set and lightly browned. Serves 6.

Chocolate Pie

50g dark cooking chocolate or 1½ tablespoons cocoa
cream pie mixture, above
½ teaspoon vanilla, or peppermint essence
1 baked, rich short pastry shell
meringue mixture.

Grate the chocolate into the thickened custard and stir until dissolved. If cocoa is used, blend in with cornflour and sugar. Flavour with essence and pour into the pastry shell. Top with meringue and bake for 10 minutes at 180°C until meringue is set and lightly browned. Serves 6.

Gooseberry Pie

4 cups gooseberries
1½ cups sugar
6 tablespoons flour
½ teaspoon cinnamon
¼ teaspoon grated nutmeg
pinch salt
⅕ cup water
1 unbaked, rich short pastry shell
meringue mixture

Top and tail gooseberries, wash and drain. Mix the sugar with flour, spices and salt in a medium saucepan. Stir in water and cook over medium heat until mixture thickens. Boil for 1 minute add gooseberries, bring to the boil and simmer for 5 minutes.
Pour gooseberry mixture into pastry shell, bake for 10 minutes at 230°C, then at 200°C for 15 minutes or longer until gooseberries are tender. Remove pie from oven, top with meringue, return to oven and bake for 8-10 minutes until meringue is lightly browned. Serves 6.

Chocolate Raisin Pie

2 cups milk
1 tablespoon cocoa
⅕ cup cornflour
2 tablespoons sugar
2 egg yolks, beaten
1 cup seedless raisins
½ teaspoon vanilla, or peppermint essence
1 baked, rich short pastry shell
meringue mixture

Warm the milk. Mix the cocoa, cornflour and sugar with a little of the milk. Mix all together and boil for a few minutes. Remove from heat, add egg yolks, raisins and flavouring. Pour into pastry shell, top with meringue and bake for 15 minutes at 180°C until meringue is set and lightly browned. Serves 6.

Gold Nugget Pie

1 cup orange juice
1 cup pineapple juice
⅕ cup sugar
4 level tablespoons cornflour
¼ cup water
1 tablespoon butter
3 egg yolks, beaten
½ cup pineapple pieces
1 baked, rich short pastry shell
meringue, made with the egg whites and
    6 tablespoons sugar

Heat the juices. Blend the sugar and cornflour to a paste with the water. Add to hot fruit juices and stir until smooth. Boil until thick and clear. Remove and add the butter, egg yolks and pineapple.
Put into pastry shell and top with meringue. Bake for 10-15 minutes at 180°C until meringue is lightly browned. Serves 4-6.

Lemon Pie

1 cup sugar
juice and grated rind 1 lemon
2 tablespoons cornflour
2 egg yolks, beaten
1 cup water
1 baked, rich short pastry shell
meringue mixture

Combine the sugar, juice, rind, cornflour, egg yolks and water, and cook over boiling water for 10 minutes. Pour into pastry shell, top with meringue and bake for 10 minutes at 180°C. Serves 6.

Pineapple Pie

1 cup crushed pineapple
¼ cup cornflour
¾ cup sugar
2 egg yolks
juice ½ lemon
1 baked, rich short pastry shell
meringue mixture

Combine the pineapple, cornflour, sugar, egg yolks, and lemon juice, and cook over boiling water for 10 minutes. Pour into the pastry shell, top with meringue and bake for 10 minutes at 180°C until meringue is lightly browned. Serves 6.

Pumpkin Meringue Pie

1 egg, beaten
2 egg yolks, beaten
1 cup brown sugar
1 cup cooked, mashed pumpkin
1 teaspoon ground ginger
1 teaspoon cinnamon
1 teaspoon allspice
1½ cups milk
1 tablespoon treacle
1 baked, rich short pastry shell
2 egg whites
¼ cup sugar

Mix together the egg, egg yolks, brown sugar, pumpkin, spices, milk and treacle. Pour into pastry shell and bake at 180°C until set.
Whip up a meringue with the egg white and sugar, pile on top of pie and bake at 180°C until meringue is set and lightly browned. Serves 6.

HOT PUDDINGS

Baked

Apple Roly-Poly

1 tablespoon butter
2 tablespoons sugar
1 egg, beaten
1 cup self-raising flour
1 cup milk
2 apples peeled, cored and sliced
1 tablespoon sugar
1 tablespoon lemon juice

Beat the butter and sugar to a cream. Add the egg and flour. Pour milk into a piedish and heat in oven. Knead pastry mixture on a floured board, roll out, spread with apples, sprinkle with sugar and lemon juice. Roll up as for jam roll and place in hot milk. Bake for 20 minutes, at 180°C, when milk should be absorbed and pudding light and well browned. Serves 6.

Apple Sago

1 cup sago, or tapioca
2½ cups water
1 tablespoon lemon juice
4 apples, peeled and cored
4 tablespoons sugar
2 tablespoons butter

Boil the sago in water until transparent. Sweeten with sugar to taste and flavour with lemon juice. Place apples in a buttered piedish, fill each centre with sugar and butter. Pour sago over and bake at 180°C for 45 minutes or until apples are tender. Serves 4.

Apple and Banana Rice

125g rice
2½ cups milk
4 apples, cored and stewed dry
3 large bananas, sliced thinly
¼ cup sugar
½ teaspoon ground cinnamon

Wash rice, cover with milk and cook in a double saucepan until milk is absorbed. Butter a piedish, add a layer of rice and cover with apples and bananas. Sprinkle with sugar and cinnamon, cover with remainder of rice and bake for 30 minutes at 190°C. Serve hot with cream or custard. Serves 6.

Apple Puff

1¼ cups milk
2 tablespoons sugar
½ teaspoon vanilla essence
1 tablespoon butter
3 tablespoons flour
3 egg yolks
3 egg whites, whipped
3 apples, peeled, cored and sliced

Bring to the boil the milk, sugar and essence. In another saucepan melt the butter, sprinkle in the flour and stir to a paste. Add hot milk slowly and stir over low heat until mixture ceases to stick to the saucepan. Cool and stir in the egg yolks, one at a time. Stir in the stiffly beaten whites. Into a deep piedish, or 23cm souffle dish, put alternate layers of the mixture and apple, finishing with the mixture. Bake for 45 minutes at 180°C. This rises to over twice its size so use a large dish. Sprinkle with icing sugar and serve with cream. Serves 6.

Simple Apple Dessert

1½ cups flour
¼ teaspoon salt
2 teaspoons baking powder
¾ cup sugar
½ cup milk
2 eggs
1 teaspoon vanilla
125g soft butter
4 apples, peeled, cored and sliced
½ teaspoon cinnamon
little extra sugar

Into a bowl sift flour, salt and baking powder. Add sugar, and milk, eggs and vanilla beaten together. Lastly beat in the butter. Mix well and pour into a 23cm square ovenware dish. Place the sliced apple on top of the dough. Sprinkle with the cinnamon and extra sugar. Bake at 190°C for 30 minutes. Serves 6.

Banana Crumble

50g butter
2 cups coarse breadcrumbs
3–4 bananas, peeled and sliced
juice 1 lemon
1 teaspoon grated lemon rind
3 tablespoons brown sugar
1 teaspoon cinnamon mixed with 1 tablespoon brown sugar

Melt butter in a shallow pan, add breadcrumbs and stir over heat until golden brown. Soak banana slices in lemon juice for a few minutes. Place layer of crumbs in bottom of a lidded 20cm ovenproof dish and add a thick layer of bananas. Sprinkle liberally with brown sugar, lemon rind and a little of the lemon juice. Continue in layers until all ingredients are used, finishing with a layer of bananas. Top with cinnamon and brown sugar

mixture. Place lid on dish, and bake at 180°C until bananas are soft. Remove lid and cook a further 5 to 6 minutes. Serves 6.

Banana Roly–Poly

1 cup milk
1 tablespoon butter
2 tablespoons sugar
1 egg, beaten
1 cup self-raising flour
4 tablespoons raspberry jam
2 bananas, mashed with 1 tablespoon sugar and 1 tablespoon lemon juice

Pour milk into a large piedish and place in oven to heat. Make a pastry dough by creaming the butter and sugar. Add the egg, and flour. Roll out on a floured board, spread thinly with jam and spread with mashed bananas. Roll up, seal ends and place in the piedish of hot milk. Bake for 20 minutes at 180°C, by which time the milk should be absorbed. Serve with custard or lemon sauce. Serves 6.

Honey Bananas With Apple Meringue

4 bananas, peeled
juice ½ lemon
1 cup honey
2 tablespoons water

Place bananas in a shallow ovenproof dish and sprinkle with juice. Pour over the honey mixed with water. Bake for 15 minutes at 200°C, basting frequently and carefully. Cover with apple meringue.
Apple Meringue
2 egg whites
pinch salt
¼ cup icing sugar
1 cup grated apple
¼ cup sugar
½ teaspoon lemon juice

Beat the egg whites until stiff with the salt. Beat in the icing sugar, then alternately beat in the apple, sugar and lemon juice. Cover the bananas and bake for a further 15 minutes. Serve hot or cold. Serves 4-6.

Grape Soufflé

2 tablespoons butter
1 cup sugar
¼ cup flour
pinch salt
2 tablespoons lemon juice
grated rind 1 lemon
3 eggs, separated
1½ cups grape juice

Cream butter and sugar, add flour, salt, lemon juice and rind. Beat egg yolks until light, add grape juice and combine with the first mixture. Lastly fold into the stiffly beaten egg whites and turn into a buttered ovenproof dish. Bake for 45 minutes at 160°C. Serve hot or cold. Serves 4.

Coconut Delight

1 cup biscuit crumbs
125g butter, softened
1 cup desiccated coconut
½ cup sultanas
125g dark chocolate
125g soft, butter caramels, chopped
¼ cup milk

Mix together the crumbs, butter, coconut and sultanas. Melt chocolate and caramels over low heat, add milk, stirring all the time until smooth. Add to biscuit mixture and blend well. Press into a 23cm piedish and chill until firm. Fill with coconut mixture and top with meringue.

Coconut Mixture
3 tablespoons brown sugar
2½ cups boiling water
50g butter
1 tablespoon desiccated coconut
2 egg yolks
2 tablespoons cornflour
juice 1 lemon

Dissolve sugar in boiling water, add butter and heat until melted. Stir in the coconut. Beat egg yolk and stir into the cornflour. Blend the two mixtures and cook until smooth and thickened. Add lemon juice.

Meringue
Beat 2 egg whites with 6 tablespoons sugar. Spread over pie and cook at 180°C until lightly browned. Serves 6.

Coconut Walnut Pudding

1 stale sponge cake, cut into fingers
3 eggs, well beaten
2 tablespoons sugar
2½ cups warm milk
½ teaspoon vanilla essence
1 tablespoon butter

Place sponge fingers in a 23cm ovenproof dish and pour over a custard made with the eggs, sugar, milk, vanilla and butter. Bake at 150°C until custard is set. Remove from oven and top with meringue.

Meringue
2 egg whites, beaten stiffly
6 tablespoons sugar
1 cup chopped walnuts
1 cup cornflakes
2 tablespoons desiccated coconut

Combine all ingredients carefully, spread over custard and brown in the oven. Serves 4–6.

Coffee Caramel Apples

6 tablespoons sugar
25g butter
1 cup cold water
1 tablespoon coffee essence
4 large apples, peeled and quartered
1 tablespoon cornflour
1¼ cups milk
2 tablespoons sugar
1 tablespoon coffee essence

Boil the sugar, butter and water until a thick cream. Add the coffee essence and stir well. Add apples and simmer until apples are golden brown and sauce is almost a jelly. Serve hot or cold with a custard made with the cornflour, milk, sugar and essence. Serves 6.

Fiji Meringue

1 cup breadcrumbs
3 bananas, peeled and thinly sliced
juice ½ lemon
½ cup pineapple pieces, drained
2 tablespoons butter
2 tablespoons sugar
2 eggs, separated
grated rind ½ lemon
½ cup flour
½ teaspoon baking powder

Butter a 20cm ovenproof dish and line with breadcrumbs. Cover with bananas, sprinkled with lemon juice, then add pineapple. Cream the butter, sugar and beat in the egg yolks. Add lemon rind and flour sifted with baking powder. Pour mixture over fruit and bake for 30 minutes at 180°C. Beat egg whites stiffly with an additional 6 tablespoons of sugar, pile on top of pie, return to oven until set and lightly browned. Serves 6.

Fruit Rice Meringue

1 cup rice
squeeze lemon juice
½ tin sweetened condensed milk
2 egg yolks, beaten
pinch salt
½ teaspoon vanilla essence
1 cup hot milk
1 teaspoon butter
3 bananas or 8 apricots, sliced
2 egg whites, whipped
6 tablespoons sugar

Cook the rice in a little water with the lemon juice. Stir in condensed milk, egg yolks, salt and vanilla. Pour into an ovenproof dish and add the hot milk and butter. Over this place the fruit and cover with the egg whites, stiffly beaten with the sugar. Bake at 180°C until set. Serve with cream. Serves 6.

Gingerbread Pudding

¼ cup sugar
50g butter
3 tablespoons golden syrup
1 teaspoon baking soda
½ cup boiling water
1 egg, beaten
1 cup flour
pinch salt
½ teaspoon cinnamon
½ teaspoon ground ginger

Mix the sugar, butter and syrup over boiling water. Beat thoroughly. Add soda, dissolved in the boiling water. Then add egg, flour, salt and spices. Turn into a piedish and bake for 35 minutes at 180°C.

Topping
⅕ cup brown sugar
2 tablespoons flour
25g butter, melted
¼ cup chopped walnuts

Mix all ingredients together and spread over gingerbread. Return to oven and bake for 10 minutes longer. Serves 6.

Preserved Ginger Pudding

1 cup wholemeal flour
pinch salt
1 teaspoon baking powder
3 tablespoons butter
3 tablespoons sugar
3 tablespoons desiccated coconut
¼ cup preserved ginger, chopped
1 egg
½ cup milk
¼ teaspoon lemon essence

Sift flour, salt and baking powder, rub in the butter, add sugar, coconut and ginger. Add egg, milk and lemon essence to make a moist batter. Bake in a pudding dish for approximately 1 hour at 180°C. Serves 4-6.

Gooseberry Spiced Pudding

2 cups gooseberries
1 cup sugar
2 tablespoons cornflour
6 tablespoons butter
1½ cups flour
1½ teaspoons baking powder
¼ teaspoon salt
½ teaspoon cinnamon
½ teaspoon ground mace
3 tablespoons sugar
⅖ cup milk

Top and tail gooseberries, cut in half and put in a shallow, buttered, ovenproof dish. Mix sugar with cornflour and sprinkle over the fruit. Dot with 2 tablespoons of the butter and put into oven to heat while preparing topping. Sift flour with baking powder, salt and spice. Rub in remaining butter and 2 tablespoons sugar. Add milk and mix to a batter. Spread over the hot fruit and sprinkle 1 tablespoon sugar on top. Bake for 30 minutes at 190°C. Serve with custard sauce. Serves 6.

Gooseberry Orange Pudding

500g gooseberries
¼ cup sugar
25g butter
1 cup plain cake crumbs
grated rind 1 orange
2 eggs, separated

Top and tail gooseberries, wash, drain and put in an ovenproof dish with sugar. Cook for 30 minutes at 180°C. Remove from oven, add butter, crumbs and rind. Mix well and lastly mix in the egg yolks. Return to oven for 10 minutes. Beat egg whites stiffly and fold in 6 tablespoons sugar. Pile on top of mixture, sprinkle with extra sugar and return to oven until meringue is lightly browned and crisp. Serves 6.

Lemon Meringue Pudding

2½ cups cubed stale bread
¼ cup lemon juice
½ cup water
2 teaspoons grated lemon rind
50g butter
¾ cup sugar
2 egg yolks, beaten
½ cup milk
2 egg whites, stiffly beaten
6 tablespoons sugar
jam, for garnish

Soak the bread cubes in lemon juice, water and lemon rind. Cream together the butter and sugar. Add the egg yolks and milk and fold into bread. Pour into a buttered ovenproof dish. Stand in a dish of hot water and bake for 35 minutes at 190°C. Remove from oven and pile on top a meringue made with the stiffly beaten egg whites and sugar. Lightly brown in oven and serve garnished with dots of jam. Serves 6.

Marmalade Apple Pudding

6 apples, peeled, cored and sliced
¾ cup brown sugar
1 teaspoon cinnamon

Place apples in a buttered, ovenproof dish. Mix sugar and cinnamon, and sprinkle over apples. Cover and bake for 20 minutes at 190°C.

Topping
2 cups flour
1 tablespoon baking powder
½ teaspoon salt
75g butter
1 egg, beaten
½ cup sugar
½ cup milk
¼ cup marmalade

Sift flour, baking powder and salt together. Cut or rub butter into dry ingredients. Make a well in the centre of flour mixture and add the egg, sugar, milk and marmalade. Mix lightly, but well, then spread batter over the top of partially cooked apples. Bake until apples are tender and topping is cooked, approximately ½ hour at 180°C. Serves 6-8.

Swiss Orange Roll

125g butter
2 cups flour
2 teaspoons baking powder
warm water, approximately ½ cup
2 large oranges, peeled and sliced thinly
1 tablespoon raw, or brown, sugar
2 teaspoons grated orange rind

Make a short crust with the butter, flour, baking powder and warm water. Roll out very thin. Place the orange over pastry, sprinkle with raw sugar and 1 teaspoon of the orange rind. Roll up, seal the edges, butter the top and over this sprinkle the remaining orange rind and a little extra sugar. Bake for 30 minutes at 200°C. Serve with the following sauce.

Sauce
2½ cups boiling water
2 tablespoons cornflour, or custard powder
juice 1 lemon
juice ½ large orange
1 tablespoon sugar
2 teaspoons grated orange rind

Thicken the water with cornflour blended with a little cold water. Add lemon juice, orange juice, sugar and orange rind. Blend well and use hot or cold. Serves 4.

Orange Crunch

2 oranges, peeled and segmented
2 tablespoons sugar
50g butter
50g sugar
1 tablespoon golden syrup
¼ cup coconut
3 tablespoons self-raising flour
milk, as required
½ cup crushed cornflakes

Place oranges in a piedish and sprinkle with the 2 tablespoons of sugar. Cream the butter with 50g sugar, add syrup, coconut, flour and add milk to make a soft batter. Pour over the oranges, sprinkle with cornflakes and a little sugar and bake for 30 minutes at 180°C. Serves 4.

Pears Frae Scotland

4 large cooking pears
50g butter, melted
¼ cup sugar
½ cup oatmeal
½ cup water
½ cup honey
¼ cup preserved ginger, sliced
pinch salt

Leave stalk and skin on pears. Dip in butter, sugar and oatmeal and place upright in an ovenproof dish. Add water, honey, ginger and salt and cook for 1 hour at 120°C. Serve with custard or cream. Serves 4.

Rhubarb Upside Down Cake

2 cups diced rhubarb
¼ cup sugar
1 teaspoon grated orange rind
2 tablespoons butter, softened
50g butter, or margarine
½ cup sugar
1 teaspoon grated lemon rind
1 egg
1 cup flour, sifted
1½ teaspoons baking powder
¼ teaspoon salt
¼ cup orange juice, or milk

Combine the rhubarb, ¼ cup sugar, orange rind and softened butter and spread on bottom of a greased, ovenproof dish. Cream together the second quantity of butter, ½ cup sugar and lemon rind. Add the egg and beat until light and fluffy. Add sifted dry ingredients, alternately with orange juice. Beat lightly and pour over rhubarb mixture. Bake for 45-50 minutes at 180°C. Invert on a flat platter and serve with cream or custard. Serves 6.

Persimmon Pudding

1 egg
½ cup sugar
1 cup flour
¼ teaspoon salt
1 teaspoon baking powder
3 tablespoons butter, melted
¼ cup milk
lemon essence
1 cup persimmon pulp

Beat the egg with sugar until frothy. Add flour sifted with salt and baking powder. Combine the butter melted in milk and the lemon essence, and stir into the mixture. Fold in fruit and turn into a greased baking dish. Bake for 30 minutes at 180°C. Serves 4.

Mocha Crumb Pudding

1½ cups stale breadcrumbs
50g butter
2 eggs, beaten
2 tablespoons sugar
2½ cups milk
1 tablespoon cocoa
1 tablespoon coffee essence
1 teaspoon vanilla essence
2 tablespoons desiccated coconut

Fry the breadcrumbs in butter until golden, then place in a piedish. Combine the eggs, sugar, milk, cocoa, coffee and vanilla essences. Mix well and pour over crumbs. Leave for an hour, then sprinkle with coconut and bake at 150°C until set. Serves 4.

Raspberry Hot Cake

125g butter
¾ cup sugar
2 eggs, beaten
1 teaspoon lemon juice
2 cups flour
2 teaspoons baking powder
pinch salt
¾ cup milk
4 tablespoons butter
¾ cup brown sugar
2½ cups raspberries

Cream the butter and sugar. Add eggs and lemon juice. Sift dry ingredients and add to the mixture alternately with the milk. Cream the 4 tablespoons butter and brown sugar. Line bottom and sides of baking tin with this mixture and over this place the raspberries. Pour cake mixture in and bake for 45 minutes at 180°C. Turn onto a dish and serve hot with whipped cream. Serves 6.

Pineapple Pudding

1 x 440g tin pineapple pieces
4 thin slices, stale bread
1 tablespoon lemon juice
2 tablespoons sugar
3 eggs, separated
1¼ cups milk

Arrange pineapple pieces in a piedish in alternate layers with the bread soaked in pineapple syrup. Sprinkle lemon juice and sugar between the layers. Beat egg yolks, mix with milk and pour over pudding. Bake for 1 hour at 180°C. Beat egg whites with ½ cup sugar until stiff, pile on top of pudding and return to oven to brown lightly. Serves 4–6.

Pumpkin Brownie

1 cup cooked, mashed pumpkin
1 tablespoon sugar
1 tablespoon butter
1 teaspoon baking soda
1 cup milk
2 cups flour
1 heaped teaspoon cream of tartar
1 egg, beaten
1 cup currants
1 cup sultanas

Blend the pumpkin with sugar and butter. Dissolve the soda in milk and add to the pumpkin. Sift in the flour and cream of tartar. Lastly add the egg and fruit. If the pumpkin is very moist use a little less milk or a little more flour. Bake in a greased dish for 1 hour at 190°C. Serves 4.

Tropical Sponge Wheel

3 tablespoons melted butter
1½ cups brown sugar
6 pineapple rings
6 cherries
3 eggs
¾ cup sugar
1 cup flour
1 teaspoon baking powder

Into a large round cake tin place the butter and brown sugar. Place one pineapple ring in the centre and arrange remaining rings around the dish. Put a cherry in the centre of each ring. Mix a sponge batter with the eggs, sugar, flour and baking powder. Pour over pineapple and bake for 20–30 minutes at 180°C. Turn out on to a warmed dish and serve with hot custard or whipped cream. Serves 6.

Steamed Puddings

Brazil Nut Pudding

1½ cups seedless raisins
½ cup diced, mixed candied fruits
1 tablespoon grated orange rind
1 medium apple, grated
½ cup orange juice
½ cup flour
¼ cup sugar
1 teaspoon baking powder
½ teaspoon baking soda
½ teaspoon salt
½ teaspoon ground cinnamon
¼ teaspoon allspice
¼ teaspoon ground cloves
¾ cup dry breadcrumbs
2 eggs, lightly beaten
⅕ cup molasses
1 cup brazil nuts, chopped
50g suet, chopped

Put raisins, mixed fruit, rind and apple in a bowl and pour over the orange juice. Leave to stand for 1 hour. Sift into a bowl the flour, sugar, baking powder, soda, salt and spices. Add breadcrumbs. Beat eggs and molasses until just blended, stir in chopped brazil nuts, chopped suet and fruit-juice mixture and blend into dry ingredients. Steam 5 hours. Serve with softened ice-cream, a hard sauce or a chilled vanilla-cream sauce. Serves 6-8.

Cauliflower Pudding

1½ tablespoons butter
1½ cups flour
¾ teaspoon baking soda
1½ teaspoons cream of tartar
pinch salt
milk, as required
½ cup sugar
2 tablespoons golden syrup
2 tablespoons butter
1 cup water

Rub butter into the sieved flour, baking soda, cream of tartar and salt. Mix to a light dough with milk and place in a greased basin. Boil sugar, syrup, butter and water and pour over batter in the basin. Steam uncovered for 30 minutes. Serves 4-6.

Chocolate Pudding

50g butter
½ cup sugar
1 egg, beaten
1 cup flour
2 teaspoons baking powder
2 tablespoons cocoa
¼ cup milk
¼ cup raspberry jam

Cream butter and sugar until light and fluffy. Add egg and beat well. Sift flour, baking powder and cocoa. Add alternately with the milk. Mix well. Turn into a medium-sized, buttered, pudding basin which has the jam in the bottom. Cover tightly and steam 1-1½ hours. Serves 4.

Chocolate Walnut Pudding

75g butter
⅕ cup sugar
3 eggs, beaten
1 tablespoon grated chocolate
2 tablespoons milk
½ cup chopped walnuts
⅕ cup flour
⅕ cup ground rice
½ teaspoon vanilla essence
1 teaspoon baking powder
pinch salt

Cream together the butter and sugar, add eggs and beat. Melt the chocolate in milk and add to the creamed mixture with the walnuts, flour, rice, essence, baking powder and salt. Blend well and pour into a greased basin, steam for 2 hours. Serves 6.

Date Pudding

1 cup flour
1 teaspoon baking powder
pinch salt
½ cup sugar
1 cup chopped dates
1 tablespoon butter
¾ cup boiling water
1 teaspoon baking soda

Sift together the flour, baking powder and salt. Stir in the sugar and dates and mix well. Place butter on top and over the mixture pour the boiling water with the soda dissolved in it. Mix well and pour into a greased basin. Steam for 1½ hours. Serves 4-6.

Eggless Plum Pudding

¾ cup suet
1 cup milk
2 cups breadcrumbs
½ cup sugar
1 cup wholemeal flour
½ cup currants
½ cup sultanas
½ cup raisins
¼ cup mixed peel
1 teaspoon ground nutmeg
1 teaspoon cinnamon
1 teaspoon allspice
pinch salt
1 teaspoon baking soda
1 cup milk

Bring suet and milk to the boil and pour over the breadcrumbs and sugar. Cool. Add remaining ingredients. Lastly the soda dissolved in milk. Mix well and put into a greased basin. Steam for 4-5 hours. Serves 6-8.

Plum and Cherry Pudding

400g sweet short pastry
1 cup cherries, stoned
1 cup small plums, stoned
sugar
cinnamon
2 tablespoons claret
custard or cream

Roll pastry out 1.2cm thick and line a greased pudding basin with ¾ of the quantity. Add the fruit and sprinkle alternated layers with sugar, cinnamon and claret. Cover with remainder of pastry and steam for 2 hours. Serve with custard, or cream. Serves 6-8.
The same mixture may be made into a pie and baked.

Marmalade Pudding

1 cup breadcrumbs
1 cup flour
1 carrot, grated
1 tablespoon sago, soaked in ½ cup milk
1 cup sultanas
2 tablespoons marmalade
1 teaspoon baking soda
pinch salt
1 tablespoon melted butter

Mix together the breadcrumbs, flour, carrot, sago, sultanas, marmalade, soda, salt and butter. Put into a greased basin and steam for 2 hours. Serves 6.

Mock Apple Pudding

250g suet pastry
2 cups ripe vegetable marrow, sliced
¾ cup raisins, or dates, chopped
⅕ cup currants
1 cup desiccated coconut
½ cup sugar
pinch nutmeg

Line a pudding basin with pastry. Put in alternate layers of marrow, raisins, currants, coconut, sugar and nutmeg. Cover with pastry, tie down and steam for 2½-3 hours. Serve with cream. Serves 6.

Raspberry Pudding

2 tablespoons sugar
2 tablespoons butter
2 tablespoons raspberry jam
1½ cups flour
1 teaspoon baking soda, dissolved in ½ cup milk
custard sauce

Place sugar, butter and jam in a saucepan and boil for 2-3 minutes. Add flour and dissolved soda. Mix well and put into a buttered basin. Steam for 2 hours and serve with sauce. Serves 6.

Ginger Pudding

125g butter
⅕ cup brown sugar
1 teaspoon allspice
1 teaspoon ginger
1 teaspoon baking soda
150ml milk, warmed
1 large egg, beaten
2 cups wholemeal flour
½ cup raisins, or preserved ginger
¼ cup golden syrup

Cream butter and sugar, add spice and ginger. Dissolve soda and golden syrup in warm milk, add beaten egg and wholemeal alternately. Add soda and milk before last of wholemeal. Add fruit and steam about 2 hours. Serves 6.

Christmas Puddings

De Luxe

1kg shredded suet
8 cups flour
500g breadcrumbs
4 cups sugar
1kg seedless raisins
500g sultanas
500g currants
250g chopped almonds
500g mixed peel
juice and grated rind 3 oranges
juice and grated rind 2 lemons
2½ cups ale
1¼ cups milk
12 eggs, beaten

Blend flour, suet, breadcrumbs and sugar. Add chopped fruit, nuts and grated orange and lemon rind. Mix in fruit juices, ale and milk. Stand some hours, then mix in beaten eggs. Press into 3, buttered, 1½ litre basins. Scald pudding cloths, dredge with flour and cover each basin. Tie on loosely leaving room for rising. Boil 5-6 hours. Boil 1-2 hours to reheat when required. Each pudding serves 8-12.

With Ale

500g butter
2 cups sugar
8 eggs
500g breadcrumbs
4 cups flour
1.5kg raisins and sultanas
250g mixed peel
125g blanched almonds, chopped
1 teaspoon ground ginger
1 teaspoon grated nutmeg
½ cup brandy
¾ cup ale

Beat together the butter and sugar and add eggs one at a time. Mix in dry ingredients, chopped fruit and lastly the brandy and ale. Place in 2 buttered, 1½ litre basins. Cover loosely. Boil for 5-6 hours. Each pudding serves 8.

With Apple

2 tablespoons butter
½ cup sugar
1 egg
2 large apples, grated
175g raisins and sultanas
1 tablespoon marmalade, or lemon peel
½ cup flour
1 teaspoon allspice
pinch salt
½ cup breadcrumbs
1 teaspoon baking soda, dissolved in
    1 tablespoon boiling water

Cream butter and sugar. Add egg, apple, fruit, marmalade or lemon peel, flour, spice, salt, breadcrumbs, then soda and water. Place in medium-sized greased basin. Cover loosely. Boil 2½ hours. Serves 6-8.

With Grapefruit

1 large grapefruit
1 cup sugar
½ cup water
500g butter, or shredded suet
1 cup brown sugar
4 eggs
1 teaspoon soda, dissolved in 2 cups milk
2½ cups flour
500g dates, chopped
500g sultanas
500g raisins
250g blanched almonds
1 teaspoon salt
2 cups breadcrumbs

Prepare grapefruit two days before making pudding. Cut the grapefruit in half and boil in slightly salted water until very tender. Pour off liquid. Make a syrup of the 1 cup of sugar and water boiled for 10 minutes. Pour over grapefruit and leave for 2 days. Remove grapefruit, drain and chop finely. Beat together the sugar, eggs and butter. Add milk and soda, then flour and all other ingredients. Place in 2 buttered, 1½ litre basins. Cover loosely. Boil or steam 5-6 hours. Each pudding serves 8.

With Marmalade

2 cups flour
250g breadcrumbs
2 cups brown sugar, or ⅔ cup golden syrup
1 cup marmalade
6 large eggs, beaten
1 teaspoon mixed spice
1 teaspoon salt
1 cup stout
½ teaspoon baking soda
500g beef suet, shredded
375g sultanas
250g raisins
375g currants
125g mixed, candied peel
125g blanched almonds, chopped
grated rind 2 lemons
juice 1 lemon

Prepare and mix all dry ingredients. Make a well in the centre and add marmalade and eggs, and stir · some of the dry ingredients into them. Heat the stout, add soda and while still frothing add to mixture, add the fruit, almonds, rind and juice and mix well. Place in 2 buttered 1½ litre basins. Cover loosely. Steam for 5-6 hours. Each pudding serves 8-12.

Without Eggs

1½ teaspoons baking soda
1 cup boiling water
1 cup shredded beef suet
1 cup breadcrumbs
1½ cups flour
150g seedless raisins
150g chopped dates
½ cup sugar
2 teaspoons mixed spice
1 tablespoon golden syrup
1 teaspoon baking powder
75g mixed, candied peel

Put soda in a cup of boiling water and mix with other ingredients. Hang in buttered and floured cloth overnight; next day boil 3 hours. Serves 8.

Rich Mixture

250g currants
250g sultanas
250g seedless raisins
250g chopped prunes
250g chopped dates
125g mixed peel
125g blanched almonds, chopped
125g figs, chopped
250g breadcrumbs
250g suet, shredded
2 cups flour
½ cup brown sugar
1 teaspoon allspice
1 teaspoon cinnamon
1 teaspoon grated nutmeg
pinch salt
6 eggs, beaten
2 tablespoons treacle
1 carrot, grated
juice and rind 2 lemons
½ cup stout, or brandy

Chop fruit and suet and add to dry ingredients. Stir in beaten eggs, treacle, carrot, juice, rind and lastly stout or brandy. Stir well and stand overnight. Place in 2 buttered 1½ litre basins. Cover loosely. Boil 5-6 hours. Reheat 2 hours. Each pudding serves 8-12.

Economical

3 cups flour
1 level tablespoon mixed spice
pinch salt
1 cup sugar
3 tablespoons dripping, or butter
150g seedless raisins, or mixed fruit
1 tablespoon mixed peel
2 tablespoons treacle
1 rounded teaspoon baking soda
1 cup milk

Sift into a basin the flour, spice and salt. Add sugar and rub in butter. Add fruit and treacle. Dissolve the soda in milk and stir into the mixture. Pour into a greased basin and boil for 2½-3 hours. Serves 4-6.

Brandy Butter:
2 level tablespoons butter
¼ cup icing sugar
1 tablespoon brandy

Cream the butter and sugar. Add brandy gradually and chill until firm. Serve with the pudding.

Sweet Soufflés

Plain Custard Soufflé

1 cup milk, scalded
3 tablespoons butter
4 tablespoons flour
4 eggs, separated
¼ cup sugar
¼ teaspoon salt

Make a white sauce with the milk, butter and flour, and pour over the egg yolks which have been beaten with the sugar and salt. Cool. Cut and fold in stiffly beaten egg whites. Pour into a medium soufflé dish and bake for 45 minutes at 180°C. Serve immediately. Serves 4–6.

Chocolate Soufflé

¾ cup milk
2 tablespoons butter
2 tablespoons flour
50g dark chocolate
⅕ cup sugar
2 tablespoons hot water
3 eggs, separated
½ teaspoon vanilla essence

Make a white sauce with the milk, butter and flour. Melt chocolate over hot water, add sugar and water and stir until smooth. Combine mixtures, add well beaten egg yolks and cool. Fold in stiffly beaten egg whites and vanilla, and bake for 45 minutes at 180°C. Serve with whipped cream. Serves 4–6.

Fruit Soufflé

1 cup chopped, stewed peaches, or apricots
custard soufflé mixture

Drain the fruit and place in bottom of a large soufflé dish. Pour over the custard mixture and bake for 45 minutes at 180°C. Serves 4–6.

Lemon Soufflé

4 eggs, separated
⅖ cup sugar
grated rind and juice 1 lemon

Beat egg yolks until pale and gradually beat in the sugar. Add rind and juice and fold in the stiffly beaten egg whites. Turn into a soufflé dish and bake for 30–40 minutes at 180°C. Serve with custard sauce. Serves 4–6.

Fruit Purée Soufflé

¾ cup fruit purée
1 tablespoon lemon juice
3 egg whites, stiffly beaten
pinch salt
sugar, to taste

Heat the fruit pulp and add lemon juice. Sweeten to taste and pour into egg whites and salt. Turn into a soufflé dish and bake for 30–40 minutes at 180°C. Serve with custard sauce. Serves 4–6.

Passionfruit Salad Soufflé

2 bananas, sliced
2 apples, grated
1 quince, grated
pulp 2 passionfruit
sugar, to taste
juice 1 lemon
1 cup milk
25g butter
1 egg yolk
2 tablespoons flour
1 egg white, stiffly beaten

In a well buttered oven dish place the fruit and cover with sugar. Add lemon juice and put dish into a hot oven to warm through. In a saucepan put the milk, butter, egg yolk and flour. Cook until thickened, stirring constantly. Cool and fold in the egg white. Pour over fruit, return to oven and cook for 15 minutes until golden brown. Serve immediately. Serves 4–6.

Two Tone Custard

2 eggs, separated
2 level tablespoons cornflour
pinch salt
¾ cup sugar
2¼ cups milk
1½ teaspoons vanilla essence
25g cooking chocolate, grated

Combine yolks with the cornflour, salt and ½ cup sugar. Gradually stir in 2 cups of milk. Cook over low heat, stirring constantly until thickened. Remove from heat and add vanilla. Pour into a greased oven dish. Put the chocolate into a saucepan with the remaining sugar and milk. Cook over low heat until chocolate melts. Beat egg whites until stiff, fold in the chocolate mixture and pour over the first mixture. Set the dish in a pan of hot water and bake for 45-60 minutes at 180°C. Serve hot or cold. Serves 6.

Sweet Sauces

Lemon Sauce

¼ cup sugar
grated rind 1 lemon
1 tablespoon cornflour
1 cup boiling water
1 tablespoon butter
1 tablespoon lemon juice

Mix sugar, rind and cornflour and add water, cook 10 minutes. Remove from stove and add butter and juice.

Brown Sauce

½ cup brown sugar
1½ tablespoons cornflour
1 cup boiling water
1 tablespoon butter
½ teaspoon vanilla essence

Prepare as for lemon sauce.

Vanilla Sauce

As for lemon sauce using 1 teaspoon vanilla in place of lemon juice and rind.

Custard Sauce

1 egg yolk
1½ tablespoons sugar
pinch salt
¾ cup milk, heated
vanilla essence

Beat egg yolk and add sugar and salt. Add hot milk, stirring constantly. Cook over hot water until mixture coats back of the spoon. Strain and add vanilla.

Chocolate Sauce

¾ cup sugar
150ml water
½ cup cocoa

Dissolve the sugar in water over a low heat. Bring to the boil and simmer a few moments. Draw off the heat and whisk in the cocoa. Mix until smooth. The sauce will be thin at first but thickens to a sauce consistency after 10 minutes.

Melba Sauce

3 tablespoons raspberry jam
½ cup water
rind and juice ½ lemon
1½ level tablespoons cornflour

Boil jam, water, rind and juice. Remove rind and add cornflour, mixed smooth in cold water. Reboil, and serve cold with puddings and fruit dishes.

Coffee Sauce

1 egg
1 egg yolk
1 tablespoon strong coffee
¼ cup sugar

Mix all together in the top of a double boiler and whisk until sauce is hot and thick. Serve with spongy puddings.

Brandy Sauce

50g butter
1 cup icing sugar
2 tablespoons brandy
2 eggs, separated
½ cup milk, or cream

Cream butter, add sugar gradually, then brandy slowly, then the well-beaten egg yolks, milk, or cream. Cook over hot water until thick, and fold into stiffly beaten egg whites.

Mock Maple Syrup

1 cup brown sugar
¼ cup water
1 tablespoon butter
½ teaspoon vanilla essence

Boil the sugar and water for 5 minutes. Add the butter and vanilla. Serve hot or cold.

Hard Sauce

100g butter
1 cup icing sugar, sieved
1 teaspoon vanilla essence

Cream the butter and add the sugar gradually continuing to cream well. Flavour with vanilla.

Sabayon Sauce

⅕ cup sugar
juice and grated rind ½ lemon
½ cup orange juice, or white wine, or sherry
2 eggs, separated

Mix sugar, rind, juices and egg yolks. Stir vigorously over hot water until it thickens. Pour over beaten egg whites and blend thoroughly.

Chocolate Sauce (Using Cocoa)

1 tablespoon cornflour
1 level tablespoon cocoa
½ cup sugar
pinch salt
1 cup hot water
1 egg, separated
2 tablespoons butter
2 teaspoons vanilla essence

Mix the dry ingredients and gradually add the hot water. Cook until thick, stirring all the time. Cool a little, add beaten egg yolk and cook for 2-3 minutes. Stir in the butter and vanilla, and finally the stiffly beaten whites. Serve hot on ice-cream.

Apple Sauce

250g apples, peeled and sliced
¼ cup water
pinch salt
1 tablespoon brown sugar
¼ teaspoon grated nutmeg
25g butter

Put the apples in a saucepan with the water, salt, sugar and nutmeg. Cook to a pulp and add butter. Beat until smooth.

COLD SWEETS

Fruit, whether fresh, tinned, bottled or stewed, forms the basis of most cold sweets. Fruit compotes are prepared by gently cooking whole prepared fruit in a small quantity of syrup, keeping the lid tightly on the saucepan or casserole. When stewing fruit, place it in boiling syrup and cook until tender. Fruit for pulping is not cooked in syrup as sugar helps to keep the flesh from breaking up. Cook in boiling water, strain or mash and reheat, then add sugar. Dried fruits are best soaked some time before cooking. Cook in unsweetened water, as sugar tends to toughen already firm skin. Add sugar once the fruit is soft and cook 2-3 minutes only.
Gelatine is used in many cold sweets. Use approximately 1 tablespoon gelatine to 2 cups of liquid. More will be necessary in hot weather if a refrigerator is not available. As gelatine is an animal protein, overcooking only toughens it; therefore it is dissolved in hot water and not boiled. Before adding hot water, dissolve in a little cold water until it swells. Gelatine will not work in the presence of fresh pineapple but cooked or tinned pineapple is suitable. It will also curdle hot milk, so when making milk jellies, dissolve the sugar and gelatine in hot water and add to cold flavoured milk.
Snow puddings are a combination of a gelatine or cornflour preparation, and whipped egg whites. Spanish cream consists of a custard, set with gelatine, and beaten egg whites. Fruit fools are custards incorporating fruit purée and sometimes whipped cream. A Bavarian cream is like a Spanish cream but has whipped cream as an additional ingredient.

Apple Cream

6 large cooking apples
sugar, to taste
stale sponge cake
2½ cups custard, sweetened
icing sugar

Stew the apples with sugar, until a pulp and set aside to cool. Line a glass dish with sponge cake and pour a little of the custard over. Beat the remaining custard into the apple and pile on top of sponge cake. Dredge with sugar. Serves 4-6.

Apple Trifle

stale sponge cake
500g apples, peeled, cored and chopped
2 eggs, separated

Line a glass dish with sponge. Cook the apples, rub through a sieve and return to saucepan with egg yolks. Stir until thick and pour over the sponge. Just before serving top with meringue of the stiffly beaten egg whites. Serve with whipped cream. Serves 4-6.

Apricot Flummery

2 tablespoons ground almonds
2 cups stewed, drained apricots
1 tablespoon sherry
½ cup apricot juice
3 tablespoons gelatine
1 tablespoon coffee essence
2½ cups milk, heated
1 cup whipped cream
chopped almonds, for garnish
apricot halves, for garnish

Mix ground almonds with the apricots, sprinkle with sherry and leave to stand for a few hours. Heat juice and dissolve gelatine. Add coffee essence to milk and combine the two hot mixtures, stirring well. Cool, then beat until thickened. Add soaked apricots and fold in cream. Pour into a wet mould and chill. Unmould and decorate with nuts and apricots. Serves 6.

Apricot Whip

1¼ cups apricot purée
4 eggs, separated
4 tablespoons sugar
2 tablespoons gelatine, dissolved in
  2 tablespoons apricot syrup
squeeze lemon juice
2-3 drops cochineal
chopped almonds, for garnish

Put the purée, egg yolks, and sugar into a large basin, stand over boiling water and whisk until it thickens. Remove from heat and strain in the gelatine. Add lemon juice and cochineal. Fold in the stiffly beaten egg whites. Fill mould and chill. Sprinkle with nuts and serve with whipped cream. Serves 4-6.

Blackberry Whip

1 chip, (punnet), blackberries, cleaned
1 cup castor sugar
1 egg white

Put berries in a basin with the other ingredients and whisk until mixture is stiff and stands in peaks. Pile into stemmed glasses and serve with sponge fingers. Serves 4.

Overnight Blackberry Shape

½ loaf stale bread
50g sugar
1 tablespoon golden syrup
250ml water
375g blackberries
500g apples, peeled, cored and sliced
whipped cream

Grease a 4 cup pudding basin, cut crusts from bread and cut slices 1.2cm thick. Cut these again into thirds. From 2 slices make a circle to fit the base of the bowl and another to fit the top. Line the sides with the strips leaving no spaces, and fit the small circle of bread at the bottom. Make the filling by dissolving the sugar and syrup in water and bring to the boil. Add berries and boil rapidly for a few seconds. Drain, keeping the syrup. Cook the apples in syrup until soft. then beat them into a purée. Reserve a few berries for garnishing and blend remainder with the apple purée. Put into the basin and cover with bread circle. Over this put a saucer and weight. Leave overnight. When required, turn out on a plate and garnish with cream and berries. Serves 4-6.

Caramel Banana Snow

1 tin sweetened condensed milk
5 cups ready-made semolina
500g bananas, mashed
2 egg whites, whipped stiffly
whipped cream
strawberries, for garnish

Boil the condensed milk in the tin for 2 hours and cool before opening. Thoroughly combine the milk with semolina and when cool add the bananas. Fold in egg whites and chill. Decorate with cream and strawberries. Serves 4-6.

Caramel Bread Custard

1 cup sugar
1 teaspoon water
4 cups milk, heated
2 cups breadcrumbs
2 eggs, lightly beaten
½ teaspoon vanilla essence
pinch salt

Make caramel by heating half a cup of the sugar in a saucepan with the water until sugar melts and browns. Add caramel to boiling milk and when dissolved, add the breadcrumbs. Allow to soak for 30 minutes. Add the eggs, remaining sugar, vanilla and salt, and turn into a buttered piedish. Bake for 1 hour at 180°C. Serve cold with whipped cream or ice-cream. Serves 4-6.

Apple Cake or Pudding (see p. 120)

Coffee Meringue Cake

4 egg whites, stiffly beaten
6 tablespoons sugar
1 tablespoon cornflour
1 tablespoon coffee essence

To the stiff egg whites add the other ingredients. Blend carefully and put into 2 sandwich tins lined with greaseproof paper. Bake for 30 minutes at 190°C. Fill with whipped cream flavoured with raspberries, passionfruit etc. Serves 4.

Chocolate Mousse

150g cooking chocolate
½ cup strong coffee
2 eggs, separated

Melt the chocolate in the coffee over low heat. Add egg yolks and stir well until thick, but not boiled. Fold in the stiffly beaten egg whites. Chill overnight and serve in glasses topped with cream. Serves 4.

Chocolate Ginger Cream

3 tablespoons cocoa
2 cups milk
1 tablespoon gelatine
⅕ cup sugar
pinch salt
2 eggs, separated
3 tablespoons shredded, preserved ginger
almond essence

Dissolve cocoa in milk, soften gelatine in a little cold water and add to milk and cocoa. Add sugar and salt and place mixture in top of double boiler, stirring until gelatine dissolves. Beat egg yolks and pour on to the hot mixture, return to heat, stirring constantly until mixture coats the spoon. Add ginger and when custard cools, the almond essence. Fold stiffly beaten egg whites into the mixture, pour into individual glasses, or one mould and chill. Decorate with cream whipped with 1 teaspoon instant coffee, and sprinkle with toasted almonds. Serves 4.

Eggless Spanish Cream

2½ cups milk
2 tablespoons custard powder
1 tablespoon sugar
1 teaspoon rennet

From the milk take enough to mix custard powder to a thin cream. Bring remainder of milk to the boil, add sugar, and slowly stir in the mixed custard powder. Set aside to cool, then stir in the rennet and allow to set. Serves 4.

Banana Tea Cake (see p. 151)

Fruit Fancy

1 packet raspberry jelly
2 cups hot water
2 bananas, peeled and sliced
1½ cups raspberries, or strawberries
1 egg, beaten
1½ cups milk
1 level tablespoon castor sugar
few drops vanilla essence
25g blanched almonds, chopped finely

Dissolve the jelly in hot water and leave to set slightly. Blend in the chopped fruit. Add the milk to the beaten egg and cook, stirring until thick, but do not boil or it will curdle. Remove from heat, stir in sugar and vanilla and cool. Pile jelly and fruit into the centre of individual dessert glasses and pour custard around. Sprinkle with almonds and serve with whipped cream. Serves 4-6.

Fruit Salad Marshmallow Cream

2 eggs whites
1 cup sugar
1 teaspoon vanilla essence
pinch salt
3 bananas, peeled and mashed

Beat all ingredients, except bananas, until stiff. Add bananas and beat until smooth. Line an ovenproof dish with the mixture and bake for 20 minutes at 190°C.

Marshmallow Filling:
1 tablespoon lemon juice
2 tablespoons orange juice
1 level tablespoon gelatine
250g marshmallows, quartered
1 cup apricot purée
½ cup whipped cream
pineapple pieces, for garnish

Heat the fruit juices, add gelatine and stir until dissolved. Add marshmallows and purée, mix well, and fold in cream. Place into prepared meringue shell, chill and serve decorated with pineapple. Serves 4-6.

Frozen Fruit Sponge

1 large sponge cake
1 teaspoon cornflour
½ cup sugar
3 eggs, separated
1 cup milk
25g butter
3 tablespoons lemon juice
grated rind 1 orange
grated rind 1 lemon
2 peaches, stoned and chopped finely
250g strawberries, chopped finely
whipped cream, for garnish
orange segments

Line a mould with waxed paper, then with slices of sponge, about 5cm x 3cm and 1.2cm thick. Mix the cornflour and sugar, add to egg yolks and beat thoroughly. Add milk and cook in the top of a double boiler, until thick and smooth. Remove from heat and add butter, lemon juice and rind. While warm add stiffly beaten egg whites, and then the chopped fruit. Pour a layer of this mixture into the lined mould and cover with more sponge slices. Continue layering until mould is full. Chill overnight. To serve, unmould, remove paper, and cover sides and top with whipped cream, flavoured with orange rind. Decorate with orange segments and whole strawberries. Serves 6.

Gingerale Salad

2 tablespoons gelatine
¼ cup cold water
½ cup boiling water
¼ cup lemon juice
2 tablespoons sugar
1 cup gingerale
1 cup stoned cherries, halved
1 banana, peeled and sliced
1 apple, peeled, cored and diced
2 oranges, peeled and segmented
¼ cup nuts, chopped

Soak gelatine in cold water for 5 minutes, then dissolve in hot water. Add lemon juice, sugar and gingerale, and when mixture begins to thicken add the fruit and nuts. Turn into moulds and chill. Serve with whipped cream. Serves 4-6.

Jellied Ice Cream Dessert

1 packet jelly crystals, any flavour
1 cup hot water
½l vanilla ice-cream, softened

Thoroughly dissolve the jelly crystals in hot water. Stir in the ice-cream until smooth mixture results. Chill for 15 minutes. Different jelly and ice-cream flavours may be used to make an attractive sweet. Serves 4.

Gooseberry Fool

750g green gooseberries
3 tablespoons white wine
3 tablespoons water
3 tablespoons sugar
1¼ cups thick custard sauce
1¼ cups whipped cream
angelica, for garnish

Stew the fruit in wine, water and sugar. When cooked, mash well, chill and fold in the custard sauce. Before serving fold in the cream. Decorate with roses of cream and pieces of angelica. Serves 4-6.

Grape Mould

500g grapes
1½ cups water
¼ cup sugar
1 lemon, quartered
2 tablespoons gelatine
½ cup whipped cream
fresh, whole grapes, for garnish

Put half the quantity of grapes in a saucepan with water, sugar and lemon. Cook gently for 5 minutes. Strain. Dissolve gelatine in the hot liquid and allow to cool. When beginning to set add the remaining grapes, skinned and seeded. Fold in the cream and pour into a wet mould. Turn out when set and garnish with whipped cream and whole grapes. Serves 4.

Grapefruit Egg Jelly

juice and rind 2 large grapefruit
½ cup sugar
1 tablespoon gelatine
2 eggs, separated
whipped cream

Put juice and rind in a measure and fill with water to make 2½ cups. Turn into a saucepan, add sugar and simmer for 10 minutes. Strain off liquid and stir in the gelatine until dissolved. Put yolks in top of a double boiler and stir in the gelatine mixture. Cook over hot water, stirring constantly until mixture thickens. Remove from heat and when cold fold in stiffly-beaten egg whites. Turn into a wet mould and leave until set. Serve with whipped cream. Serves 4.

One Egg Pavlova

1 egg white
1 cup sugar
1 teaspoon vinegar
pinch salt
2 tablespoons hot water
1 teaspoon baking powder
few drops vanilla essence

Put egg white, sugar, vinegar, salt and water in a bowl and beat well over hot water until fluffy. Add baking powder and vanilla, and leave for a few minutes. Spread mixture on to some wet greaseproof paper and cook for 1-1½ hours at 100°C. Serves 4-6.

Orange Delight

2 tablespoons gelatine
2½ cups warm water
⅕ cup castor sugar
juice and thinly pared rind 2 oranges
2 egg whites, stiffly beaten
orange segments, for garnish

Dissolve the gelatine in a little warm water, then add remaining water. Put in a saucepan with the sugar and orange rind. Stir over a low heat until sugar is dissolved. Add juice and bring to boil. Simmer for a few minutes, strain, and leave to cool. Add to the egg whites and whisk until stiff and frothy. Pour into a wet mould. When set, turn out carefully and decorate with whipped cream and orange segments. Serves 4.

Passionfruit and Banana Shape

3 eggs, separated
½ cup sugar
juice ½ lemon
2 teaspoons gelatine
pulp 4 passionfruit
3 bananas, mashed
1 cup cream, whipped

Beat the egg yolks, sugar and lemon juice, and cook over hot water until thick. Remove from heat and add the gelatine dissolved in ½ cup of boiling water. Stir in the passionfruit pulp and bananas and allow to cool. Fold in the stiffly-beaten egg whites and cream, and pour into moulds. Chill. Serves 4-6.

Passionfruit Foam

2 cups water
1 cup sugar
2 tablespoons cornflour
pulp 12 passionfruit
2 eggs, separated

Bring the water and sugar to the boil and thicken with cornflour mixed with a little cold water. Cook for 5 minutes and add pulp. Fold in the stiffly beaten egg whites while mixture is still hot. Beat until light and foamy, cool and serve with a custard sauce made with the egg yolks. Serves 6.

Pastel Snow Puddings

Foundation Recipe

5 tablespoons cornflour
¾ cup sugar
⅛ teaspoon salt
2 cups boiling water
flavouring
2 egg whites, beaten stiffly

Blend the cornflour, ½ cup of the sugar and salt in the top of a double boiler. Gradually stir in the boiling water and cook over a low direct heat, stirring constantly until mixture is smooth and thickened. Place over boiling water, cover and cook for 7 minutes, stirring occasionally. Remove from heat, stir in flavouring, cover and cool completely, stirring occasionally. Fold in the egg whites, and remaining sugar into the cornflour mixture and pour into dessert glasses. Chill and serve with a chilled custard made with the egg yolks. Serves 4.

Orange Snow

foundation mixture (above)
¾ teaspoon grated orange rind
½ cup orange juice
2 tablespoons lemon juice
few drops vanilla essence

To the cooked mixture add the rind, juices and essence. Cover and cool. Serves 4.

Lemon Snow

foundation mixture
½ teaspoon grated lemon rind
¼ cup lemon juice
¼ cup water
few drops green food colouring

To the cooked mixture add the rind, juice, water and colouring. Serves 4.

Pineapple Delight

2 tablespoons gelatine
½ cup cold water
½ cup sugar
1 tablespoon lemon juice
2 cups crushed pineapple, heated
1¼ cups whipped cream, or 2 beaten egg
   whites

Soak the gelatine in water. Add the sugar, juice and dissolved gelatine to the heated pineapple. Chill, stirring occasionally. When it begins to thicken, fold in the cream or egg whites. Serves 4.

Peach Ginger Trifle

1 x 15cm sponge cake, cut into small pieces
1 x 425g tin peaches
1 cup preserved ginger, chopped
2 teaspoons gelatine, dissolved in a little hot
   water
½ cup cream
sugar, to taste

Place the cake in a serving dish. Spoon the peach syrup over to moisten. Arrange fruit over the cake and fill cavities with ginger. Add the dissolved gelatine to the cream with sugar to taste and beat until thick. Spoon this over the peaches and sprinkle with remaining ginger. Serves 4.

Peach Shortcake

1 egg, separated
pinch salt
½ cup sugar
½ cup milk
½ teaspoon vanilla essence
1 cup flour
½ teaspoon baking powder
1 tablespoon butter, melted
½ cup cream, whipped
1 x 450g tin peaches, drained

Beat the egg white, add salt, sprinkle in the sugar and beat until thick. Add the egg yolk, milk and essence. Stir in the flour sifted with baking powder and lastly add the butter. Press into a deep sandwich tin and bake for 20 minutes at 190°C. When cool, split in two and join together with flavoured whipped cream. Pipe more cream on top and decorate with sliced peaches. Serves 4-6.

Peasant Girl Pudding

250g breadcrumbs
½ cup brown sugar
50g butter
750g cooking apples, peeled, cored and .
   chopped
squeeze lemon juice
sugar, to taste
½ cup cream, whipped
50g grated chocolate, for garnish

Mix the breadcrumbs and sugar together and fry in hot butter until crisp. Cook the apples to a pulp with very little water and lemon juice. Add sugar to taste. Put alternate layers of crumb mixture and apple into a glass dish, finishing with a layer of crumbs. When pudding is quite cold, spread with whipped cream and grated chocolate. Serves 4-6

Plum Cream

⅛ teaspoon salt
½ cup sugar
1 tablespoon gelatine
food colouring, optional
½ cup plum juice
1 cup stewed and sieved plums, unsweetened
1 cup whipped cream, or ½ cup whipped
   cream and ½ cup made custard.

Add the salt, sugar, gelatine and colouring to the plum juice, and stir over low heat until dissolved. Pour into the sieved plums, stirring well. When mixture is cold, fold in the whipped cream, pour into a mould and chill. When set, unmould and serve with cream. Serves 4-6.

Cold Plum Pudding

⅕ cup brown sugar
1 tablespoon butter
4 tablespoons flour
1 teaspoon cocoa
2½ cups milk
1 tablespoon coffee essence
2 egg yolks, beaten
½ cup each of raisins, dates, figs and lemon
   peel

Melt the sugar with butter. Add flour, cocoa and milk and cook until thickened. Blend in coffee essence and egg yolks. Mix in the dried fruit. Set in a mould, then turn out and cover with marshmallow topping. Serves 4.

Marshmallow
2 egg whites, beaten stiffly
4 tablespoons sugar
½ cup hot water
2 teaspoons gelatine

Beat the sugar into the stiff egg whites and add the gelatine dissolved in hot water. Whip again and pour over the mould.

Rice Royal

1½ cups biscuit crumbs
¼ teaspoon cinnamon
150g melted butter
¾ cup sugar
1 tablespoon gelatine
¼ cup cold water
3 eggs, separated
3 cups milk
⅖ cup cooked rice
2 teaspoons vanilla essence
pinch ground nutmeg
pinch salt

Combine the crumbs with cinnamon, butter and 2 tablespoons of the sugar. Press into a sandwich tin and chill. Soften the gelatine in cold water and dissolve over boiling water. Beat egg yolks with ½ cup sugar and add to the milk. Stir over a medium heat until mixture coats the spoon. Cool slightly and add rice, vanilla, nutmeg and gelatine. Chill until mixture begins to thicken. Add salt to egg whites and whip until stiff but not dry. Gradually beat in the remaining sugar, then fold into the rice mixture. Pile on to crumb crust and chill overnight. Serve with fruit. Serves 6.

Syrup Mould

1½ tablespoons golden syrup
4½ tablespoons sugar
¾ cup water
1 tablespoon butter
pinch cream of tartar
¾ cup milk
1 tablespoon gelatine, dissolved in
   3 tablespoons hot water

Heat the syrup, sugar and water, stirring until dissolved. Add butter and cream of tartar and boil for 7 minutes. When lukewarm, stir in the milk and when cool add the dissolved gelatine. If the mixture is too hot it will curdle. Pour into a rinsed mould and set. Turn out and decorate with fruit. Serves 4-6.

Spanish Cream

2 tablespoons gelatine
4 cups milk
3 eggs, separated
4 tablespoons sugar
sherry, or other flavouring to taste

Soak the gelatine in milk. Put in a saucepan and bring to the boil, stirring all the time. Beat the egg yolks with sugar, add to the milk and stir until thickened but not boiling. Remove from heat and add the stiffly-beaten egg whites and flavouring. Stir well and pour into a rinsed mould. When set, turn out and serve with fruit. Serves 4-6.

Strawberry Shortcake

3½ cups flour
3 teaspoons baking powder
50g butter
50g lard
2 tablespoons sugar
1 egg, separated
½ cup milk
375g strawberries, chopped
½ cup cream, whipped
whole strawberries, for decoration

Sift the dry ingredients and rub in the fat. Beat the egg yolk lightly with milk, pour into the dry ingredients and mix to a soft dough. Roll out to 1.2cm thickness, cut into 8cm rounds (12). Bake in pairs for 15 minutes at 200°C. Wrap in a cloth until cold. Combine the whipped cream and stiffly-beaten egg white. Add the chopped berries to three quarters of the cream mixture for filling, sweetening to taste. Fill the shortcake rounds and decorate with remaining cream and whole berries. Raspberries, loganberries or peaches may be substituted. Serves 6.

Crust for Chilled Pies

Chocolate Crunch Crust

1½ cups crushed cornflakes
3 tablespoons sugar
3 tablespoons cocoa
¼ teaspoon cinnamon
few drops vanilla essence
4 tablespoons melted butter

Mix all ingredients together, pack into a 20cm pie dish and chill.

Coconut Biscuit Crust

1½ cups coconut
¾ cup fine biscuit crumbs
⅕ cup sugar
½ cup flour
125g soft butter

Combine all ingredients and press into an ovenproof dish. Bake for 25 minutes at 160°C.

Ginger Crumb Crust

1½ cups fine ginger biscuit crumbs
¼ cup icing sugar
125g melted butter

Combine all ingredients and press into a tin lined with greaseproof paper. Allow to set.

Nut Meringue Crust

2 egg whites, stiffly beaten
1 cup rolled oats
1 cup coconut
½ cup chopped walnuts
½ cup chopped almonds
5 tablespoons sugar

To the stiff egg whites add the oats, coconut, nuts and sugar. Line a meat tin with greaseproof paper, wet with cold water and spread with a thin layer of butter. Spread mixture on to this and bake for 45 minutes at 150°C. Serve cold with stewed fruit and cream.

Peanut Butter Crust

1 cup fine wholemeal
½ teaspoon salt
3 tablespoons peanut butter
1 teaspoon baking powder
⅕ cup milk

Combine the dry ingredients, rub in the peanut butter and stir in the milk. Roll out, making slits in the top. Bake for 20 minutes at 180°C.

Pink Coconut Meringue Crust

2 egg whites, stiffly beaten
5 tablespoons castor sugar
1 teaspoon cochineal
1 teaspoon orange essence
1 cup shredded coconut
chopped walnuts, for decoration

Combine all ingredients, press into an ovenproof dish, cover with walnuts and bake for 1 hour, at 150°C. Serve with stewed peaches or strawberries.

Vinegar and Meringue Crust

2 egg whites, stiffly beaten
5 tablespoons castor sugar
1 tablespoon vanilla essence
1 small teaspoon vinegar
1 cup cornflakes
½ cup finely chopped brazil, or hazel nuts

Combine all ingredients, stir well and bake for 1 hour at 150°C. Serve with fruit salad.

Ice-Cream and Frozen Desserts

When making ice-cream always turn the refrigerator to its coldest point. Rich creamy ice-creams are harder to freeze than lighter mixtures containing gelatine or cornflour. Sugar hinders rapid freezing so should not be used in excess. Mixtures are usually taken out when half frozen, beaten in a chilled bowl and returned to the freezer until frozen. The dial may then be switched to normal refrigerator temperature. Do not over freeze.
If fruit is added to ice-cream it must be pulped and sweetened or the fruit juices will freeze hard. Berries, the most common fruit used, are pulped with a potato masher, sprinkled with sugar and stirred until the sugar is completely dissolved.

Ice-Cream

1 tin unsweetened, condensed milk
1 tablespoon gelatine
1 tablespoon cold water
1 teaspoon vanilla
2 tablespoons sugar

Refrigerate the tin of milk the day before using. Empty milk into a large bowl. Dissolve the gelatine in water and when thick, stand in hot water to melt. Cool, but do not allow to set. Add remaining ingredients and gelatine to the milk and beat well until the consistency of whipped cream. The amount will double itself in the beating. Freeze and do not stir. Serves 6.

Simple Ice-Cream

½ cup cream
½ cup top milk
½ tin sweetened, condensed milk
few drops vanilla essence, or 150g melted
    chocolate

Beat the cream and milk until stiff, add the
condensed milk and beat lightly. Stir in vanilla, or
chocolate, and pour into freezing trays. Freeze for 2
hours. Serves 4.

Delicious Vanilla Ice-Cream

1 tin sweetened, condensed milk
1½ cups cream, whipped
1½ cups milk
few drops vanilla essence

Combine all ingredients carefully and pour into
freezing trays and freeze until the mixture begins to
set. Turn into a bowl, beat and return to
refrigerator to finish freezing. Serves 4.

Fresh Fruit Ice-Cream

1 tablespoon gelatine
½ cup water
½ tin sweetened, condensed milk
125g tin reduced cream
1 cup crushed fresh fruit, sweetened with
    ¼ cup icing sugar

Soak the gelatine in a little cold water, then add the
balance of half a cup as hot water to dissolve
thoroughly. Mix together the condensed milk and
reduced cream, and pour dissolved gelatine into
this mixture. Add the fresh fruit, mix well and
pour into freezing trays to freeze. When partially
set, like custard, remove from refrigerator, scrape
into a bowl and beat for ½ minute. Smooth out
and return to freezing tray and freeze. Serves 4-6.

This ice-cream is equally delicious when made with
any one of the following fruits, or they may be
mixed to make a delightful fruit salad ice cream:
Strawberries, bananas, pineapple, cherries, oranges,
apricots, passionfruit, raspberries and peaches.

Cornflour Ice-Cream

½ cup cornflour
1 cup sugar
5 cups milk, scalded
5 cups whipped cream

Mix the dry ingredients and add to the milk. Cook
until slightly thickened. Cool. Add whipped cream
in proportion of 1 cup of mixture to 1 cup of
cream. Pour into freezing trays and stir twice
during freezing process. Serves 12.

Vanilla Ice-Cream with Condensed Milk

1 tin condensed milk
3½ cups water
3 egg yolks, beaten
½ teaspoon sugar
1 teaspoon vanilla essence
juice 1 lemon

Boil milk and water together. Mix the yolks with
sugar, vanilla and lemon juice. Add the milk and
water and stir until thick. Freeze. Serves 4.

Chocolate Ice-Cream

1 tablespoon cocoa
¼ cup sugar
1 tablespoon custard powder
1¼ cups milk
2 tablespoons butter, melted
½ cup cream, or top milk

Make a custard with the cocoa, sugar, custard
powder and milk. Stir in the butter and pour into a
bowl with the cream. Beat well and freeze.
Serves 4.

Raspberry Ice-Cream

250g raspberry jam
1 cup milk
few drops cochineal
juice ½ lemon
1¼ cups cream, whipped

Mix together the jam and milk and pass through a
sieve. Add colouring and strain in lemon juice.
Add mixture carefully to the whipped cream and
blend. Pour into freezing trays and freeze, stirring
twice during the process. Serves 6-8.

Strawberry Ice-Cream

1 tablespoon gelatine, dissolved in
    2 tablespoons cold water
1 tablespoon lemon juice
500g sieved strawberries
¼ cup castor sugar
few drops cochineal
1¼ cups cream, whipped

Add dissolved gelatine, lemon juice and sugar to
the sieved fruit. Freeze until pulpy, then add the
whipped cream and colouring. Beat and freeze,
beat again and freeze until required. Serves 4-6.

Banana Ice-Cream

1 cup mashed bananas
2 tablespoons lemon juice
1 cup milk
1 teaspoon grated lemon peel
2 egg yolks, lightly beaten
½ cup honey
¼ cup sugar
2 egg whites, stiffly beaten

Blend together the bananas, lemon juice, milk, peel, egg yolks and honey. Pour into freezing trays and freeze until almost set. Turn into a bowl and beat until creamy. Gradually beat the sugar into the egg whites and fold into the banana mixture. Return to freezing tray and freeze until firm. Serves 4.

Marshmallow Ice-Cream

1 teaspoon gelatine
4 tablespoons cold water
2 tablespoons sugar
4 heaped tablespoons powdered milk
1¼ cups milk
2 tablespoons sweetened, condensed milk
pulp 4 passionfruit

Soak gelatine in cold water and dissolve over low heat, add sugar and stir until dissolved, and mixture is boiling. Pour into a bowl, cool, then beat until thick. Combine the powdered milk, fresh and condensed milk and add to the marshmallow mixture. Beat well and pour into freezing trays and freeze until hard around the edges. Transfer to a bowl and beat until thick, then add pulp. Return to trays and freeze. Serve with fruit salad. Serves 4-6.

Pineapple Ice-Cream

½ cup cream
½ cup top milk
2 tablespoons icing sugar
2 tablespoons skim milk powder
few drops pineapple essence
1 x 300g tin crushed pineapple

Whip the cream until thick, then add top milk and continue whipping. Add the sugar, milk powder and essence, and beat until thick. Put crushed pineapple in a freezing tray and pour over ice-cream mixture. Freeze for at least 2 hours. Does not require further beating. Serves 4.

Apple Mousse

500g cooking apples, peeled, cored and chopped
1¼ cups water
1 cup sugar
juice 1 lemon
1 egg white, beaten stiffly
1¼ cups cream, whipped

Stew the apples with water, sugar and lemon juice until pulpy. Rub through a sieve and cool, then place in a freezing tray for 30 minutes. Fold together the whipped egg white and cream and fold into the cooled apple purée. Return to freezing tray and freeze. Serves 4-6.

Royal Peach Sherbet

4 tablespoons sugar
1 teaspoon flour
pinch salt
½ cup milk
1 egg, beaten
½ cup peach pulp
2 tablespoons chopped crystalised, or drained cherries
½ teaspoon vanilla essence
½ cup chopped marshmallows
1¼ cups whipped cream

Blend half the sugar with flour and salt. Gradually add milk, stir until boiling, then simmer for 2-3 minutes. Pour slowly on the egg beaten with the remaining sugar, mix well and cool. Add peaches, cherries, vanilla and marshmallows, lastly folding in the whipped cream. Freeze in freezing trays and when thickened, stir to mix fruit evenly throughout. Return to freezer. Serves 4-6.

Raspberry Cream

1 x 450g tin raspberries, drained
16 marshmallows
1 cup cream, whipped
½ cup chopped dates or nuts, or coconut

Place raspberries and marshmallows in the top of a double boiler until marshmallows have melted. Cool. Fold in the fruit or nuts, then the cream, and freeze in freezing trays until firm. Serves 4-6.

Peach Melba

1 x 450g tin peaches, or fresh peach halves
vanilla ice-cream
whipped cream
Melba Sauce (See Toppings)

Arrange fruit in dessert glass with servings of ice-cream and top with cream and sauce.

Banana Mousse

6 bananas, mashed
¼ cup castor sugar
juice 1 orange
juice ½ lemon
½ cup prepared custard
½ cup cream, whipped
2 egg whites, beaten stiffly

To the mashed bananas add the sugar and juices, mix well and chill. When cool, stir in the custard, cream and egg whites and freeze. Serves 4-6.

Fig Freeze

6 ripe figs, peeled and chopped
¼ cup glacé cherries, chopped
¼ cup mixed nuts, chopped
juice ½ lemon
5 tablespoons powdered milk
3 tablespoons sugar
2½ cups milk, slightly warmed
2 teaspoons gelatine, melted in a little warm
　　water
few drops vanilla essence

Combine the figs, cherries, nuts and lemon juice, mash with a fork and chill in the refrigerator. Mix the powdered milk and sugar, then add the warm milk. Beat well. Add gelatine gradually, then essence, making sure the powdered milk and sugar are thoroughly dissolved. Pour mixture into a freezing tray and freeze. Turn into a chilled bowl and beat until quantity doubles. Gradually whisk in the fruit and nut mixture, mix well, pour into trays and return to freezer. Serves 6.

Marshmallow Pears

18 marshmallows
4 tablespoons pear juice
1 cup crushed, stewed pears
3 tablespoons chopped, preserved ginger
1 tablespoon lemon juice
1 cup stiffly-whipped cream

Steam the marshmallows in juice over hot water until melted. Add the stewed pears, ginger and lemon juice. Cool. When quite cold and slightly stiffened, carefully combine the mixture with cream. Pour into freezing trays and freeze. Serves 4-6.

Ice-Cream Toppings

Butterscotch
¾ cup brown sugar
2 tablespoons golden syrup
2 tablespoons butter
¼ cup top milk

Over hot water melt the sugar, syrup and butter. Add milk and cook for 15 minutes.

Chocolate
50g dark chocolate, grated
¼ cup hot water
2 tablespoons butter
1 tablespoon cream, or top milk
few drops vanilla essence

Melt the chocolate in hot water. Add butter, cream and vanilla, and stir well. Serve hot.

Melba
1 cup raspberry purée
75g sugar
1 teaspoon cornflour
¼ cup redcurrant jelly

Heat the purée, sweeten with sugar and thicken with cornflour. Stir until clear. Add jelly, or dilute the required amount of raspberry jam with a little hot water.

Strawberry, blackcurrant, loganberry, blackberry and boysenberry jams all make excellent sauces for ice-creams.

CAKES

Cakes rise and are made light by beating in air and by the use of leavening agents, the popular ones being baking powder and baking soda. These work when moisture and heat are present, their action being to liberate tiny bubbles of carbon dioxide which aerate the mixture. Baking powder consists of baking soda, an acid, and a buffer substance, usually cornflour. The acids in baking powder differ; some are tartaric, others phosphate. The housewife soon learns which she prefers. Baking soda will not aerate a cake on its own and requires the presence of an acid agent. Sour milk, cream of tartar, treacle or golden syrup may be used. Self-raising flour has a leavening agent present in the flour so no added powders are needed. Although this makes baking a little easier, it does not keep well unless kept in a cool dry place.

- Use 2 level teaspoons baking powder to each cup of flour.
- After the first egg, reduce the baking powder by ½ teaspoon for each egg.
- If baking soda and sour milk are used, allow ½ teaspoon soda to each cup of sour milk. In addition, allow 1 teaspoon baking powder to each cup of flour.
- If baking soda and treacle or golden syrup are used, allow ½ teaspoon soda to 1 cup treacle.
- If using cream of tartar, allow ½ teaspoon soda and 1 teaspoon cream of tartar to each cup of flour.
- To each cup wholemeal flour allow 2½ teaspoons baking powder.

Apple Cake or Pudding

125g butter
125g sugar
2 eggs
225g flour
1 teaspoon baking powder
½ teaspoon mixed spice
½ teaspoon cinnamon
½ teaspoon ground cloves
1 tablespoon cornflour
½ cup milk

Cream the butter and sugar. Add the eggs and beat well. Sift in the flour, baking powder, spices and cornflour. Fold in the milk and beat carefully until smooth. Spread in a 23cm square tin.

Topping
2 apples, peeled, cored and sliced
2 tablespoons brown sugar
1 cereal biscuit, crumbed
½ cup chopped raisins
juice ½ lemon
2 tablespoons butter

Arrange apple slices over the cake, sprinkle with sugar, biscuit crumbs, raisins and lemon juice and dot with butter. Cook for 40 minutes at 180°C. When cold, cut into squares and serve as cake, or leave in the tin for 10 minutes, cut into pieces and serve hot with cream as a pudding. Serves 6-8.

Apple Sauce Cake

125g butter
125g castor sugar
1 egg, beaten
1 cup apple sauce
2½ cups flour, sifted
½ teaspoon salt
1½ teaspoons baking soda
1 teaspoon cinnamon
1 teaspoon ground ginger
1 cup hot water

Cream the butter and sugar. Add egg and sauce and fold in the sifted dry ingredients. Lastly add hot water, pour into a greased 21cm baking tin and bake for 40-50 minutes at 180°C.

Almond Ring Cake

125g butter
125g flour
1 level teaspoon baking powder
pinch salt
3 cereal biscuits, crushed
175g sugar
25g desiccated coconut
1 teaspoon vanilla essence
1 tablespoon cocoa
1 cup milk
chocolate icing, flavoured with either vanilla
    or peppermint
chopped almonds, or walnuts, for decoration

Rub butter into the flour, baking powder, salt,
crushed biscuits, sugar, coconut, vanilla and cocoa.
Mix thoroughly, then blend in the milk. Bake in a
well-buttered 18cm ring tin for 45 minutes at
180°C. When cool, ice with chocolate icing and
sprinkle with nuts.

Banana and Ginger Cake

75g butter
¾ cup brown sugar
1 egg, well beaten
1 cup flour
1 teaspoon baking powder
2 ripe bananas, mashed
½ cup chopped, preserved ginger
1 teaspoon baking soda, dissolved in a little
    hot water
chocolate icing
2 tablespoons chopped, preserved ginger, for
    decoration

Cream the butter and sugar. Add the egg and sift
in the flour and baking powder. Add the bananas
and ginger and lastly mix in the soda. Pour into a
greased deep, 18cm round sandwich tin and cook
for 50 minutes at 180°C. When cold ice with
chocolate icing and sprinkle with chopped ginger.

Blackberry Cake

125g butter
1 cup brown sugar
3 eggs, separated
½ teaspoon baking soda
½ teaspoon cinnamon
250g flour
2 teaspoons baking powder
1 cup blackberry jam
2 tablespoons sour cream or yoghurt
½ cup chopped nuts and raisins

Cream the butter and sugar and add the beaten egg
yolks. Sift in the dry ingredients and then add the
jam, milk, nuts and raisins and beaten egg whites.
Divide into 2 x 20cm sandwich tins and bake for
40 minutes at 180°C.

Butter Crunch Cake

Crunch Mixture
125g butter
125g sugar
½ cup dry breadcrumbs
½ cup finely chopped nuts

Mix the butter and sugar until crumbly, add
breadcrumbs and nuts, and mix well. Press this
mixture on to the bottom and sides of a baking
pan, approximately 20cm x 30cm.

Cake Batter Filling
1 cup sugar
75g butter
2 eggs, well beaten
250g flour
2½ teaspoons baking powder
½ teaspoon salt
⅔ cup milk
1 teaspoon vanilla essence
¼ teaspoon almond essence

Cream the butter and sugar. Add eggs and mix
well. Add the sifted dry ingredients in thirds,
alternately with the milk and flavouring. Pour into
a 20cm x 30cm sponge roll tin and bake for 50
minutes at 180°C. Let stand for 5 minutes before
turning out on to a cake rack.

Chocolate Health Cake

125g butter
250g sugar
1 tablespoon golden syrup
1 teaspoon baking soda
1 teaspoon baking powder
1 cup flour
½ cup semolina
½ cup wholemeal flour
1 tablespoon cocoa
1 cup hot milk

Melt the butter and sugar, add syrup and beat well.
Add soda to the warm mixture, and then the dry
ingredients alternately with the hot milk. Bake in a
deep, 20cm round tin for 20–30 minutes at 200°C.

Filling
2 tablespoons butter
2 tablespoons boiling water
2 tablespoons sugar

Combine all ingredients and beat well until
creamy.

Icing
1 cup icing sugar
1 tablespoon coffee essence
few drops vanilla essence
½ cup chopped walnuts, for decoration

Combine sugar and essences, mix well, ice the cake
and sprinkle with nuts.

Caramel Cake

125g butter
1 cup sugar
1 egg, beaten
1 tablespoon golden syrup
1 cup milk
1 level teaspoon baking soda
1½ cups flour
1 teaspoon baking powder
pinch salt
few drops vanilla essence
½ cup raisins
1 tablespoon cocoa
caramel frosting
½ cup chopped nuts, for decoration

Cream the butter and sugar, add the egg, and mix well. In a small saucepan melt the syrup and milk, and add the soda. Add this to the previous mixture. Sift in the flour, baking powder, salt and essence. Pour half of this mixture into a greased· 18cm square tin and spread with raisins. Stir the cocoa into the remaining mixture, blend well and pour lightly on top of the first mixture. Bake for 45-60 minutes at 190°C. Ice with caramel frosting and sprinkle with nuts.

Caramel Frosting
2 tablespoons butter
4 tablespoons brown sugar
1 tablespoon milk
icing sugar

Cook butter and sugar over low heat for 2 minutes. Add milk and bring to boil. Cool and add enough icing sugar to make of spreading consistency. This is a delicious frosting.

Chocolate Potato Cake

50g dark chocolate
125g butter
¾ cup castor sugar
⅖ cup cooked, mashed potato, loosely packed
⅕ cup cocoa
2 eggs
1½ cups self-raising flour, sifted
½ teaspoon salt
⅕ cup milk

Put chocolate over hot water to melt. Cream butter, add sugar and potato, beat well. Add melted chocolate and sifted cocoa, add eggs one at a time beating well after each addition. Fold in flour and salt alternately with milk. Spoon mixture into two greased, 20cm sandwich tins. Bake for 25-30 minutes at 180°C. Cool. Sandwich layers together with whipped cream and top with chocolate icing.

Chocolate Sponge

3 eggs, beaten
1 cup sugar
1 cup flour
1½ teaspoons baking powder
1 tablespoon cocoa
75g butter, melted in 6 tablespoons boiling milk

Blend together the eggs and sugar. Sift in the dry ingredients and mix. Lastly add the butter, melted in milk. Pour into 2 x 18cm greased sandwich tins and bake for 20 minutes at 180°C.

Chocolate Malt Sponge

75g butter
1 tablespoon malt extract
2 tablespoons milk
3 eggs, beaten
1 cup sugar
1 tablespoon cocoa
1 cup flour
1 teaspoon baking powder
pinch salt

Warm the butter, malt and milk. Combine eggs and sugar, beat well, then trickle the warm mixture onto the eggs. Fold in the sifted dry ingredients and bake in 2 x 20cm round sandwich tins for 30 minutes at 180°C. Ice and fill with chocolate icing.

Chocolate Cake (Sour Milk)

1 tablespoon butter
1 cup brown sugar
1 egg
2 tablespoons cocoa
1 teaspoon soda
pinch salt
1 cup flour
1 cup sour cream or yoghurt
few drops vanilla essence

Cream the butter and sugar, add the egg and beat well. Add the sifted dry ingredients alternately with the milk. Add essence, pour into a buttered, deep, 9cm round tin and bake for 30 minutes at 180°C.

Chocolate Rhapsody Cake

125g butter
250g sugar
2 eggs
250g flour, sifted
2 teaspoons baking powder
pinch salt
½ cup milk
1 teaspoon grated orange rind
1 tablespoon orange juice
2 tablespoons cocoa
good pinch soda
2 tablespoons milk

Cream the butter and sugar. Add the eggs one at a time, beating well. Add flour, baking powder and salt alternately with milk. Divide into 2 equal portions. Add orange rind and juice to one portion. Mix cocoa, soda and the tablespoon of milk and add to the second portion. Place alternate spoonfuls of the two mixtures into 2 well-greased and floured 18cm sandwich tins and bake for 30 minutes at 180°C.

Icing
1½ tablespoons butter
3 tablespoons milk
2 cups icing sugar
1 tablespoon cocoa
1 teaspoon grated orange rind
2 tablespoons orange juice

Heat the butter and milk, and stir in the icing sugar. Divide in two, add cocoa to one half, the orange rind and juice to the other. Join cakes with orange icing and cover top and sides with chocolate icing. Decorate as desired.

Coffee-Apricot Cake

125g butter
1 cup sugar
3 eggs
1 tablespoon golden syrup
250g flour
2 teaspoons baking powder
¼ teaspoon salt
½ teaspoon vanilla essence
1 tablespoon coffee essence
milk, to mix, approximately ½ cup
3 tablespoons apricot jam
¼ cup chopped walnuts

Cream the butter and sugar, add eggs one at a time and beat well. Add syrup, dry ingredients and vanilla, lastly adding the coffee essence and milk. Grease and flour a 23cm square tin. Put half the mixture in, spread with jam and sprinkle with nuts. Add remaining mixture and bake for 45 minutes at 180°C. Ice with coffee icing and decorate with walnut halves.

Coffee Cake

225g self-raising flour
pinch salt
175g butter
1 cup brown sugar
1 tablespoon coffee essence
3 eggs
50g chopped walnuts
1-2 tablespoons milk

Sift flour and salt together. Cream butter and sugar, beat in coffee essence. Lightly beat eggs and beat into butter mixture a little at a time beating each addition in well before adding next. Fold in flour and chopped walnuts adding enough milk to make a medium soft consistency. Divide mixture between 2 x 20cm sponge sandwich tins. Bake for 25 minutes at 190°C.

Coffee Butter Cream Filling
100g butter
175g icing sugar
1 tablespoon coffee essence
few walnut halves

Cream butter until soft, beat in sieved icing sugar and coffee essence. Use half the cream to sandwich layers together and the remainder to frost the top of the cake. Decorate with walnut halves.

Sultana Crumb Cake

175g butter
2 cups flour
1 cup sugar
1 cup milk
1 egg, beaten
2 teaspoons baking powder
1 cup sultanas
1½ teaspoons mixed spice

Rub the butter into the flour and sugar. Mix to a fine texture and take out 1 cup of this mixture. To the rest add the milk, egg, baking powder, sultanas and spice. Pour into a greased 23cm square tin, scatter the retained portion of crumb mixture over the top and bake for 45-60 minutes at 180°C.

Daffodil Cake

125g butter
¾ cup sugar
3 eggs
grated rind 2 oranges
1½ cups flour
2 teaspoons baking powder
pinch salt
milk to mix

Cream butter and sugar until light and fluffy. Beat eggs gradually into creamed mixture, add orange rind. Sift flour, baking powder and salt. Stir gently into the creamed mixture adding milk as necessary to make a soft, dropping consistency. Divide mixture between 2 x 20cm sandwich tins, greased or lined with paper. Bake for 20-30 minutes at 180°C. When cold fill with orange butter icing and leave top plain or ice with orange glace icing as desired.

Coffee Ginger Cake

250g gingernuts
50g butter
50g sugar
1 tablespoon coffee essence
1 egg, well beaten
coffee butter icing
½ cup walnut halves

Finely crush some of the biscuits and break the rest into small pieces. Simmer together the butter, sugar, essence and egg. Mix in the biscuits, knead into a 3cm x 30cm roll, wrap in greaseproof paper and leave in refrigerator overnight. Ice with coffee butter icing and decorate with walnut halves.

Crumb Cake

4 tablespoons butter
1½ cups flour
1 cup sugar
pinch salt
2 teaspoons baking powder
1 egg, beaten
few drops vanilla essence
½ cup milk

Rub the butter into the flour and sugar. Add salt and baking powder, mix well and take out 1 cup of this crumb mixture. To the rest add the egg, vanilla and milk. Pour into a greased 20cm round tin with a loose base and sprinkle with remaining crumb mixture. Bake for 40 minutes at 180°C.

Feather Mint Cake

1 cup flour
1½ teaspoons baking powder
¾ cup castor sugar
pinch salt
3 tablespoons cooking oil
4 egg yolks
½ teaspoon peppermint essence
⅓ cup cold water
4 egg whites
¼ teaspoon cream of tartar

Sift flour with baking powder, sugar and salt into a bowl. Make a well in the centre and in this place the oil, egg yolks and peppermint essence. Add water and draw in the flour gradually and beat to a smooth butter. Whisk the egg whites until stiff with the cream of tartar, pour the egg yolk mixture over the surface of the whites and using a metal spoon mix lightly until blended. Turn into a 23cm tube tin and bake for 50-55 minutes at 160°C. When cooked, invert the tin onto a wire rack and leave until cool. Loosen cake from tin, ice and decorate as desired.

Genoa Cake

225g butter
grated rind 1 lemon
1 cup sugar
5 eggs
2½ cups flour
1 teaspoon baking powder
pinch salt
350g sultanas
100g glacé cherries
75g candied peal
50g almonds

Cream butter, add lemon rind and sugar and beat again until light and soft. Beat in each egg with a tablespoon of flour, sift the remaining flour with the baking powder and salt and fold ⅕ into the mixture. Stir in sultanas, halved cherries and finely shredded peel. Fold in remaining flour and turn the mixture into the tin and bake at 150-160°C for 1½-2 hours.

Ginger Cake

125g butter
125g sugar
3 tablespoons golden syrup
2 eggs, beaten
250g wholemeal flour
1 teaspoon ground ginger
1 teaspoon mixed spice
1 teaspoon baking soda, mixed with ½ cup milk
50g chopped, preserved ginger
50g sultanas
50g chopped walnuts

Cream together the butter, sugar and syrup. Add the eggs alternating with the dry ingredients. Add the soda dissolved in milk and finally the fruit and nuts. Mix well, pour into a greased 21cm x 19cm square shallow tin and bake for 40 minutes at 180°C.

Golden Peach Cake

125g butter
1 cup sugar
2 eggs, beaten
2 cups flour
½ teaspoon baking powder
1 teaspoon baking soda
1 cup unsweetened, sieved cooked peaches

Cream together the butter and sugar and add the eggs. Sift in the dry ingredients, then the cold peach purée. Pour into 2 greased 20cm sandwich tins and bake for 30 minutes at 180°C.

Filling
2 peaches peeled, stoned, and mashed
½ cup water
1 level tablespoon gelatine

124

Cook the peaches in water until very soft. Remove from heat and add gelatine. When mixture starts to set, whip until thick and put between cakes. Dust with icing sugar.

Golden Date Cake

125g butter
1 cup sugar
2 eggs
1 tablespoon golden syrup
2 teaspoons baking powder
250g flour
1 cup chopped dates
1 tablespoon coffee essence
few drops lemon essence
milk, to mix

Cream together the butter and sugar, and add the eggs, syrup and remaining ingredients. Pour into a greased, deep, round, 21cm tin and bake for 40 minutes at 180°C. Ice with lemon icing when cold.

Grapefruit Cake

250g butter
250g sugar
1 tablespoon golden syrup
2 eggs
1 teaspoon baking soda
1 teaspoon vinegar
250g flour
pinch salt
1 teaspoon mixed spice
2 cups mixed fruit
juice and grated rind 1 grapefruit

Melt the butter and sugar and stir in the syrup. Add eggs and beat well. Stir in soda and vinegar and sift in the flour, salt and spice. Add the fruit, juice and rind, mix well and bake in a greased, lined, 23cm tin for 2 hours at 180°C.

Leap Year Ring Cake

125g butter
1 cup sugar
2 eggs, well beaten
juice and grated rind 1 orange
1 cup flour
1 teaspoon baking powder
pinch salt
½ cup desiccated coconut

Cream the butter and sugar. Add the eggs, juice and rind, mix well, then blend in the flour, baking powder, salt and coconut. Line a 20cm ring tin with greased paper, pour in mixture and bake for 30 minutes at 180°C. When cold ice with gem icing.
Gem Icing
1 cup icing sugar
1 level tablespoon butter
1 teaspoon vanilla essence
pinch salt
1 tablespoon milk

Cream together the sugar and butter, add the essence and salt, mix well adding milk, and ice the cold cake. Sprinkle with toasted coconut.

Madeira Cake

175g butter
175g sugar
rind ½ lemon, finely grated
3 eggs, well beaten
175g flour
1 teaspoon baking powder

Cream butter and sugar, add lemon rind. Add eggs alternately with sifted dry ingredients. Place in greased 23cm tin. Bake approximately 1 hour at 180°C.

Madeira Seed Cake

250g butter
1 cup sugar
3 eggs, separated
juice and grated rind 1 lemon
1 teaspoon caraway seeds
1½ cups flour
pinch salt
1 teaspoon baking powder
½ cup milk

Cream together the butter and sugar, then add the egg yolks, juice, rind and seeds. Sift in the flour, salt and baking powder alternately with the milk. Fold in stiffly beaten egg whites, pour into a greased, 21cm tin and bake for 45 minutes at 180°C. The top may be sprinkled with sugar and a strip of lemon rind in the centre.

Mocha Cake

125g butter
1 cup sugar
3 eggs, separated
2 cups flour
2 teaspoons baking powder
½ cup milk
1 teaspoon vanilla essence
100g blanched almonds, toasted and chopped
    finely

Cream together the butter and sugar, add egg yolks, then the stiffly-beaten egg whites, flour, baking powder, milk and vanilla. Beat lightly together and bake in a 23cm x 35cm sponge roll tin for 40 minutes at 180°C. When cold, cut in narrow, oblong pieces, cover all sides with icing and roll in almonds.

Icing
125g butter
2 cups icing sugar
1 tablespoon milk
½ teaspoon vanilla essence

Cream together all the ingredients.

Never-Fail Sponge

3 eggs
½ cup sugar
¾ cup flour
pinch salt
25g butter
3 tablespoons hot water

Beat eggs and sugar until very thick and fluffy. Sift flour and salt together and gently fold into the egg mixture. Lastly fold in the butter, melted in the hot water. Divide between 2 x 18cm sandwich tins that have been greased and floured. Bake at 190°C for 20 minutes.

Orange Cake

50g butter
1 cup sugar
2 eggs
1¼ cups flour
1 teaspoon cream of tartar
½ teaspoon baking soda
pinch salt
1 tablespoon milk
juice and grated rind 1 orange

Cream together the butter and sugar. Add eggs and beat well. Sift in the flour, cream of tartar, soda and salt. Add alternately with milk, juice and rind and blend well. Pour into a greased 20cm round tin and bake for 45 minutes at 180°C. Ice with orange icing when cold.

De Luxe Orange Cake

125g butter
125g sugar
2 eggs
juice and grated rind 1 orange
175g flour
1 teaspoon baking powder
75g desiccated coconut

Butter a 20cm square tin and sprinkle with 2 tablespoons of coconut. Cream together the butter, sugar, eggs and most of the juice and rind. Add flour, baking powder and rest of coconut, blending well. Use a little milk if the mixture is too stiff. Pour into prepared tin and bake for 30 minutes at 180°C. Leave cake in the tin for an hour, then place on buttered paper on a wire rack. Ice the coconut side with orange icing made with the balance of orange juice and rind. Orange essence may be substituted.

Peach Slice Cake

125g butter
1 cup sugar
1 teaspoon salt
1 egg, beaten
1 teaspoon baking soda
1 teaspoon ground ginger
1 teaspoon ground cloves
1 teaspoon cinnamon
½ teaspoon ground nutmeg
1 cup drained, cooked and sieved peaches
2 cups flour
1 teaspoon baking powder
½ cup walnuts, chopped

Cream together the butter, sugar and salt. Beat in the egg. Stir the soda and spices into the peach purée and add to the first mixture. Blend in the sifted dry ingredients, lastly adding the nuts. Stir well and pour into a buttered 23cm x 35cm tin. Sprinkle top with 1 tablespoon of sugar and cinnamon and bake for 1 hour at 180°C.

Peanut Cake

3 eggs
¾ cup sugar
500g peanuts, minced
1 teaspoon baking powder
pinch salt

Beat together the eggs and sugar, then fold in the nuts, baking powder and salt. Pour into a greased 23cm x 35cm sponge roll tin and bake for 30 minutes at 180°C. When cold ice with chocolate icing.

Raisin Cake

1 cup sugar
125g butter
1 egg
1 cup cold apple purée
1 cup raisins, chopped
2 cups flour
½ teaspoon allspice
½ teaspoon cinnamon
½ teaspoon ground nutmeg
pinch salt
1 teaspoon baking soda, dissolved in
   2 tablespoons warm milk

Cream together the butter and sugar. Add the egg, beat well, then add the remaining ingredients. Mix well and bake in a 20cm greased tin for 40-50 minutes at 180°C.

Golden Peach Cake (see p. 124)

Pineapple Cake

2 tablespoons butter
1 tablespoon sugar
1 egg, beaten
1 cup flour
½ teaspoon cream of tartar
¼ teaspoon baking soda
1 x 350g tin crushed pineapple

Cream together the butter and sugar. Add the egg and mix well. Add the sifted dry ingredients and blend well. Roll out thin and spread in a greased 23cm square tin. Cover with pineapple and topping and bake for approximately 30 minutes at 180°C. Cut into fingers or squares.

Topping
2 cups desiccated coconut
1 egg, beaten
1 cup brown sugar

Blend together all the ingredients and spread over pineapple.

Prune Cake

125g butter
1 cup sugar
3 eggs
1½ cups flour
1 teaspoon cream of tartar
1 teaspoon baking soda
1 teaspoon cinnamon
1 teaspoon mixed spice
1 cup cold, cooked prunes, chopped
4 tablespoons prune juice

Cream together the butter and sugar, then add eggs one at a time, beating well after each one. Add the sifted dry ingredients, then the prunes and juice. Blend well, pour into a greased 20cm tin and bake for 1 hour at 160°C.

Seed Cake

250g butter
2 cups sugar
4 eggs, separated
3 cups flour
¼ teaspoon salt
1 tablespoon baking powder
1 tablespoon caraway seeds
1 cup milk

Cream together the butter and sugar, add the well-beaten egg yolks one at a time, and beat again. Stir in the sifted flour, baking powder and salt, alternating with the seeds and milk. Fold in the stiffly-beaten egg whites. Bake in a 25cm round, greased tin for 1-1½ hours at 180°C.

Rhubarb Cake

125g butter
1 cup light brown sugar
2 eggs, well beaten
1 cup stewed rhubarb, drained
1 cup raisins
1 teaspoon baking soda, dissolved in
   2 tablespoons rhubarb juice
1½ cups flour
½ teaspoon cinnamon
½ teaspoon ground ginger
pinch salt
2 cloves

Cream together the butter and sugar. Add the eggs, then stir in the rhubarb, raisins, soda and sifted dry ingredients. Blend well and spread in a 23cm tin. Stick in the cloves and bake for 1 hour at 180°C. When cold remove the cloves and ice.

Icing
1 tablespoon butter
2 tablespoons brown sugar
1 tablespoon golden syrup
pinch ground nutmeg

Cream together the butter and sugar and stir over low heat. Add the syrup and nutmeg and, when setting, spread over the cake.

Wholemeal Simnel Cake

Almond Paste
50g ground almonds
50g castor sugar
50g icing sugar
1 egg, well beaten

Mix all ingredients to a firm paste.

Cake
500g mixed fruit
250g sultanas
250g butter, chopped
1 teaspoon ground cinnamon
1 teaspoon ground cloves
1 teaspoon allspice
1 teaspoon vanilla essence
75g cherries
3 eggs
1½ cups raw sugar
2½ cups wholemeal flour
2 teaspoons baking powder

Cover mixed fruit and sultanas with water in a saucepan. Bring to boil and simmer for 5 minutes. Strain off water, add butter and spices, essence and cherries. Beat eggs with sugar, blend and add flour and baking powder. Mix with fruit mixture. Place half of mixture into a 20cm square cake tin. Place a layer of almond paste on top. Cover with remainder of cake mixture. Bake for 1½ hours at 150°C.

Chocolate Rhapsody Cake (see p. 123)

Simnel Cake

250g butter
1 cup sugar
4 eggs
2½ cups flour
50g ground rice
1 teaspoon baking powder
100g candied peel
50g crystallized cherries
500g currants
whole, blanched almonds, optional

Cream butter and sugar, add eggs one at a time beating well. Sift flour, ground rice and baking powder together. Chop peel and cherries and blend well with currants. Add flour and fruit alternately to the butter mixture. Put half cake mixture into tin. Place almond paste on top and spoon remaining cake mixture on top. Level off mixture. Bake for 30 minutes at 160°C, then lower heat to 150°C-140°C for a further 1½ to 2 hours. While cake is cooking roll out the other piece of almond paste to fit the circle. Tip onto the hot cake using paper and press lightly. Stud top layer of almond paste with whole blanched almonds if desired. Return cake to oven for about 15 minutes until almond paste is faintly browned.

Almond Paste
250g ground almonds
⅕ cup castor sugar
½ cup icing sugar
1 egg, beaten
1 tablespoon melted butter

Grease and paper line a 20cm round cake tin. Mix the almonds and sugars. Add egg and blend in with the melted butter. Knead the paste well. Roll out half the quantity to a 20cm circle, setting aside the remainder until cake is baking.

'William Tell' Apple Cake

2 apples, peeled and sliced thinly
2 tablespoons sugar
¼ teaspoon ground nutmeg
1 tablespoon sherry, or brandy
125g butter
1 cup sugar
2 egg yolks
½ cup golden syrup
1 teaspoon baking soda, dissolved in
    1 tablespoon boiling water
1 cup flour
pinch salt
½ teaspoon ground ginger
½ teaspoon cinnamon

Sprinkle the apples with sugar, nutmeg and sherry and leave for at least 1 hour. Cream together the butter and sugar and beat in the egg yolks and syrup. Stir in the foaming soda. Sift in the remaining dry ingredients, mix well and pour into a greased, 20cm round cake tin. Gently insert the apple slices into the mixture and bake for 45-60 minutes at 180°C. Use as a pudding with custard, or ice with lemon icing as a cake.

Fruit Cakes

Fruit cakes, with the exception of a few special recipes such as eggless cakes, are made by the creaming method. The softened butter is beaten with the sugar until light and fluffy, and the eggs are beaten in one by one until the mixture is like whipped cream. Should the mixture curdle at this stage, a little flour helps to smooth it. The fruit should be clean, chopped and floured, and may be added after the flour and liquid.

Once the dry ingredients are added no further beating is necessary; thorough mixing is carried out by lightly mixing with a wooden spoon. An electric mixer should not be used after the eggs have been beaten in unless the mixer has a special blending attachment.

Very little rising is necessary in fruit cakes; if too much is used the cake will sink in the middle. Well-lined tins are necessary and a piece of heavy paper may be put over the top of the cake to prevent burning. Have the paper 5-7.5cm higher than the rim of the cake tin. The oven should be moderately hot to begin with and after 30-45 minutes it should be turned down; it is better for an oven to be too cold rather than too hot as excess heat causes burnt fruit and makes the cake rise in the middle and crack. Always leave a fruit cake to cool in the tin and do not remove the paper until the cake is to be eaten or iced.

Viennese Fruit Cake

125g butter
¾ cup sugar
2 eggs
1 cup milk
2 tablespoons golden syrup
2¼ cups flour, sifted
1 teaspoon cinnamon
2 teaspoons baking powder
1 teaspoon mixed spice
pinch salt
¾ cup fruit mincemeat

Cream together the butter and sugar. Add the eggs, then fold in the milk and syrup alternately with the dry ingredients. Grease and line the bottom of a 20cm tin and fill with the mixture. Bake for 1-1¼ hours at 180°C. When cold, cut in half and fill with fruit mincemeat. Top with lemon icing and decorate with walnuts.

Chocolate Fruit Cake

1 cup warmed, stewed apples
125g butter, softened
1 cup brown sugar
100g raisins
100g sultanas
50g chopped walnuts
2 cups flour, sifted
1½ teaspoons baking soda
1 teaspoon cream of tartar
½ teaspoon mixed spice
1½ tablespoons cocoa

Mix the apples with butter, then beat in the sugar, fruit, nuts and sifted dry ingredients. Blend well and bake for 45 minutes at 180°C. Ice with thick chocolate icing and decorate with walnuts.

Christmas Cake

250g sultanas
250g currants
250g raisins
125g mixed peel
50g glacé cherries
50g blanched almonds, chopped
250g candied pineapple, chopped
250g preserved ginger, chopped
4 cups flour, sifted
¼ teaspoon salt
2 teaspoons mixed spice
2 teaspoons baking soda
250g butter
1½ cups brown sugar
grated rind 1 lemon
4 eggs
1¼ cups milk
1 teaspoon coffee essence
3 teaspoons dark jam

Wash and dry thoroughly the dried fruits, except pineapple and ginger. Sift flour, salt, soda and spice into a large bowl and rub in the butter until crumbly. Stir in the sugar and lemon rind, add fruit and almonds and mix well. Whisk eggs, add milk and coffee essence, then stir in jam. Make a well in the centre of the dry ingredients and pour in the liquid. Stir well and set aside.
Prepare a 20cm square tin with 2 layers of greased, greaseproof paper, and an additional piece of paper for covering. Pour the cake mixture into the tin, making a depression in the centre for a flat icing surface. Bake for 2 hours at 160°C, then remove the top paper and cook for 1 hour longer, reducing the heat to 140°C. Leave in the tin until cold.

Economical Fruit Cake

50g butter
4 tablespoons shredded suet
1 cup sugar
2 eggs
2 tablespoons golden syrup
2 cups flour
1 teaspoon baking powder
pinch salt
½ cup milk
few drops essence, vanilla, lemon or almond
500g mixed fruit

Cream together the butter, suet and sugar. Beat in the eggs and syrup, then the sifted flour, baking powder and salt, added alternately with the essence and milk. Lastly add the fruit, mix well and bake for 30 minutes at 160°C, then reduce to 140°C for 1½ hours. When cold, ice with vanilla butter icing if desired.

Eggless Dundee Cake

275g butter, or margarine
pinch salt
½ cup water
125g mixed peel
50g blanched almonds, chopped
250g sultanas
250g currants
50g glacé cherries, chopped
finely grated rind 2 lemons
finely grated rind 2 oranges
1 x 310g tin sweetened, condensed milk
¾ level teaspoon baking soda
2½ cups flour
50g blanched almond halves

Put all ingredients except the soda and flour in a saucepan, bring to boil and simmer for 3 minutes, stirring continuously. Cool, add the soda and flour, and blend well. Pour into a 20cm square cake tin, place whole blanched almonds on top and bake for 3 hours at 150°C. Leave for 5 minutes before turning out.

Wholemeal Fruit Cake

250g butter
1 cup sugar
4 eggs
3 cups wholemeal flour
1 cup white flour
1 teaspoon baking powder
½ cup milk
500g sultanas
50g lemon peel, chopped
50g preserved ginger, chopped
few drops lemon essence

Cream together the butter and sugar, then beat in the eggs one at a time. Add the sifted flour, baking powder, milk, fruit and essence. Mix well and bake in a lined, 20cm round tin for 2 hours at 150°C.

Eggless Fruit Cake

4 cups flour
1 teaspoon mixed spice
125g butter, or margarine
500g seedless raisins
250g sultanas
50g candied peel
1 cup brown sugar
75g blanched almonds, chopped
1 teaspoon baking soda
1¼ cups milk
1 tablespoon black treacle

Sift the flour and spice into a bowl and rub in the
fat. Stir in the fruit, peel, sugar and most of the
almonds. Dissolve the soda in 1 tablespoon of the
milk and add with the remaining milk and treacle
to the other ingredients. Beat thoroughly. Line a
tin with greased greaseproof paper, turn mixture
into the tin and scatter remaining almonds on top.
Bake for 2-2½ hours at 150°C.

Rich Fruit Cake

500g currants
250g raisins
500g sultanas
175g mixed peel, chopped
125g glacé cherries, chopped
125g blanched almonds, chopped
3 cups flour
300g butter
1¼ cups castor sugar
8 eggs
2 teaspoons mixed spice
pinch salt
grated rind and juice 1 lemon
milk, as required

Cover the prepared fruit and nuts with some of the
flour. Beat the butter and sugar until light and
creamy, then carefully beat in the eggs one at a
time. Should the mixture curdle, stir in a little of
the flour. Sift in the remaining flour, spice and salt
into the mixture and add the floured fruit. Mix
thoroughly then add lemon juice, rind and
sufficient milk to make a stiff batter. Line a 23cm
tin with 3-4 layers of greaseproof paper and drop
mixture in. Smooth top with a spatula and bake for
30 minutes at 160°C, reducing heat to 140°C for a
further 3½-4 hours.

Fruit Cake

175g butter
¾ cup sugar
3 eggs
500g sultanas
250g raisins
125g mixed peel
125g glacé cherries, chopped
½ cup milk
1 tablespoon marmalade
1 tablespoon golden syrup
2 cups flour
½ teaspoon baking powder
½ teaspoon mixed spice
½ teaspoon curry powder

Beat together the butter and sugar, then beat in the
eggs one at a time. Add fruit gradually and
continue beating. Add the milk, marmalade and
syrup warmed together and lastly the sifted dry
ingredients. Bake for approximately 3 hours at
150°C, reducing heat after the first half hour.

Rich Wedding Cake

1kg butter
4 cups brown sugar
12 eggs
2 teaspoons baking soda
½ cup sour milk
2 cups treacle
800g currants
1 kg raisins
250g mixed peel, chopped
125g blanched almonds, chopped
2 cups flour
2 teaspoons cinnamon
½ nutmeg, grated
½ teaspoon pepper
2 teaspoons ground cloves
2 teaspoons mixed spice
1 teaspoon mace
brandy, optional

Cream together the butter and sugar, then beat in
the eggs one at a time. Dissolve the soda in milk
and add to the mixture with the treacle. Stir in the
floured fruit and nuts, then the sifted flour and
spices. Extra flour may be added if necessary to
make a stiff batter. Add brandy if desired.
Pour mixture into well-lined 18cm x 20cm square
tins and bake for 3-4 hours, at 160°C, reducing to
140°C after the first half hour.

Overnight Fruit Cake

250g butter
1 cup brown sugar
4 eggs
1 tablespoon treacle
1 tablespoon coffee essence
2½ cups flour
1 teaspoon cinnamon
½ teaspoon ground nutmeg
½ teaspoon ground cloves
½ teaspoon ground allspice
1kg mixed fruit
grated rind ½ lemon
¼ teaspoon baking soda
1 tablespoon brandy

Cream together the butter and sugar. Add the eggs, beating well after each one. Beat in the treacle and coffee essence, then the sifted flour and spices. Lastly add the fruit, floured if desired, and the rind. Leave overnight. The following day, add the soda dissolved in the brandy and blend well. Line a tin with 2 layers of greaseproof paper and bake for 3-4 hours at 140°C.

Sultana Fruit Cake

250g butter
1 cup sugar
4 eggs
2 cups flour
500g sultanas
125g mixed peel, chopped
125g glacé cherries, halved
125g nuts, chopped
1 teaspoon baking powder
1 teaspoon vanilla essence

Cream together the butter and sugar, then beat in the eggs one at a time. Flour the fruit with some of the measured quantity. Add baking powder to the remaining flour and sift into the cake mixture. Add the fruit, nuts and essence, and blend well. Line a 23cm tin with 2 layers of greaseproof paper, pour in the cake mixture and bake for 2-3 hours at 150°C.

ICINGS AND FILLINGS

Almond Icing

ground almonds
icing sugar
few drops almond essence
1 egg white, beaten

Mix to a paste equal quantities of almonds and sugar, bound with egg white and flavoured with almond essence.

Mock Almond Paste

125g breadcrumbs
250g icing sugar
few drops almond essence
1 egg white, beaten

Mix all ingredients well to make a stiff paste, and press on top of cake. Let stand for an hour to dry, then ice.

Brown Sugar Icing

345g brown sugar
1 cup water
1 egg white, beaten
few drops vanilla essence
chopped nuts, optional

Boil the sugar and water until the mixture spins a thread. Pour over the egg white and beat until thick. Add vanilla and nuts.

Butter Cream Icing

4 tablespoons butter
250g icing sugar
cream, as required
1 teaspoon vanilla essence

Cream the butter, gradually adding the sugar. Beat until light and fluffy. If necessary add a little cream to make the desired consistency. Mix in the essence.

Chocolate Butter Cream Icing

To the basic recipe above add 90g melted, unsweetened chocolate, or 2 tablespoons cocoa. Nuts may be added also.

Orange Butter Cream Icing

To the basic recipe add the grated rind, pulp and juice of ½ an orange and ½ tablespoon lemon juice. If too thin, add a little more icing sugar and beat well.

Coffee Butter Cream Icing

To the basic recipe add 2 tablespoons coffee essence and sprinkle top with chopped, blanched almonds which have been browned in the oven.

Fruit Butter Icing

To the basic recipe add 1 tablespoon strawberry juice and a few drops of red colouring. Sprinkle with coconut.

Caramel Frosting

2 tablespoons butter
4 tablespoons brown sugar
1 tablespoon milk
icing sugar, as required

Cook butter and sugar over low heat for 2 minutes. Add milk and bring to the boil. Cool and add enough icing sugar to make a spreading consistency.

Chocolate Marshmallow Frosting

185g sugar
⅓ cup water
6-8 marshmallows
1 egg white, beaten
few drops vanilla essence
90g dark chocolate
½ teaspoon butter

Boil the sugar and water without stirring until syrup spins a thread. Melt the marshmallows in this syrup, then pour slowly over the egg white. Add vanilla and beat until thick. Spread thickly over cake. Melt the chocolate with butter and spread thinly over the frosting when cool.

Fondant Icing

410g sugar
¾ cup water
pinch cream of tartar

Make a syrup with 90g of the sugar and ¼ cup of water. Boil for 5 minutes and put aside. With the remaining sugar and water make another syrup, adding the cream of tartar and boiling until the consistency of a soft ball in cold water. Pour into a large platter and cool. Work with a wooden spoon until creamy. Add 5 teaspoons of the first syrup and cool in a covered dish. Heat in a double boiler before using.

Ginger Icing

2 teaspoons golden syrup, warmed
2 teaspoons butter
½ teaspoon ground ginger
155g icing sugar, sifted

Combine all ingredients and mix well.

Mocha Frosting

155g icing sugar
2 teaspoons cocoa
2 tablespoons butter
2 teaspoons vanilla
2 tablespoons hot coffee

Mix all ingredients thoroughly.

Orange Icing

220g sugar
¾ cup water
1 egg white, beaten to a froth
½ teaspoon cream of tartar
½ teaspoon grated orange rind
1 tablespoon orange juice

Boil together the sugar and water until it spins a thread when lifted on the spoon. Pour the syrup slowly on to the egg white, beating continuously. Add the rind and juice and beat until a spreading consistency.

Banana Butter Filling

185g icing sugar, sifted
90g butter
1 ripe banana, mashed
30g ground almonds
15g angelica, chopped
3 drops vanilla essence

Cream together the sugar and butter until soft and fluffy. Add the banana, almonds, angelica and vanilla and blend thoroughly.

Pineapple Frosting

2 tablespoons pineapple juice
2 tablespoons butter
2 teaspoons lemon juice
315g icing sugar

Bring the pineapple juice to the boil, remove from heat and add butter and lemon juice. When butter has melted, slowly add the sugar beating well until it is a good spreading consistency.

Seven Minute Frosting

1 egg white, unbeaten
220g sugar
3 tablespoons cold water
½ teaspoon flavouring
½ teaspoon baking powder

In the top of a double boiler place the egg white, sugar and water, and beat for 7 minutes over heat. Add the flavouring and baking powder and beat again.

Variations
Chocolate Frosting
To the basic recipe add 60g melted, dark chocolate 2 minutes before removing from heat.

Coffee Frosting
To the basic recipe add 3 tablespoons strong cold coffee instead of water.

Marshmallow Frosting
After the basic frosting thickens add 8 marshmallows, chopped finely and beat until melted.

Orange and Honey Filling

60g butter
90g castor sugar
1 tablespoon honey
1 teaspoon grated orange rind
1 tablespoon orange juice

Beat all ingredients thoroughly until the consistency of thick cream. Vary the flavour by using 1 tablespoon of lemon curd in place of the orange rind and juice.

Iced Wafer Filling

125g cooking fat
125g icing sugar
few drops vanilla essence

Melt the fat in a saucepan and cool a little before adding the sugar and vanilla. Beat well.

Nutty Chocolate Filling

60g dark chocolate, melted
45g butter, softened
icing sugar, as required
60g finely-chopped walnuts

Cool the melted chocolate and beat in the butter. Add enough sugar to make a soft spreading consistency and finally mix in the walnuts.

Fudge Chocolate Filling

1 egg yolk
3 tablespoons cream, or top milk
125g sugar
125g dark chocolate, broken
1 tablespoon butter

In a saucepan, thoroughly mix the egg yolk, cream, sugar, chocolate and butter. Cook until bubbles appear. Remove from heat and beat until thick. To make chocolate curls to decorate the top of the cake, slightly warm the bar of chocolate and cut off long shavings from the smooth side of the bar and they will curl up.

Lemon and Coconut Filling

30g butter
125g castor sugar
grated rind and juice 1 lemon
1 egg, beaten
60g desiccated coconut

In a small saucepan melt the butter. Add the sugar, rind and juice and stir in the egg. Cook slowly over gentle heat, stirring continuously until mixture thickens. Cool slightly, then stir in the coconut.

Tutti-Frutti Filling

90g sugar
1 tablespoon cream, whipped
60g raisins, minced
60g nutmeats, minced
60g figs, minced

Add the sugar to the whipped cream and beat thoroughly, then stir in the fruit and nuts.

Lemon Cream Filling

3 tablespoons cornflour
125g sugar
½ cup boiling water
1 egg yolk, beaten
2 tablespoons lemon juice
grated rind ½ lemon
1 tablespoon butter

Mix the cornflour and sugar, and add the water. Cook in the top of a double boiler until thick and smooth, stirring continuously. Stir the mixture into the beaten egg, return to saucepan and cook for 2 minutes longer. Remove from heat and add the lemon juice, rind and butter. Cool, then use as a spread with thinly sliced bananas, if desired.

Orange Cream Filling

60g sugar
1½ tablespoons flour
¼ teaspoon salt
2 teaspoons grated orange rind
½ cup orange juice
2 teaspoons butter
1 egg yolk, beaten
1 teaspoon lemon juice

Put the sugar, flour and salt in the top of a double boiler and mix. Add the orange rind and juice, then the butter and egg yolk and cook until thick and smooth, stirring continuously. Remove from heat and add lemon juice.

BISCUITS AND SMALL CAKES

Biscuits

Almond Biscuits

125g butter
½ cup sugar
1 egg, beaten
few drops almond essence
1½ cups flour
1 teaspoon baking powder
blanched almonds, for decoration

Cream together the butter and sugar. Beat in the egg and essence, then sift in the flour and baking powder. Mix well, roll into small balls, flatten with a fork and press an almond into the centre of each. Bake for 15–20 minutes at 180°C. These biscuits keep very well.

Cherry and Almond Biscuits

¾ cup icing sugar, sifted
75g ground almonds
25g walnuts, chopped
½ teaspoon baking powder
1 egg white, stiffly beaten
glacé cherries for decoration

Into a bowl put the sugar, almonds, walnuts and baking powder. Mix with the stiff egg white and put ½ teaspoon lots on greased greaseproof paper on an oven tray. Place a cherry in the centre of each and bake for 20 minutes at 150°C. To remove biscuits easily, slip paper on to a damp cloth, remove biscuits and return to a hot tray for a minute to dry and crisp.

Condensed Milk Biscuits

125g butter
2 tablespoons sugar
2 teaspoons sweetened, condensed milk
1 teaspoon vanilla essence
1 teaspoon baking powder
1 cup flour

Mix all the ingredients in the order given, and form into small balls. Place on a cold baking tray, press lightly with a floured fork and bake for 20 minutes at 180°C.

Chocolate Banana Drops

150g butter
1 cup sugar
2 eggs, beaten
1 teaspoon vanilla essence
150g dark chocolate, melted
2¼ cups flour, sifted
2 teaspoons baking powder
¼ teaspoon baking soda
½ teaspoon salt
2 ripe bananas, mashed

Cream together the butter and sugar, add the eggs and vanilla. Mix in the chocolate, then all the dry ingredients alternately with the bananas. Drop in teaspoon lots 4cm apart on an ungreased baking tray. Bake for 12-15 minutes at 180°C.

Chocolate Coconut Biscuits

125g butter
¾ cup sugar
1 cup coconut
¾ cup flour
1 egg, beaten
1 tablespoon cocoa
60g walnuts, chopped
pinch salt
few drops vanilla essence

Mix all ingredients in the order given and put in small teaspoon lots on a cold baking tray. Bake for 15 minutes at 180°C. When cold, ice with chocolated and decorate with walnut pieces.

Chocolate Tip Fingers

¼ cup castor sugar
100g butter
1 egg, beaten
1 cup flour
½ cup cornflour
½ teaspoon almond essence
apricot jam, for filling
50g dark chocolate
1 tablespoon water

Cream together the sugar and butter, and beat in the egg. Sift in gradually the flour and cornflour and add the almond essence. Mix well and pipe 8cm strips on to a greased baking tray. Bake for 12 minutes at 180°C. When cold join with jam. Melt the chocolate with water in the top of a double boiler and when dissolved dip each biscuit end in the chocolate and leave to set before storing.

Crunchies

125g butter
¾ cup brown sugar
1 tablespoon golden syrup
2 tablespoons milk
1 cup flour
1 teaspoon baking soda
pinch salt

Cream together the butter and sugar. Melt the syrup in milk and add to the first mixture. Sift in the flour, soda and salt, mix well and place teaspoon lots on a greased baking tray. Bake for 15 minutes at 180°C. Leave plenty of room between biscuits as they spread. If desired they may be rolled up when removed from oven and used as brandy snaps.

Crunchy Mallow Biscuits

3 cereal biscuits, crushed finely
¾ cup sugar
2 tablespoons cocoa
1 cup coconut
1 cup flour
1 teaspoon baking powder
125g vegetable fat
2 level tablespoons gelatine
1 cup boiling water
2 cups sugar
few drops vanilla essence

Mix the crushed biscuits, sugar, cocoa, coconut, flour and baking powder. Melt the fat and mix into the dry ingredients. Press the mixture into a greased tin and bake for 10-15 minutes at 150°C. Allow to cool. Dissolve the gelatine in boiling water and pour over the sugar. Beat until the mixture thickens, adding vanilla. Pour over biscuit and leave to set before cutting into fingers.

Chocolate Snowballs

½ x 400g tin sweetened, condensed milk
1 tablespoon cocoa
¼ cup sugar
1 egg, beaten
250g wine biscuits, crushed
150g mixed fruit
50g desiccated coconut

Melt together the milk, cocoa and sugar. Beat in the egg, remove from heat and add the biscuit crumbs and fruit. Roll into small balls and dip in coconut. Leave to set.

Date Fingers

125g butter
½ cup brown sugar
1¼ cups flour, sifted
pinch salt
½ teaspoon baking soda
1¼ cups rolled oats
¼ cup warm water

Cream together the butter and sugar and work in the flour, salt, soda and oats. Add the warm water to make a stiff dough. Divide mixture into 2 portions and roll each thinly. Spread date filling on one half and cover with the other half. Cut into fingers and bake for 20-25 minutes at 180°C. When cold, ice if desired.

Date Filling
250g pitted dates, chopped
¼ cup cold water
½ teaspoon cinnamon
1 teaspoon lemon juice

Mix all ingredients in a saucepan and cook until smooth. Cool before spreading.

Easy Biscuits

125g butter
½ cup sugar
2 tablespoons condensed milk
1 cup flour
1 teaspoon baking powder
50g raisins, peanuts or chocolate chips

Beat together the butter and sugar, then add the milk, flour, baking powder and finally the raisins. Roll into small balls, flatten with a fork and bake for 15 minutes at 180°C.

Fairy Hedgehogs

4 large ripe bananas, mashed smoothly
⅕ cup castor sugar
75g ground almonds
3 tablespoons drinking chocolate
¼ teaspoon almond essence
1 teaspoon peanut butter
50g chopped almonds, for decoration

To the mashed bananas add all the remaining ingredients except the almonds. Mix well and place in teaspoon lots on a baking tray. Stick chopped almonds over the outside and bake for 20 minutes at 180°C.

Fridge Biscuits

250g butter
2 cups brown sugar
2 eggs, beaten
3½ cups flour
1 level teaspoon baking soda
½ teaspoon salt
few drops vanilla essence
125g walnuts, chopped

Cream together the butter and sugar, add eggs, sifted dry ingredients and nuts. Mix well and form into a long roll about the size of a rolling pin, and wrap in greaseproof paper. Refrigerate until quite firm, then slice thinly and bake for 15 minutes at 180°C. If dough becomes soft and difficult to slice, it may be re-chilled.

Ginger Nuts

125g butter
⅔ cup treacle
2 cups flour
2 teaspoons ground ginger
1 teaspoon allspice
1 cup sugar

Melt the butter with the treacle and add the sifted dry ingredients. Blend well and roll into small balls. Flatten slightly and bake for 20 minutes at 180°C.

Hokey Pokey Biscuits

125g butter
1 cup sugar
1 tablespoon milk
1 tablespoon golden syrup
1 teaspoon baking soda
1 cup flour
pinch salt

Cream together the butter and sugar. Warm the milk and syrup, stir in the soda until it foams, then add to the butter and sugar. Beat in the flour and salt and mix well. Roll into small balls, place on a cold tray, press with a fork and bake for 10 minutes at 180°C. Makes approximately 40 biscuits.

Lady's Fingers

125g butter
1 cup sugar
1 egg
1½ teaspoons vanilla essence
2½ cups flour, sifted
2 teaspoons baking powder
¼ cup milk

Cream together the butter and sugar, add the egg, vanilla, flour, baking powder and milk, and mix well. Pat out on a sugared board, cut into 6cm strips and roll each lightly with the hands. Bake for 10-15 minutes at 190°C. Do not use a rolling pin.

Marzipan Bars

75g butter
3 tablespoons water
½ cup castor sugar
2 tablespoons apricot jam
¾ cup semolina
1 teaspoon almond essence
¼ teaspoon lemon essence
¼ teaspoon vanilla essence

Melt the butter in water without boiling. Add the sugar and jam, bring to the boil and stir in the semolina. Simmer gently, stirring continuously, until thick. Remove from heat and beat in the essences. When cool, roll out and cut into bars. If desired, before rolling add green or pink colouring to a portion of the mixture to obtain a marbled effect.

Meg's Biscuits

125g butter
½ cup sugar
1 cup flour
1½ teaspoons golden syrup
1 teaspoon baking powder
½ cup cornflour
¾ cup walnuts, chopped

Cream together the butter and sugar, mix in the other ingredients and roll into small balls. Put on a cold greased baking tray and cook for 15 minutes at 160°C.

Melting Moments

250g butter
⅕ cup icing sugar
½ cup cornflour
1½ cups flour
few drops vanilla essence

Cream together the butter and sugar, then add the cornflour, flour and vanilla. Mix well and put in teaspoonful lots on a greased baking tray. Bake for 15 minutes at 180°C. When cool join with vanilla icing.

Orange Cream Biscuits

1 cup flour
½ cup castor sugar
pinch salt
2 tablespoons full-cream milk powder
½ teaspoon baking powder
grated rind ½ orange
125g butter
1 egg yolk beaten

In a bowl mix the flour, sugar, salt, milk powder, baking powder and orange rind. Rub in the butter and bind with the egg yolk. Roll out, cut into shapes and bake for 15 minutes at 160°C. When cold join together with orange filling.

Orange Filling
1 teaspoon butter
¾ cup icing sugar
pinch salt
1 teaspoon orange juice

Mix all ingredients thoroughly.

Passionfruit Crunchies

175g butter
½ cup icing sugar, sifted
pulp 4 passionfruit
1½ cups self-raising flour
1 cup cornflour
pinch salt

Cream together the butter and sugar, add passionfruit pulp and the dry ingredients. Mix well and drop teaspoon lots on a cold baking tray. Bake for 15 minutes at 180°C. Leave to cool on the tray, then join or frost with icing flavoured with more passionfruit pulp.

Raspberry Rolls

250g butter
¾ cup sugar
2 eggs, beaten
4 cups flour
2 teaspoons baking powder
raspberry jam
desiccated coconut

Cream together the butter and sugar, add beaten eggs, then stir in the dry ingredients. Mix well, roll out thinly, spread with jam and sprinkle with coconut. Form into a roll and with a sharp knife cut off 5mm rounds. Place on a cool baking tray and bake for 15 minutes at 180°C.

10-In-One Biscuits

250g butter
½ cup sugar
1 egg, beaten
2 cups flour
2 teaspoons cream of tartar
1 teaspoon baking soda
2 level tablespoons golden syrup

Cream together the butter and sugar, beat in the egg, then the sifted flour and cream of tartar. Dissolve the soda in syrup and stir into the first mixture. Mix well and place teaspoon lots on a greased baking tray. Bake for approximately 12 minutes at 180°C.

Ginger Crisps

To the basic 10-in-one recipe add 1 level tablespoon ground ginger.

Coconut Biscuits

Add ½ cup desiccated coconut to the basic 10-in-one recipe. Roll into balls, flatten slightly and dip into coconut.

Peanut Shorties

Add 1 cup crushed, partly-roasted peanuts to the basic 10-in-one recipe.

Almond Biscuits

Add 1 teaspoon almond essence to the 10-in-one recipe, roll mixture into balls, flatten and place a blanched almond on top of each biscuit.

Walnut Biscuits

Add 1 cup chopped walnuts to the 10-in-one recipe.

Caraway Biscuits

Add 1 teaspoon or more, caraway seeds to the 10-in-one recipe.

Afghans

Substitute 1 tablespoon cocoa for 1 tablespoon flour in the 10-in-one recipe and add 1 cup cornflakes. When cold, ice with chocolate icing.

Coconut Kisses

Add 1 cup desiccated coconut to the 10-in-one recipe. When cooked and while hot, stick together in pairs with jam.

Date Buns

Before baking place a pitted date on each spoonfu of 10-in-one mixture, then cover with a little of the biscuit mixture. An almond may be put inside the date first.

Peanut Brownies

Add 1 tablespoon cocoa and 1 cup peanuts to the 10-in-one recipe.

Small Cakes and Tartlets

Almond Ginger Cakes

4 level tablespoons treacle
⅓ cup brown sugar
50g butter
2 cups flour
1 teaspoon baking powder
2 teaspoons ground ginger
pinch mixed spice
pinch salt
1 egg
½ cup milk
blanched almonds, for decoration

Melt together the treacle, sugar and butter. Into a bowl sift the flour, baking powder, ginger, spice and salt. Beat the egg and milk and stir into the treacle mixture. Add to the dry ingredients and mix well. Half fill greased patty tins and place an almond on each. Bake for 20 minutes at 180°C.

Almond Shortbread

2 tablespoons butter
½ cup castor sugar
1 egg yolk, beaten
1¼ cups ground almonds
pinch salt
1 cup flour

Cream together the butter and sugar. Add the egg yolk and mix in the almonds, salt and flour. Work to a paste with the hands, roll into fingers and bake for 30 minutes at 150°C. Keeps well.

Apple and Raspberry Turnover

50g butter
1 cup flour
½ cup milk
2 teaspoons vinegar
2 cups grated apple
raspberries
sugar

Rub the butter into the flour and mix to a soft dough with the milk mixed with vinegar. Using as little flour as possible roll out 3 times and leave for 30 minutes. Cut into 8cm squares, place 2 tablespoons of grated apple and a few raspberries in the centre of each square. Sprinkle with a little sugar, bring the 4 corners together and pinch in the centre. Brush with milk and sprinkle with sugar. Bake for 10 minutes at 200°C.

Banana Bubbles

1 cup sugar
½ cup water
3 eggs, beaten
1½ cups flour
1 teaspoon baking powder
4 ripe bananas, sliced
2 tablespoons castor sugar
½ cup mock cream
icing sugar

Boil the sugar and water together for 5 minutes, then add this syrup to the beaten eggs, whisking well for several minutes. Add the flour and baking powder and mix well. Place teaspoons into greased patty tins and bake for 10 minutes at 190°C. When cold, split open and fill with a mixture made from the bananas, sugar and cream. Sprinkle each cake with icing sugar.

Butter Tarts

200g sweet, short pastry
1 cup mixed dried fruit
1 cup brown sugar
1 egg, beaten
1 teaspoon vanilla essence
1 tablespoon butter, softened

Line greased patty tins with pastry and fill with a mixture of fruit, sugar, egg, vanilla and butter. Bake for 20 minutes at 190°C.

Cherry Cakes

125g butter
½ cup brown sugar
1 egg yolk, beaten
1 cup flour, sifted
glacé cherries, for decoration

Cream together the butter and sugar, and stir in the egg yolk. Add the flour and knead until soft and pliable. Roll into small balls and place on greased baking trays. Flatten with a fork and press half a cherry on top. Bake for 15 minutes at 180°C.

Coconut Cakes

1 egg white, stiffly beaten
½ cup sugar
¼ teaspoon salt
½ teaspoon vanilla essence
¼ cup desiccated coconut
¼ cup walnuts, chopped
1 cup cornflakes

To the beaten egg white gradually add the sugar, salt, vanilla, coconut, walnuts and cornflakes. Place in teaspoon lots on a greased tray and bake for 20-30 minutes at 150°C.

Chocolate Caramel Tarts

125g butter
¾ cup brown sugar
1 tablespoon golden syrup
1 egg, beaten
1½ cups flour, sifted
1 tablespoon cocoa
1 teaspoon baking powder

Cream together the butter and sugar, and beat in the syrup and egg. Mix in the flour, cocoa and baking powder. Roll out thinly, cut into rounds and line greased patty tins. Bake for 10-15 minutes at 180°C, then cool. Fill with prepared and cooled caramel filling and ice with chocolate icing. Decorate with walnut halves.

Caramel Filling
2 tablespoons butter
1 x 310g tin sweetened, condensed milk
2 tablespoons golden syrup
¼ cup brown sugar
1 egg yolk

Cook all the ingredients in the top of a double boiler until thick and smooth.

Chocolate Cream Roll

1 cup cream, whipped
1 tablespoon sugar
1 tablespoon cocoa
20 chocolate wafers
3 tablespoons chopped walnuts

To the thickened cream add the sugar and cocoa and continue beating until stiff and forms peaks. Spread the wafers with two thirds of the cream mixture and stack the biscuits together in a row, standing the biscuits on edge like a loaf of sliced bread. Frost all over with remaining cream and sprinkle with nuts. Chill for at least 3 hours. Cut roll diagonally to achieve a striped effect.

Chocolate Drops

250g dark chocolate
2 tablespoons sultanas
2 teaspoons desiccated coconut
2 teaspoons butter
2 tablespoons chopped, glacé cherries, pineapple or ginger, optional.

Melt all the ingredients together in the top of a double boiler. Cool, then drop teaspoon lots on a cold tray. Leave to harden. Omit the coconut if the cherries, etc. are added.

Coffee Meringues

2 egg whites
1 teaspoon strong coffee essence
¼ cup castor sugar
whipped cream, for filling

Beat the egg whites with coffee essence until stiff, then fold in the sugar lightly. Drop spoonful lots on a cold, greased tray and bake for approximately 1¼ hours at 80-90°C, until meringues are dry and can be lifted off the tray. Store in an airtight container. One hour before serving join together with whipped cream. Makes 12.

Cornflake Meringues

½ cup sugar
2 egg whites, stiffly beaten
2 cups cornflakes
¼ cup walnuts, chopped

Fold sugar lightly into the stiff egg whites. Add the cornflakes and walnuts and mix carefully. Put teaspoon lots on greased greaseproof paper, on a baking tray and bake at 80-90°C for 1-1¼ hours or until light brown and crisp. Cool and store in an airtight container. Before serving join together with whipped cream. Makes 12-15.

Cream Puffs

Method I
125g butter
1¼ cups water
1½ cups flour, sifted
4 eggs
1¼ cup cream, whipped
icing sugar

Heat the butter and water in a saucepan and when boiling, add the flour. Remove from heat and beat in the eggs one at a time, then beat well for 5 minutes. Drop teaspoon lots on a lightly buttered baking tray and bake for 45 minutes at 190°C. When cold, open cases, fill with whipped cream and dust with sugar.

Method II
125g butter
1 cup water
125g flour
pinch salt
4 eggs
whipped cream

Boil together the butter and water and while boiling add the flour and salt. Boil until the mixture leaves the side of the saucepan. Cool and add the eggs, beating well after each one. Continue beating until smooth and shiny, then drop heaped teaspoon lots on greaseproof paper on a tray and bake for 15 minutes at 230°C reducing to 190°C for a further 25 minutes. When cold, open cases and fill with whipped cream. Do not open oven door while cooking. Makes 24-30.

Date Treats

125g butter
2 tablespoons brown sugar
1 egg, well-beaten
½ teaspoon vanilla essence
2 cups flour
1 teaspoon baking powder
pinch salt
24 pitted dates, stuffed with walnut halves

Cream the butter and sugar, then beat in the egg and vanilla. Sift the flour, baking powder and salt, and stir into the mixture, making a fairly dry dough. Turn on to a floured board, knead into a round shape and cut into 4cm rounds with floured cutter. Place a stuffed date on half the rounds, glaze lightly and cover with remaining rounds. Place on a greased baking tray and bake for 10-12 minutes at 180°C. When cold, top with lemon icing and walnut pieces.

Pineapple Rock Cakes

4 cups flour
pinch salt
1 cup sugar
600g butter
2 cups ground rice
1 cup chopped, glacé pineapple
1 egg
milk, as required

Sift together the flour and salt. Rub in the sugar, butter and rice. Add the pineapple, egg and milk, if mixture will not hold together. Mix well and place tablespoon lots in cone shapes on a cold, greased tray. Sprinkle with castor sugar and bake for 10 minutes at 200°C. These store well.

Malt Log

125g butter
1 cup icing sugar
1 egg white
2 teaspoons cocoa
1 teaspoon vanilla essence
25 malt biscuits

Cream together the butter and sugar, add the egg white, cocoa and vanilla, and beat well. Place 5 biscuits side by side on a flat board. Ice thickly with the mixture and cover with 5 more biscuits. Continue layering and cover top and sides with the icing. Mark with a fork to create a log effect. Leave for 2-3 days before serving.

Swiss Tarts

stale cake
¼ cup sugar
juice and grated rind 1 lemon
3 tablespoons butter, melted
50g mixed fruit
1 egg white, beaten
brandy, optional

Crumble the cake into a bowl. Stir in the sugar, juice, rind, butter and fruit. Add the egg white, keeping the yolk for the pastry. A little brandy can be added to taste.

Pastry
1 cup flour
1 tablespoon cornflour
3 tablespoons castor sugar
125g butter
1 egg yolk
raspberry icing
walnut halves, for decoration

Sift the flour, cornflour and sugar into a bowl. Rub in the butter until crumbly and mix to a soft dough with the egg yolk. Roll out thinly, cut with a fluted cutter and line 12 patty tins. Put a teaspoon of filling into each case, smooth flat and bake for 15 minutes at 190°C. Loosen from tins and when cold, ice and top with walnut halves.

Doctor Jim's Cakes

125g butter
¾ cup raw sugar
2 eggs, beaten
1 teaspoon molasses
¼ teaspoon salt
1¼ cups ground almonds
juice ½ orange
½ cup wholemeal flour
1 cup flour
1 teaspoon baking powder
50g raisins
75g sultanas

Cream together the butter and sugar. Add the eggs, molasses, salt, almonds and juice. Beat well, then add the wholemeal and white flour and baking powder. Finally beat in the fruit and bake in greased patty tins for 15 minutes at 180°C.

Lamingtons

1 cup sugar
2 eggs
1 cup flour
1 teaspoon baking powder
1 tablespoon cocoa, dissolved in 2 tablespoons boiling water
1½ cups icing sugar
desiccated coconut

Beat the sugar and eggs to a cream. Add the flour and baking powder, pour into a greased roll tin and bake for 10 minutes at 200°C. Make a chocolate icing with the cocoa and sugar. When sponge is cold, cut into squares, dip into the icing and roll in coconut.

One Egg Meringues

1 egg white
1 cup castor sugar
1 teaspoon vinegar
2 tablespoons boiling water
1 teaspoon baking powder

Whip the egg white and beat in the sugar. Stand the bowl over boiling water, and add the vinegar and boiling water. Continue beating until mixture peaks. Add the baking powder and place in tablespoon lots on a greased tray which has been sprinkled with cornflour. Bake for 1 hour at 100°C.

Vanity Fair Cakes

125g butter
½ cup sugar
2 eggs, beaten
1⅕ cups wholemeal flour
1 teaspoon baking powder
50g sultanas
50g glacé cherries

Cream together the butter and sugar. Add the eggs, alternating with the dry ingredients, lastly adding the fruit. Mix well and bake in greased patty tins for 12 minutes at 180°C. When cold ice with butter icing and decorate with cherry halves.

Shortcakes and Cut Slices

Apple Meringue Squares

150g butter
⅖ cup sugar
2 egg yolks, beaten
⅖ cup fine soft breadcrumbs
2 teaspoons grated lemon rind
1⅕ cups flour
1½ teaspoons baking powder
¼ teaspoon salt
2 cooking apples, peeled, cored and sliced
¼ teaspoon cinnamon
2 tablespoons sugar
75g walnuts, finely chopped
2 egg whites
pinch salt
¼ cup sugar

Cream together the butter and sugar. Add the egg yolks, breadcrumbs and rind. Mix well and sift in the flour, baking powder and salt. The dough should be stiff. Spread half the dough in the bottom of a greased baking dish and add the apple slices. Sprinkle with cinnamon, sugar and 25g of the walnuts. Cover with the remaining dough and bake for 25 minutes at 190°C. Cool. Beat the egg whites with salt until stiff, adding the sugar gradually. Spread on top of the cake and sprinkle with remaining walnuts. Brown quickly in the oven.

Apricot and Almond Shortcake

125g dried apricots, soaked overnight in water
½ cup sugar
squeeze lemon, or orange, juice
1½ cups flour
½ cup ground almonds
2 tablespoons castor sugar
½ teaspoon baking powder
pinch salt
1 tablespoon butter
1 egg yolk, beaten
pastry strips

Slice the apricots and cook until soft. Mash together with the sugar and lemon juice. Sift into a bowl the flour, almonds, sugar, baking powder and salt, then rub in the butter and mix with the egg yolk. Press into a sandwich tin and spread with the apricots. Cross hatch with pastry strips, cover with a meringue made with the remaining egg white and a little sugar. Bake for 30 minutes at 180°C.

Blackcurrant Shortcake

125g butter
½ cup sugar
1 egg yolk
2 tablespoons milk
1½ cups flour
1 teaspoon baking powder
pinch salt
blackcurrants
sugar
thin piece lemon rind

Cream together the butter and sugar. Add the egg yolk and milk, then sift in the flour, baking powder and salt. Roll out half the mixture to fit a greased sandwich tin. Sprinkle with a little cornflour or ground rice, to prevent juice escaping. Fill with prepared fruit, sweeten with sugar and place rind on top. Cover with remaining pastry and decorate with pastry leaves. Bake for 30 minutes at 180°C.

Yoghurt Gingerbread (see p. 152)

Caramel Squares

75g butter
¾ cup sugar
2 egg yolks
1¾ cups flour
1 teaspoon baking powder
½ x 400g tin sweetened, condensed milk
2 tablespoons golden syrup
1 teaspoon vanilla essence
2 egg whites, whipped with 4 tablespoons sugar

Cream together the butter and sugar. Add one egg yolk, flour and baking powder. Press into a flat tin. Mix the milk, syrup, second yolk, 1½ tablespoons flour and vanilla, and spread on the shortbread mixture. Top with the meringue and bake for 45 minutes at 180°C. Cut into squares when cold.

Chocolate Cream Bars

500g tin full-cream milk powder
4 tablespoons cocoa
7 tablespoons sugar, dissolved in 1 cup boiling water

Mix the ingredients thoroughly.

Cream Filling
1½ cups icing sugar
1 teaspoon vanilla
1 tablespoon sweetened condensed milk

Mix the ingredients to a stiff paste. Place a layer of the chocolate mixture in a flat tin, then spread with a layer of cream filling and cover with the remaining chocolate mixture. Leave overnight to set. Cut into bars.

Ginger Caramel Squares

150g butter
½ cup brown sugar
1 cup flour
1 teaspoon baking powder
2 tablespoons desiccated coconut
25g mixed nuts and raisins

Melt the butter and sugar, then add the other ingredients. Mix well and bake in a greased tin for 30 minutes at 150°C.

Icing
50g butter
1 cup icing sugar
1 teaspoon golden syrup
½ teaspoon ginger

Cook all ingredients slowly for 5 minutes, then spread on cake.

Choc-Pep-Mallow Squares

125g butter
1 cup sugar
1 egg, beaten
1¾ cups flour
1 teaspoon baking powder
pinch salt
few drops vanilla essence

Cream together the butter and sugar, add the egg, then the other ingredients. Mix well and spread evenly in a buttered sponge-roll tin. Bake for 30 minutes at 180°C.

Marshmallow
1½ cups water
2 tablespoons gelatine
1½ cups sugar
few drops vanilla essence
1½ cups icing sugar

Boil the water, gelatine and sugar for 8 minutes. Cool in a bowl, then add the vanilla and icing sugar. Beat until thick and white and spread on the cold cake. When set cover with a thin peppermint icing and when this has set, cover with chocolate icing. Sprinkle with chopped nuts if desired.

Coconut Peach Shortcake

2 tablespoons butter
½ cup sugar
1 egg, beaten
1 teaspoon grated lemon rind
1 tablespoon milk
1½ cups self-raising flour, sifted
pinch salt
310g tin peaches, drained

Cream the butter and sugar, add the egg and mix well. Flavour with rind and stir in milk alternately with the flour and salt. Mix well and spread in a greased shallow tin. Arrange the fruit on top.

Topping
1 egg white, stiffly beaten
½ cup sugar
1 cup desiccated coconut
½ cup crushed cornflakes

To the beaten egg white add the sugar and beat until thick. Fold in the coconut and cornflakes and spread mixture over the peaches. Bake for 30 minutes at 180°C. Can also be served as a dessert with ice-cream or custard.

Foam Nut Squares

125g butter
¼ cup sugar
½ cup brown sugar
2 eggs, separated
2 tablespoons cold water
½ teaspoon vanilla essence
¼ cup milk
2 cups flour
2 teaspoons baking powder

Cream together the butter and sugar until light and fluffy. Add the egg yolks, water, vanilla, milk, flour and baking powder. Mix well and spread in a well-greased tin.

Topping
2 egg whites, stiffly beaten
1½ cups brown sugar
50g chopped walnuts

To the stiff egg whites fold in the sugar gradually, beating well after each addition. Spread over the mixture in the tin and sprinkle with nuts. Bake for 30-40 minutes at 170°C. Cut into squares while warm.

Ginger Squares

2 cups flour
1 teaspoon baking powder
125g butter
½ cup sugar
3 tablespoons chopped preserved ginger
milk, as required

Into a bowl sift the flour and baking powder. Cream together the butter and sugar and stir into the flour. Add the ginger and milk to make a moist dough. Press into a greased, square tin and bake for 20 minutes at 180°C.

Ginger Icing
2 tablespoons butter
3 teaspoons golden syrup
½ teaspoon ground ginger
4 tablespoons icing sugar

While crust is cooking, melt the butter and syrup and add the ginger. Stir in the sugar, mix well and spread over the crust while warm. Cut into squares when cold.

Ginger Creams

250g gingernut biscuits, crushed finely
125g butter, melted
½ cup cream
½ cup sweetened, condensed milk
2 teaspoons gelatine, dissolved in
   1 tablespoon hot water
juice 2 lemons

Combine the biscuit crumbs and butter and press

into a sponge-roll tin. Beat together the cream and condensed milk, then add the dissolved gelatine and lemon juice. Spread over the crumb base and leave to set. Cut into squares.

Ginger Crunch

125g butter
2 cups flour
½ teaspoon baking powder
1 teaspoon ground ginger
¼ teaspoon salt
¾ cup brown sugar
2 teaspoons golden syrup, warmed

Rub the butter into the sifted dry ingredients. Add the sugar and syrup, mix well and press into a greased, square tin. Bake for 15 minutes at 180°C. Ice while warm and cut into squares when cool.

Ginger Icing
2 teaspoons golden syrup
2 teaspoons butter
½ teaspoon ground ginger
1 cup icing sugar

Mix together all ingredients and spread over the cake.

Chocolate Mint Squares

1 cup sugar
2 eggs, beaten
75g butter, melted
2 tablespoons cocoa
¼ cup flour
½ teaspoon baking powder
50g chopped walnuts
1 teaspoon vanilla essence
16 chocolate mints

Beat the sugar into the eggs, add the butter and cocoa and mix well. Add the sifted dry ingredients, nuts and vanilla. Bake in a greased tin for 35 minutes at 180°C. Remove from oven and place mints on top. Return to oven for a few minutes, swirling with a knife as they melt to create a design. When cold, cut into squares.

Malt Raisin Squares

375g butter, softened
2 tablespoons sugar
2 cups flour
1 tablespoon malt
150g seedless raisins, moistened with
   2 teaspoons lemon juice

Cream together the butter and sugar, then sift in the flour, add the malt and mix well. Spread half this mixture in a tin and scatter over the fruit. Cover with remaining mixture and bake for 15-20 minutes at 180°C. Can be used as a cake or dessert served with custard.

Cherry and Almond Shortcake

250g butter
1 cup castor sugar
1 egg yolk
pinch salt
1 teaspoon baking powder
1½ cups flour, sifted
50g crystallised cherries, halved
25g blanched almonds, halved
1 egg white
2 tablespoons sugar
2 tablespoons desiccated coconut

Cream together the butter and castor sugar, add the egg yolk, salt, baking powder and flour. Mix with a knife, then lightly roll out into a square on a floured board. Press in the cherries and almonds and cover with a meringue made with the egg white, sugar and coconut. Bake for 20-30 minutes at 150°C. Cut into fingers.

Night and Day Shortcake

75g butter
¼ cup sugar
1 egg, beaten
1 cup flour, sifted
1 teaspoon baking powder
raspberry jam

Cream together the butter and sugar, add the egg and mix well. Fold in the flour and baking powder and press mixture into a greased tin. Spread with jam and cover with top layer mixture.

Top Layer
50g butter
⅕ cup brown sugar
1 egg
1 tablespoon golden syrup
1 tablespoon milk
2 tablespoons desiccated coconut
1 teaspoon vanilla essence
¾ cup flour
1 teaspoon baking powder
50g chopped walnuts
150g sultanas

Cream together the butter and sugar. Add the egg, syrup, milk, coconut and vanilla. Fold in the flour, baking powder, walnuts and sultanas. Spread over first layer and bake for 35-40 minutes at 180°C. Cool in the tin and when cold ice with lemon icing. Sprinkle with grated chocolate or coconut.

Nut and Date Bars

3 tablespoons butter
1 cup castor sugar
3 eggs, separated
125g chopped walnuts
500g pitted dates, chopped
1 cup flour, sifted
¼ teaspoon salt
1 teaspoon baking powder
½ teaspoon vanilla essence
icing sugar

Cream together the butter and sugar. Add egg yolks one at a time, beating well after each. Add walnuts, then the dates, flour, salt and baking powder. Lastly fold in the stiffly-beaten egg whites and vanilla. Bake for 30-40 minutes in a greased shallow tin at 180°C. Cut in bars when cold and dust with icing sugar.

Oatmeal Date Squares

1¼ cups rolled oats
1¼ cups flour
½ cup brown sugar
1 teaspoon baking soda
175g butter

Combine the dry ingredients in a bowl and rub in the butter until mixture is crumbly. Press half into a sponge-roll tin, cover with cooled date filling and cover with remaining crumb mixture. Bake for 30 minutes at 180°C.

Date Filling
300g pitted dates, chopped
1 cup boiling water
1 tablespoon brown sugar
1 tablespoon lemon juice, or lemon essence

Combine all ingredients in a saucepan and cook until smooth.

Tamarillo Shortcake

125g butter
1½ cups flour
1 tablespoon cornflour
1 teaspoon baking powder
pinch salt
1 egg yolk, beaten
500g tamarillos, peeled and cooked
squeeze lemon juice
meringue, optional

Rub the butter into the sifted dry ingredients. Beat in the egg yolk and a little milk if necessary. Roll out half the mixture and line a greased sandwich tin. Cover with tamarillo purée and lemon juice. Cover with the remaining crust and decorate with pastry leaves. Bake at 180°C until lightly browned. May be topped with meringue made with the egg white, stiffy-beaten with 2 tablespoons castor sugar.

Walnut Caramel Squares

125g butter
½ cup sugar
1 egg, beaten
1 cup flour
1 teaspoon baking powder
50g chopped walnuts
few drops vanilla essence
chocolate icing
walnut halves, for decoration

Cream together the butter and sugar. Add egg and beat well. Mix in the dry ingredients, walnuts and vanilla. Spread in a shallow tin, cover with caramel topping and bake for 25-30 minutes at 180°C. When cold ice thinly with chocolate icing, mark into squares and decorate each square with a walnut half. Cut through when icing has set.

Caramel Topping
½ x 400g tin sweetened, condensed milk
1 tablespoon golden syrup
1 tablespoon butter

Combine all ingredients in a saucepan, melt and allow to cool before spreading.

Cereal Shortcake

150g butter
¼ cup sugar
1 tablespoon golden syrup
3 cereal biscuits, crumbled
1 cup flour, sifted
1 teaspoon baking powder
1 tablespoon cocoa

Cream together the butter and sugar, add the syrup and mix well. Add the cereal biscuits, flour, baking powder and cocoa. Press into a greased shallow tin and bake for 15 minutes at 180°C. Ice while hot.

SCONES, GEMS AND LOAVES

Apple Scones

125g butter
1 cup sugar
1 egg, beaten
1 cup milk
1 teaspoon baking soda
4 cups flour
2 teaspoons cream of tartar
2 apples, peeled, cored and sliced

In a large bowl cream together the butter and sugar, add the egg, then the milk, soda, flour and cream of tartar. Roll out the mixture, place half on a floured baking tray and spread with apple. Cover with the other half and bake for 30 minutes at 220°C. Makes 24.

Apple Scones (Wholemeal)

3 tablespoons butter
4 cups wholemeal flour
2 tablespoons brown sugar
2 teaspoons cream of tartar
1 teaspoon baking soda
pinch salt
1 egg, beaten
1 cup milk
500g apples, peeled, cored and sliced thinly

Rub the butter into the wholemeal, add the other dry ingredients, the egg and milk to make a soft dough. Roll out 1cm thick. Place half the dough on a baking sheet, cover with a layer of apple and cover with remaining dough. Bake for 30 minutes at 200°C. Cut into squares and serve with whipped cream. Makes 24.

Apple Loaf

2 large apples, peeled and grated
4 tablespoons sugar
2 eggs, beaten
3 cups self-raising flour, sifted
4 teaspoons baking powder
½ cup milk

Combine the apple and sugar, then add the eggs and flour. If too stiff add a little milk. Bake for 40-50 minutes at 180°C.

Banana Tea Cake

1½ cups flour
1 teaspoon baking powder
½ teaspoon salt
2 tablespoons sugar
125g butter
1 egg, well-beaten
5 tablespoons milk
4 firm bananas, sliced thinly
2 tablespoons melted butter
2 tablespoons sugar
¾ teaspoon cinnamon
1 teaspoon grated orange rind

Sift together the flour and baking powder. Add salt and sugar, and rub in the butter, egg and milk, and stir until mixture is well blended. Turn into a greased sponge-roll tin and spread evenly. Place banana slices over this and brush with melted butter. Mix the sugar, spice and rind and sprinkle over the bananas. Bake for 30 minutes at 180°C. Butter and serve hot, or as dessert served with whipped cream.

Bran Muffins

2 cups flour
1 cup sugar
4 teaspoons baking powder
2 cups bran
1 cup sultanas
2 tablespoons melted butter
1¾-2 cups milk

Into a bowl sift the flour, sugar and baking powder. Add the bran and sultanas, mix thoroughly, make a well in the centre and pour in the butter and enough milk to make a soft batter. Mix well but do not beat too much. Drop into greased muffin tins and bake for 15 minutes at 220°C. Serve hot with butter. Makes 24.

Savoury Cheese Scones

2 cups flour
4 teaspoons baking powder
½ teaspoon salt
pinch thyme
75g butter
¾ cup rolled oats
1 cup milk
60g cream cheese
1 teaspoon Worcestershire sauce

Sift together the flour, baking powder, salt and thyme. Rub in the butter and add the oats. Mix to a scone consistency with milk and roll out 1.5cm thick. Spread lightly with the cream cheese mixed with sauce and cut into shapes. Bake for 15 minutes at 220°C. Serve with butter, which may have chopped parsley blended into it. Makes 12.

Savoury Corn Scones

2 cups flour
2 teaspoons baking powder
1 teaspoon salt
1 teaspoon dry mustard
2 tablespoons butter
1 cup drained sweetcorn
milk, as required, approximately ¾ cup

Sift together the flour, baking powder, salt and mustard. Rub in the butter, add corn and mix with milk. Knead lightly on a floured board and roll out to 1.5cm thick. Cut into shapes, place on a hot greased tray and glaze with milk. Bake for 15 minutes at 220°C. Serve with butter blended with mustard, minced ham, or beef, and chopped parsley. Makes 12.

Cheese Oatcakes

25g dripping or shortening
50g self-raising flour
125g oatmeal
50g cheese, grated
5½ tablespoons cold water, to mix

Rub the dripping into the sifted flour and oatmeal. Add the cheese and mix to a stiff dough with water. Roll out 6mm thick, place lots on a tray and bake for 15-20 minutes at 180°C. Makes 15.

Coconut Bread

3 cups flour
3 teaspoons baking powder
pinch salt
1 cup desiccated coconut
1 cup sugar
2 eggs, beaten
½ cup cream and ½ cup milk , to mix

Sift together the flour, baking powder, salt and coconut. Add the sugar and eggs and mix to a soft scone dough with the cream and milk, knead on a floured board, place in 2 x 22cm greased loaf tins, and bake for 1½ hours at 180°C. Serve as sandwiches with a fruit filling such as sliced strawberries, bananas or other fruit.

Date and Walnut Loaf

¾ cup chopped walnuts
1 cup chopped dates
4 cups flour, sifted
4 teaspoons baking powder
1 teaspoon salt
1 cup sugar
2½ cups milk

To the nuts and fruit add the sifted dry ingredients. Make a well in the centre and blend in the milk. Place in 2 x 22cm greased loaf tins and bake for 55 minutes at 180°C.

Crumb Girdle Cakes

2 cups thick, sour milk, or yoghurt
1 cup water
2 cups dry breadcrumbs
1 teaspoon baking soda
1 teaspoon salt
1½ cups flour
2 teaspoons baking powder
2 tablespoons butter, melted
2 tablespoons golden syrup

Pour the milk and water into a bowl, stir in the breadcrumbs and leave one hour in a cool place. Stir in the soda, dissolve in a little cold water, and beat well. Add other ingredients, beat well, then cook on a greased girdle. Brown on both sides and serve with butter and honey, or golden syrup. Makes 48.

Eggless Buns

225g butter
1 cup sugar
½ cup golden syrup
2 level teaspoons ground ginger
1 level teaspoon baking soda
¾ cup milk
3 cups flour
225g sultanas, or raisins
½ cup choppped walnuts

In a saucepan boil the butter, sugar, syrup and ginger. Add the soda dissolved in milk and then flour, fruit and nuts. Mix well, drop lots on a cold greased tray and bake for 20 minutes at 180°C. These keep well. Makes 24.

Flapjacks

1 cup flour
2 teaspoons baking powder
pinch salt
1 egg
¾-1 cup milk

Sift the dry ingredients into a bowl. Make a well in the centre and drop in the egg and sufficient milk to make a pikelet batter consistency. Beat well and cook on a hot greased girdle as for pikelet, only larger. Serve hot with butter and syrup. Makes 12.

Never-Fail Fruit Loaf

1 cup milk
1 tablespoon golden syrup
1 teaspoon baking soda
1 teaspoon baking powder
2 cups flour, sifted
2 level tablespoons sugar
1 tablespoon marmalade
1 cup mixed fruit and nuts

Warm together the milk and syrup. Dissolve the soda in one tablespoon of cold water, add to the remaining ingredients and blend in the milk and syrup. Cook in a greased loaf tin for 1 hour at 180°C.

Economical Gingerbread

2½ cups flour
1 cup sugar
2 teaspoons ground ginger
1 teaspoon cinnamon
125g butter
1 cup golden syrup
1 teaspoon baking soda
1 cup milk

Sift all the dry ingredients except the soda. Melt the butter with the syrup and dissolve the soda in the milk. Make a well in the dry ingredients and blend in the liquids, beating vigorously for 2-3 minutes. Pour into a greased 23cm tin and bake for 1 hour at 180°C.

Fruit Gingerbread

2 cups flour
2 teaspoons ginger
1 teaspoon mixed spice
½ teaspoon baking soda
2 tablespoons golden syrup
2 tablespoons butter
1 egg
2 tablespoons sugar
½ cup mixed fruit

Into a bowl sift the flour, ginger, spice and soda. Warm together the syrup and butter. Beat the egg with the sugar and add with the other liquid to the dry ingredients. Finally add fruit, mix well and pour into a well-greased 22cm loaf tin. Bake for 45 minutes at 180°C.

Yoghurt Gingerbread

1 cup flour
1 cup wholemeal flour
pinch salt
3 teaspoons ground ginger
½ teaspoon ground nutmeg
½ teaspoon mixed spice
1 egg, beaten
125g butter
¾ cup treacle
¾ cup yoghurt or sour milk
1½ level teaspoons baking soda, dissolved
  in 1 tablespoon boiling water

Sift together the dry ingredients. Beat the egg and melt the butter and syrup together. Make a well in the dry ingredients and drop in the egg, yoghurt, warmed butter and treacle, and lastly the dissolved soda. Mix well. The mixture tends to be wet. Pour into a pan and bake for 45-60 minutes at 180°C.

Old English Gingerbread Cake

3½ cups flour
1 tablespoon sugar
2 teaspoons ground ginger
pinch salt
1 teaspoon baking soda
1 cup treacle
125g butter, melted
2 eggs, beaten

Sift together the flour, sugar, ginger and salt. Into the centre pour the soda, dissolved in the treacle melted with the butter. Beat in the eggs and bake in a greased 20cm round tin for 50 minutes at 180°C.

Billy Ginger Loaf

125g butter
350g flour
1 cup sugar
1 teaspoon ground ginger
¼ teaspoon ground nutmeg
pinch salt
¾ cup golden syrup, or treacle
1 teaspoon baking soda
1 cup warm milk
1-2 eggs

Rub the butter into the dry ingredients, then add the syrup and the soda dissolved in milk. Lastly stir in the eggs. Grease a 6-cup billy or steamer and pour in the mixture. Cover and bake or steam for 1 hour.

Ginger Gems

1 cup wholemeal flour
1 teaspoon baking powder
1 teaspoon ground ginger
pinch salt
1 egg, beaten with 6 tablespoons milk
2 tablespoons melted butter
25g brown sugar, melted with 2 tablespoons golden syrup

Mix the flour, baking powder, ginger and salt. Blend in the egg, butter and milk, then the sugar and syrup. Bake in hot, greased gem irons for 12-15 minutes at 180°C. Makes 12.

Ginger Scones

2 cups flour
pinch salt
2 teaspoons baking powder
2 tablespoons butter
½ cup milk
¼ cup chopped, preserved ginger
¼ cup butter
½ cup brown sugar

Into a bowl sift the flour, salt and baking powder. Melt the butter with sufficient milk to make a stiff dough. Press half into a sponge sandwich tin and cover with ginger. Mix the butter and sugar and sprinkle on top. Lightly roll out the other portion of dough and place on top pressing to the edge. Brush with milk and bake for 20 minutes at 220°C.

Ginger Walnut Muffins

2 cups flour
2 teaspoons baking powder
pinch salt
75g shredded, preserved ginger
25g chopped walnuts
50g butter
1 cup milk
1 tablespoon golden syrup, warmed
1 egg, beaten

Into a bowl sift the flour, baking powder and salt. Add the ginger and nuts, and rub in the butter. Beat in the milk, syrup and lastly the egg. Mix well, roll out and cut into shapes. Bake on a greased tray for 15 minutes at 200°C. Makes 12.

Honey and Coconut Loaf

1 tablespoon honey
1 cup milk
2 tablespoons golden syrup
½ teaspoon baking soda
2 cups wholemeal flour
¾ cup desiccated coconut
1 teaspoon baking powder
½ cup mixed fruit and nuts
pinch salt
few drops almond essence
few drops vanilla essence

Warm together in a saucepan, the honey, milk, syrup and soda. Place this mixture with the other ingredients in a bowl and mix thoroughly but do not beat too much. Bake in a greased 23cm loaf tin for 45-50 minutes at 180°C.

Oatcakes

1 cup water
250g butter, softened
5 cups oatmeal
1 cup brown sugar
1½ teaspoons baking soda, dissolved in 2
  tablespoons boiling water

Bring to the boil the water and butter, and stir into the combined remaining ingredients. Mix well, roll out thinly on a floured board and cut into shapes. Bake on greased trays for 15-20 minutes at 180°C. Serve hot with butter. Makes 30.

Rolled Oats Wafers

125g butter
¾ cup brown sugar
1 egg
1 tablespoon golden syrup
2 cups rolled oats
¾ cup flour
1 teaspoon baking powder
pinch salt
few drops vanilla essence

Cream together the butter and sugar, add the egg and syrup, then the oats and flour sifted with the baking powder. Mix to a firm dough, roll out 1cm thick and sprinkle with oats. Cut into 5cm round biscuits and bake on a greased tray for 20-30 minutes at 180°C. Makes 24.

Pancakes

125g flour, sifted
1 egg
1 cup milk
2 tablespoons melted butter
½ teaspoon baking powder

Into the sifted flour blend the egg, milk and butter, lastly adding the baking powder. Cook in hot butter, turning when set. Remove to a hot dish and add lemon juice and sugar before folding. Jam may be substituted for sugar. Makes 12.

Quick Nut Loaf

4 cups flour
4 teaspoons baking powder
1 teaspoon salt
½ cup sugar
½ cup chopped walnuts
1 egg, beaten
2 cups milk

Sift together the flour, baking powder, salt and sugar. Add walnuts. Into the centre blend the egg and milk and mix thoroughly. Put into greased 22cm loaf tins and bake for 1 hour at 180°C.

Cream Pancakes

2 cups flour
⅛ teaspoon salt
2 teaspoons baking powder
2 eggs, beaten
1 cup milk
½ cup cream

Sift together the flour, salt and baking powder. Add the eggs beaten with the milk and cream. Beat well, then cook on a hot greased griddle or frying pan. Serve with fresh fruit and sprinkle with castor sugar. Makes 15.

Pikelets

1 egg
3 tablespoons sugar
1 tablespoon melted butter
1½ cups flour
2 teaspoons baking powder
1 cup milk

Beat together the egg and sugar. Add the butter and beat again. Beat in the flour, baking powder and milk alternately, then cook on a hot griddle rubbed over with a small salt bag. This is easier than grease. Makes 24.

Pinwheels

3 cups flour
3 teaspoons baking powder
½ teaspoon salt
1 tablespoon sugar
2 tablespoons melted butter
1 cup water
3 tablespoons brown sugar
1 cup currants
1½ teaspoons cinnamon

Make an ordinary scone mixture with the flour, baking powder, salt, sugar, butter and water to mix to a soft dough. Roll out to an oblong shape 1.5-2cm thick. Butter it liberally and sprinkle over the brown sugar, currants and cinnamon. Roll up and seal the edge with water. Cut off 2.5cm slices and bake on a greased tray for 15-20 minutes at 220°C. Makes 12.

Pumpkin Scones

25g butter
½ cup sugar
1 egg
1 cup cooked, mashed pumpkin
3½ cups flour
4 teaspoons baking powder
1 teaspoon nutmeg
1 teaspoon cinnamon
pinch salt
¼ cup milk

Cream together the butter, sugar and egg. Mix in the cold pumpkin and the sifted dry ingredients. If necessary add milk to make a scone consistency. Roll out lightly, cut in to shapes and place on a greased tray. Bake for 15 minutes at 220°C. Makes 15.

Rice Gems

1 cup cooked rice
2 cups wholemeal flour
½ teaspoon baking powder
pinch salt
1 tablespoon golden syrup
1 egg, beaten
1 cup milk

Blend together all ingredients and bake in very hot, greased gem irons for 15 minutes at 180°C. Makes 24.

Lemon Butter Filling
2 tablespoons butter
1 tablespoon honey
1 teaspoon lemon juice
grated rind 1 lemon

Cream together all the ingredients.

Rusks

125g butter
125g castor sugar
1½ teaspoons salt
4 teaspoons baking powder
3½ cups wholemeal flour
2 eggs, beaten
½ cup milk and water

Cream together the butter and sugar. Add salt, baking powder and wholemeal. Mix to a smooth paste with a knife, using the eggs and sufficient milk and water to make a fairly firm dough. Roll out .5cm thick, cut into 5cm rounds and bake on a greased tray for 15 minutes at 200°C. Makes 70.

Sultana Loaf

1 cup flour
1 teaspoon baking powder
1 tablespoon sugar
½ tablespoon butter
½ cup sultanas
¼ cup mixed peel
1 egg
½ cup milk

Mix the ingredients in the order given, as for scones, only making a slightly wetter consistency. Bake in a small loaf tin for 50 minutes at 180°C.

American Waffles

2 cups flour, sifted
3 teaspoons baking powder
½ teaspoon salt
3 eggs, separated
1¼ cups milk
¼ cup melted shortening

Mix the dry ingredients, add well-beaten egg yolks and milk, beating until smooth. Add shortening and lastly the stiffly-beaten egg whites. Bake in hot waffle irons until golden. Makes 15.

YEAST COOKERY

Yeast is the aerating agent used in bread, buns and bread rolls. Many hesitate to try it but if a few factors about its use are clearly understood it becomes a very easy matter to bake with it.
First, yeast is a living plant requiring moisture and warmth before it will grow and liberate its aerating gases. When not in use it should, therefore, be stored in a cool dry place. As it will not keep indefinitely, only small quantities should be purchased at a time.
Secondly, excess heat kills the action of yeast, so all the rising must take place before the food is cooked. Most mixtures are left to rise twice, the second time until they become the size of the desired loaf, etc. This is called 'proving'. If a mixture is left too long and becomes too big it may be kneaded down and put to prove again.
Yeast is always dissolved before being added to any mixture. When mixed with sugar it liquefies, or it may be dissolved in a little lukewarm, not hot, water. It should be stirred into a warmed mixture. This is done by dissolving sugar, salt and fat in hot milk or water and cooling to lukewarm; and by warming the flour and utensils used. Endeavour to keep the mixture at blood heat. Once the dough is made it should be kept warm; if it takes too long to rise the result may be a soured bread.
Kneading takes place to incorporate air and to blend all the materials. Mixtures should be kneaded until they are elastic; when dented with the finger the dent will quickly disappear. In the second kneading, the dough is formed into the desired shapes, remembering that they will become bigger when proven.
A very hot oven is necessary to kill the yeast and cook the starch in the flour. When baked the bread will be nicely browned, will crackle if you listen to it, sound hollow when tapped, and will have shrunk from the sides of the tin. When baking a loaf the oven temperature may be turned down to a moderate heat after about 15-20 minutes. The crust may be softened or glazed as desired. When done, turn out and cool on a wire rack.
Dried yeast will keep indefinitely but takes a little longer to act. It is best to follow the instructions accompanying the preparation.
Two rounded teaspoons dried yeast equal 1 cake compressed yeats.

Yeast Bread

2 tablespoons sugar
2 teaspoons salt
2 teaspoons butter
2½ cups boiling water
2 cakes compressed yeast
1kg flour
½ cup lukewarm water

Into a large bowl put the sugar, salt and butter. Add the boiling water, or a mixture of water and milk. Stir until sugar and butter melt, set aside and cool until lukewarm. Break yeast into a bowl and stir in ½ cup of water. Add to the first mixture but not until it cools. Sift in the flour, adding just enough to make a dough that can be handled without sticking to the hands. Turn on to a floured board and knead until elastic. Grease the sides of the bowl and replace dough. Paint the top with lukewarm water, or cover with a buttered piece of greaseproof paper, put a clean tea towel over the bowl and place in a warm, not hot, place to rise. Leave until doubled in bulk, then knead again and form into 2 loaves. The dough will rise again so the loaves should be smaller than required. Put into well-greased loaf tins and set aside to prove. Bake for 45 minutes at 220°C.

To soften crust
When cooked, remove the loaf from the oven and rub with a buttered piece of greaseproof. Return to oven for two minutes, then rub the crust again.

To glaze crust
When cooked, remove from the oven and brush with milk and sugar – 1 part sugar to 2 parts milk. An alternative glaze is made from egg white diluted with 1 tablespoon of water. Return to the oven for 5 minutes.

Wholemeal Bread

3 cakes compressed yeast
½ cup lukewarm water
3 cups hot milk
2 tablespoons treacle
1 tablespoon salt
700-750g wholemeal flour, or a mixture of wholemeal and white flour

Make as for white bread, above, adding treacle once some of the flour has been stirred into the milk. Have the dough too stiff to be handled with a wooden spoon but sticky to knead by hand. Flour hands frequently rather than adding flour to the dough. Bake as for white loaf.

Fruit Loaves

To either white or wholemeal bread add 2 cups fruit. Increase sugar to ½ cup in the white loaf and add 2 tablespoons in the brown one. Seeded raisins, sultanas, chopped nuts and peel, currants and even glacé cherries may be incorporated in this loaf. This mixture may be made into buns if desired.

Plaited Loaf

Use plain, wholemeal or potato yeast loaf. Each loaf will take about 500g dough. Knead risen dough on a floured board and divide into 3 pieces. Shape these into long strips and join all three at one end with a little milk. Plait and seal the other end. Put on greased oven slide, put to prove and bake as usual.

Parker House Rolls

½ cup milk
1 tablespoon sugar
2 tablespoons butter
1 teaspoon salt
2 tablespoons warm water
1 tablespoon yeast
1½ to 2 cups unsifted flour

Warm the milk and stir in sugar, butter and salt. Cool to lukewarm. Measure the warm water into a warm bowl, crumble yeast into the water and stir to mix. Add the lukewarm milk mixture and stir thoroughly. Stir in one cup of the flour, beat until smooth using a wooden spoon. Add another cup of flour or sufficient to make a soft, slightly sticky dough. Turn onto a lightly floured surface and knead thoroughly for 10 minutes or until dough is smooth and elastic. Place in a lightly greased warm bowl and cover with a clean damp cloth. Leave to rise in a warm place until doubled in bulk and springy to touch. Punch the dough down and reform into a ball. Cover and leave to rise another 15 minutes. Roll the dough into a 22cm round. Cut into rounds with a large scone cutter. Make a crease to one side of each round. Brush each with melted butter. Fold the larger side to the edge and gently press down. Place on a lightly greased oven tray. Bake at 200°C for 15 to 20 minutes.

Chelsea Buns

750g bread dough
2 tablespoons softened butter
2 tablespoons brown sugar
150g currants, or sultanas
1 teaspoon cinnamon, or mixed spice
milk, or water, for sealing

Knead the bread dough on a floured board and roll out into an oblong 1.5-2cm thick. Spread with the butter and sugar and sprinkle with fruit and spices. Roll up as for a jam roll and seal the edge with milk or water. Cut off 2.5cm rounds and stand cut side down on a well-buttered oven slide or roasting dish, allowing a little room for expansion. Leave to prove for 20-30 minutes and bake for 15-20 minutes at 220°C.

Potato Yeast Rolls

1 cup scalded milk
100g butter
75g sugar
1 cup cooked, mashed potatoes
700-750g flour
2 eggs, beaten
2 cakes compressed yeast
½ cup lukewarm water
1½ teaspoon salt

Mix the milk, butter and sugar. Stir in the potatoes and stand until lukewarm. Add 125g of the flour and the eggs. Add the yeast dissolved in the warm water and thoroughly mix all the ingredients. Cover and set aside until the mixture is risen and is full of air bubbles. Add more flour and knead the dough until it is elastic. Cover and set aside to rise until it doubles in bulk. Turn on to a floured board and knead again. It is now ready to be made into plain buns, rolls, Chelsea buns, plaited loaves or Parker House rolls.

Hot Cross Buns

4 cups flour
1 teaspoon salt
½ teaspoon mixed spice
½ teaspoon ground cinnamon
½ teaspoon nutmeg
¼ cup castor sugar
1½ cakes compressed yeast
250ml warm mixed milk and water
1 teaspoon castor sugar
1 egg
50g butter, melted
100g clean currants
50g mixed peel, chopped

Sift flour, salt, spices and sugar into a warm mixing bowl. Stir the yeast into the warm mixed milk, water and teaspoon of sugar. Stir the yeast liquid, egg, melted butter, currants and peel into the centre of the dry ingredients. Mix and turn out onto a lightly floured surface. Knead well until dough is smooth. Shape into a round and leave, covered with a damp cloth, in a warm place to rise until doubled in bulk. Turn out the dough, flatten, and knead again. Divide into 12 pieces and shape into buns. Place on a lightly greased baking tray and leave in a warm place until puffy. To make the crosses slash the buns with a knife. Bake at 220°C for 15 to 20 minutes.

Glaze
2 tablespoons milk
2 tablespoons sugar
2 tablespoons water

Dissolve all ingredients together then boil for 2 minutes. Brush over buns while still hot.
Makes 12.

Crumpets

2 cups flour
½ teaspoon salt
1½ cakes compressed yeast
150ml milk
200ml water
1 teaspoon sugar

Sift the flour and salt into mixing basin and make a well in the centre. Blend the yeast with the warm milk and water. Pour the yeast liquid into the centre of the flour. Using a wooden spoon, gradually work in all the flour and beat the mixture to a smooth batter. Leave in the basin covered with a cloth, in a warm place for about 30-40 minutes, until the mixture is light and frothy. Pour into a jug. Grease the griddle or frying pan and some egg poaching rings. Warm the griddle thoroughly on a moderate heat. Half fill the rings with mixture poured from the jug. Cook over moderate heat for about 5 minutes, until bubbbles begin to appear on the surface. Reduce heat and cook until the bubbles have burst and the rings can be slipped off easily. Turn crumpets over to cook for a few minutes on the other side. Serve spread with butter. Makes 12.

Cheese-Topped Buns

4 cups flour
2 teaspoons sugar
2 cakes compressed yeast
½ cup warm water
1¼ cups tepid milk
1 teaspoon salt
90g mixed peel, chopped
2 tablespoons grated tasty cheese

Sift half the quantity of flour into a bowl. Mix the sugar and yeast with slightly warmed water and stir into the flour with the milk, mixing well. Cover and leave to rise for 30 minutes in a warm place. Stir in the salt, peel and remaining flour. Turn onto a floured board and knead well. Set aside again until it doubles in bulk. Knead again and shape dough into buns. Leave to rise again, then bake at 220°C until golden brown, approximately 15-20 minutes. Glaze with melted cheese and sprinkle with walnuts. Return to the oven for 5 minutes.

Doughnuts

2 tablespoons butter
½ cup warm milk
2 teaspoons sugar
½ teaspoon salt
1 egg, beaten
1 cake compressed yeast, dissolved in a little
  sugar or lukewarm water
2 cups flour
jam, for filling
lard, or cooking oil, for deep frying
castor sugar

Melt the butter in milk and stir in the sugar and salt. Stir until dissolved and leave to cool until lukewarm. Add the egg and dissolved yeast. Mix to a soft dough with the flour and leave to rise. Turn on to a floured board and knead well. Break off small pieces, roll out and put a spoonful of jam in the centre of each. Roll up and seal edges. Set aside to prove in a warm place, then deep fry for approximately 5 minutes. Drain and toss in castor sugar while still warm.

SUPPER SAVOURIES

Angels on Horseback

12 large oysters
juice 1 lemon
cayenne pepper
12 strips bacon

Squeeze lemon juice over the oysters and sprinkle with cayenne. Put each oyster in a piece of bacon, roll up and pack tightly in a piedish. Bake at 220°C until crisp. Serve on toast. Serves 4.

Apricot Salad Savouries

250g cream cheese, softened
milk, or cream as required
½ cup chopped walnuts
pinch salt
1 x 450g tin apricot halves, drained
round water crackers
mayonnaise
parsley, for garnish
shredded lettuce

Mash the cream cheese and add sufficient milk or cream to make smooth. Mix in walnuts and salt, then form into balls, allowing 1 for each apricot half. Arrange each apricot half on a cracker spread with mayonnaise and place a cheese ball in each apricot hollow. Garnish with parsley and arrange on shredded lettuce.

Cheese and Bacon Tartlets

1 egg
½ cup milk
75g cheese, grated
1 small onion, grated
50g bacon, chopped
salt
pepper
8 small vol-au-vent cases

Beat together the egg and milk. Mix in the cheese, onion, bacon, salt and pepper. Put into pastry cases, sprinkle with grated cheese and bake for 15 minutes at 200°C. Garnish with parsley. Makes 8.

Cheese Surprises

150g butter
50g cheese, grated
salt
pepper
pinch dry mustard
125g flour
cold water, as required

Melt 60g of butter in a saucepan. Add the cheese, salt, pepper and mustard. Cool. Mix the flour and remaining butter, adding a pinch of salt. Mix with a little cold water, to make a stiff dough. Roll out thinly, spread with most of the cheese mixture on half the pastry and fold over the other half. Then spread the top with the remaining cheese mixture. Cut into fingers and bake for 15 minutes at 220°C. Makes 12.

Corn Tartlets

2 cups thick white sauce
salt
pepper
chopped parsley
1 x 300g tin sweetcorn, drained
8 medium baked pastry cases
90g cooked green peas

Season the sauce with salt, pepper and parsley. Add the corn, heat and spoon into pastry cases. Surround with peas and heat as required. Makes 10.

Madras Eggs

6 hard-boiled eggs
2 teaspoons chutney
1 teaspoon curry powder
salt to taste
watercress, shredded
1 tablespoon lemon juice

Halve the eggs lengthwise. Remove the yolks and mix in a bowl with the chutney, curry powder and salt. Stuff the egg whites with this mixture and place on a bed of cress seasoned with the lemon juice. Makes 12.

Marmite Biscuits

50g butter
75g flour
100g cheese, grated
½ teaspoon Marmite
¼ teaspoon dry mustard
pepper
1 egg yolk
1 tablespoon milk

Combine all the ingredients, mix to a stiff paste, roll out and cut into strips. Bake for 7 minutes at 220°C. Spread with Marmite and chopped celery or mint. Makes 12-14.

Festival Savouries

Pastry:
350g butter
3 cups flour
½ teaspoon salt
1 teaspoon baking powder
1 egg
water, as required

Rub the butter into the sieved flour, salt and baking powder. Mix to a firm dough with the egg and a little water. Divide the mixture in half.

Rings:
¾ cup ground walnuts
1 teaspoon Marmite
1 tablespoon melted butter

Roll out half of the pastry thinly into 2 equal pieces. Spread 1 piece with a mixture of walnuts, Marmite and butter. Cover with remaining pastry and roll lightly. Cut into 5cm rounds and stamp out the centre with a smaller cutter. Bake on a greased tray for 15 minutes at 220°C. Makes 10.

Crescents:
1 small can sardines, mashed
salt to taste
⅛ teaspoon cayenne pepper
1 teaspoon lemon juice

Roll out the 2nd portion of pastry and cut into 5cm rounds. Combine the sardines, salt, pepper and juice and place 1 teaspoon of this mixture on each round. Fold in half, seal the edges and curve to form crescents. Bake for 15 minutes at 220°C. Makes 10.

Suns:
50g cheese, grated
½ teaspoon salt
2 teaspoons Worcestershire sauce
½ teaspoon mustard
pinch saffron

Roll out all left-over pastry into an oblong piece. Combine the cheese, salt, sauce, mustard and saffron, spread evenly over the pastry and roll up like a jam roll. Cut off 6mm rounds and bake for 15 minutes at 210°C. Serve hot or cold. Makes 10.

Macaroni Delight

100g butter
3 tablespoons flour
450ml milk
salt and pepper
1 onion, grated
6 rashers rindless bacon
225g macaroni, cooked
100g cheese, grated
parsley

Melt half the butter and stir in the flour. Blend in the milk and season. Cook, stirring until sauce thickens. Add onion and three bacon rashers, chopped and fried in the remaining butter. Cut the rest of the bacon into strips.
Stir the macaroni, fried bacon and half the cheese into the sauce. Spoon into a baking dish. Top with remaining cheese and bacon strips. Cook at 375°C for about 40 minutes. Garnish with parsley. Serves 4.

Oyster Mornay in Savoury Cases

Mornay Filling:
3 tablespoons butter
3 tablespoons flour
salt, to taste
1½ cups oyster liquor
½ cup milk or cream
1 tablespoon finely-chopped parsley
1 teaspoon lemon juice
2 tablespoons grated cheese
36 oysters
8 large, or 24 small, cooked vol-au-vent cases

Melt the butter, add the flour and salt, and cook for a minute, then add the oyster liquor and milk, and stir until boiling. Add the parsley, lemon juice and cheese, and finally the drained oysters. Spoon into vol-au-vent cases.

Savoury Cases:
30 small tomatoes
salt
pepper

Scoop out the tomato pulp and season the cases with salt and pepper. Stuff with the oyster mornay mixture and reheat in the oven before serving.

Salmon Tartlets

250g cream cheese
220g tin salmon, mashed
100ml cream
125g butter, softened
1 tablespoon parsley, finely-chopped
ground black pepper
lemon juice to taste
24 bread cases, baked

Beat all filling ingredients together until smooth. Place spoonfuls into bread cases and garnish with lemon and parsley. Makes 24.

Sardine Rolls

250g short pastry
2 tins sardines, drained
1 egg, beaten
breadcrumbs
grated cheese, optional

Roll out the pastry thinly and cut into 8cm x 4cm rectangles. Place a sardine on each rectangle. Wet the edges of the pastry, roll up and seal. Brush with the egg, roll in crumbs and fry. Drain on kitchen paper before serving. Sardines may be dipped in cheese before rolling up. Salmon or asparagus may be substituted for sardines. Makes 12-15.

Sardine Patties

1 celery heart, chopped finely
1 tablespoon anchovy paste
salt
pepper
baked pastry cases
1 can sardines, drained

Combine the celery, paste, salt and pepper and fill the pastry cases. Top with half a sardine and serve. Makes 8.

Savoury Boats

Pastry Cases:
125g flour
½ teaspoon baking powder
pinch salt
2 tablespoons grated cheese
pinch cayenne pepper
¼ teaspoon mustard
25g butter
1 egg yolk
cold water, as required

Combine the flour, baking powder, salt, cheese, pepper and mustard. Rub in the butter and form a paste with the egg yolk and a little water. Knead lightly, roll out thinly and line boat-shaped patty tins. Prick the cases and bake for 15 minutes at 190°C.

Fillings:
Flaked salmon, flavoured with lemon juice and cayenne, and bound with a little white sauce.
Creamed corn with snippets of grilled bacon added.
Left-over chicken and ham bound with white sauce.

Savoury Butters

Devilled:
Mix equal quantities Worcestershire and tomato sauce with half the amount meat extract. Beat into softened butter and add chopped parsley to taste.

Anchovy:
Cream butter with squeeze lemon juice, add anchovy paste (or other fishpaste to taste) and work in well.

Sardine:
Cream butter with squeeze lemon juice, a few drops of onion juice and a few mashed sardines.

These savoury butters are delicious for filling sandwiches, spreading on hot toast or on hot crumpets.

Savoury Pikelets

1 egg, beaten
¾ cup milk
125g flour
1 tablespoon grated onion
2 tablespoons grated tasty cheese
1 tablespoon chopped parsley
1 tablespoon melted butter
1 teaspoon baking powder

To the egg add alternately the milk and flour. Stir in the onion, cheese, parsley, butter and baking powder. Cook quickly on a hot griddle. Makes 18.

Savoury Puffs

125g butter
1 cup water
125g flour
4 eggs
¼ teaspoon salt
100g cheese, grated

Bring to the boil the butter, water and salt. Add the flour quickly. Beat well and add the eggs, beating until mixture is smooth and shiny. Put small teaspoon lots on a cold greased tray, sprinkle with cheese and bake for 30-35 minutes at 190°C. Makes 30.

Savoury Filling:
3 tablespoons butter
3 tablespoons flour
1 cup milk
¼ teaspoon cayenne pepper
salt
2 tablespoons mayonnaise
250g cooked, finely-diced, poultry or pork

Melt the butter, add the flour and stir until smooth. Add the milk gradually, stirring until boiling, Season and cool. Add the mayonnaise and meat, mix well and fill coooked, cold cases. Serve on lettuce leaves.

Savoury Wheels

125g flour
125g butter
1 teaspoon vinegar
milk, as required
100g chopped bacon
1 cup cold, mashed potato
½ cup chopped onion
salt
pepper

Sieve the flour into a bowl and rub in the butter.
Add the vinegar and sufficient milk to make a
fairly stiff dough. Roll out and spread with a
mixture of bacon, potato, onion, and seasoning to
taste. Roll up and cut off 5cm slices. Place on a
cold, greased tray and bake for 15-20 minutes at
220°C. Makes 10-12.

Stuffed Eggs Printanier

6 hard-boiled eggs
2 radishes, finely chopped
watercress leaves, finely chopped
salad dressing
salt
pepper

Cut the eggs in half lengthwise. Remove yolks and
mix with the chopped radish and watercress. Add
the dressing and season to taste. Stuff the eggs and
decorate with a radish floweret. Makes 12.

Toasted Sandwiches

Mix chosen ingredients and spread thickly on a
slice of bread. Cover with another slice of bread
and butter the top. Toast under grill, butter side
uppermost.

Tomato and Cheese:
250g tomatoes, sliced
50g cheese, grated
salt
pepper
½ teaspoon dry mustard
butter

Chicken and Ham:
50g cooked, minced chicken
50g cooked, minced ham
1 tablespoon chopped parsley
salt
pepper
butter

Salmon:
1 x 200g tin salmon
1 teaspoon chopped capers
2 tablespoons cream
salt
pepper
butter

Two-Way Savoury

450g flour
1 teaspoon salt
1 teaspoon baking powder
350g butter
cold water, as required
750g pork sausages, skinned
1 large apple, peeled, cored and sliced
1 large onion, finely chopped
salt
pepper
2 cups cooked, minced rabbit
1 cup breadcrumbs
1 onion, sliced
1 tablespoon chopped parsley
¼ cup stock
milk

Into a bowl sift the flour, salt and baking powder.
Rub in the butter and mix to a firm dough with
cold water. Line a large baking dish and divide
with a strip of pastry down the middle. In one half
place the sausages and cover with apple, onion, salt
and pepper. On the other half place the rabbit
meat, breadcrumbs, onion, parsley, stock, salt and
pepper. Cover with the remaining pastry, prick the
top, brush with milk and bake for 1 hour at 200°C.
Serve hot or cold. Serves 4-6.

162

Fruit Fancy (see p. 111)

PICNIC IDEAS AND SANDWICHES

Barbecue Pancakes

Batter:
125g flour
¼ teaspoon salt
pinch pepper
pinch mixed herbs
1 egg
1¼ cups milk

Sift together the flour, salt and pepper. Add the herbs and break in the egg. Pour in half the milk, beating well to prevent lumps, then add the remaining milk. Melt sufficient fat to cover the bottom of the pan, pour in sufficient batter to cover the bottom thinly and cook gently until it bubbles on top. Turn and cook other side. Place the filling on half the pancake and fold over.

Filling:
4 rashers bacon, finely-chopped
½ cup white sauce
½ cup cooked peas
salt
pepper
1 tablespoon chopped parsley

Fry the bacon until crisp. Add to the white sauce with the peas, salt, pepper and parsley. Mix well and keep hot until ready to serve.

Egg and Bacon pie

Pastry:
250g flour
1 teaspoon baking powder
50g butter
50g lard
milk, to mix

Sift together the flour and baking powder, rub in the butter and lard and mix with milk to form a fairly stiff dough. Halve the pastry, roll out 1 piece and line a 23cm pie dish.

Filling:
3-4 eggs, beaten
1 onion, finely chopped
salt
pepper
4 rashers bacon, chopped
3-4 tomatoes, peeled and chopped
50g cheese, grated

Put the eggs on top of the pastry then sprinkle with the remaining ingredients. Cover with the second portion of pastry, rolled out, and bake at 200°C until golden brown.

Ham and Green Pea Shortcake

185g flour
¼ teaspoon salt
¼ teaspoon pepper
2 teaspoons baking powder
½ teaspoon dry mustard
50g butter
1 egg, well-beaten
50g cheese, grated
milk, to mix

Mix all the dry ingredients and rub in the butter. Add the egg and cheese, and mix to a soft dough using a little milk if required. Turn on to a floured board, halve the dough and roll out the 2 portions to fit a 20cm sandwich tin. Place 1 round in a greased tin and spread with a little softened butter. Cover with the 2nd round of pastry and bake for 30 minutes at 220°C, until golden brown. Lift off the top half and cool.

Filling:
155g minced ham
4 tablespoons white sauce
1 cup cooked, green peas
1 hard-boiled egg, chopped

Combine all the ingredients and spread on to the bottom pastry. Cover with the top piece and press lightly. Reheat in the oven and serve. Serves 4-6.

Jellied Chicken Cake

2 hard-boiled eggs, sliced thickly
250g cold, cooked chicken, chopped
500g streaky bacon, chopped
2 tablespoons parsley
salt
pepper
grated rind 1 lemon
15g gelatin
1¼ cups chicken stock

Line the well buttered bottom of a baking dish with the egg slices. Add the chicken, bacon, parsley, seasoning and rind. Place a few slices of egg along the sides of the dish and continue layering the filling ingredients. Dissolve the gelatin in the stock and pour over the contents. Refrigerate for a few hours, turn out and serve with salad. Serves 4-6.

Meat Loaf

500g minced beef
1 egg, beaten
125g breadcrumbs
1 cup milk
3-4 rashers bacon, chopped
1 large onion, grated
1 large carrot, grated
salt
pepper
2 tablespoons tomato sauce

Mix all the ingredients and bake in a greased loaf tin for 1 hour at 200°C. Serves 4-6.

Minted Meat Pie

250g short pastry
2 tablespoons chopped mint
2 tablespoons chopped parsley
1½ cups cold, chopped potato
½ cup cooked, chopped carrot
¼ cup cooked, green peas
1 cup cooked meat, chopped
2 eggs, beaten
3 tablespoons tomato sauce
50g cheese, grated

Roll out half the pastry to fit a 23cm piedish. Spread with the mint, parsley, vegetables and meat, pour over the eggs and sprinkle with the sauce. Cover with the remaining, rolled-out pastry and sprinkle with the cheese. Bake for 30 minutes at 200°C. Serves 4-6.

Mutton and Mushroom Pie

1 large onion, chopped
1kg stewing chops
1¼ cups water
salt
pepper
125g button mushrooms
250g flaky pastry
1 egg, beaten
15g gelatin
1 tablespoon chopped parsley

Brown the onion in a little fat then add to the water with the chops and season to taste. Cook until meat can be removed from the bones. Strain off the gravy, cut up the meat and place in a piedish. Add the prepared mushrooms. Remove the fat from the gravy, add water if necessary to make 1¼ cups and pour half this quantity on to the meat. Cover with pastry, decorating the edges. Make a slit in the centre, brush with egg and bake for 30 minutes at 200°C. Melt the gelatin in the remaining gravy, add the parsley and pour into the pie through the slit, using a funnel. Serve hot or cold. Serves 4.

Picnic Loaf

1 loaf bread
butter
cold meat, or cooked sausages
chutney
beetroot, or tomatoes
1¼ cups savoury jelly

Cut a slice off the top of the loaf and take out most of the bread leaving 2cm around the crust. Butter the inside of the loaf and then pack with layers of chopped, cold meats, chutney, beetroot or tomatoes. Pour over each layer a little jelly and allow to set. Replace the top, buttered slice and press down firmly. Wrap the loaf in greaseproof paper and secure with tape. Serves 4-6.

Picnic Roll

185-250g minced, corn beef
2 rashers bacon, minced
3 small onions, minced
500g skinned, pork sausages, minced
1 egg, beaten
sprinkle pepper
flour, as required
1 tablespoon butter
½ cup hot water

Combine the meat, bacon, onion and sausage meat. Bind with the egg, season and form into a roll with a little flour. Into a casserole put the butter and water. Place the roll on greaseproof paper and place in the casserole. Cover and bake for 45-60 minutes at 200°C, removing the lid for the last 10 minutes. Serves 4-6.

Picnic Sandwich

500g flour
1 teaspoon baking powder
½ teaspoon salt
250g lard

Make a pastry with the flour, baking powder, salt and lard. Divide into 2 portions and line a large roasting dish with one portion.

Filling:
500g mincemeat
salt
pepper
125g well-seasoned stuffing
3-4 onions, chopped and fried
3-4 tomatoes, peeled and sliced
3-4 eggs

Season the meat and put half the quantity on top of the pastry in the dish. Over this spread the stuffing and cover with the rest of the mince. Cover with the prepared onions and tomatoes, and break the eggs over the mixture. Season and cover with the remaining pastry. Bake for 1-1½ hours at 150°C. Serves 4-6.

Pork and Apple Pie

500g lean pork, minced, or pork sausage meat
2 tablespoons bacon fat
½ cup minced onion
1 teaspoon mixed herbs
salt
pepper
1 x 300g tin green peas, drained
3 apples, peeled, cored and sliced
1 cup water
250g short pastry

Roll the meat in flour and brown in hot bacon fat. Add the onion, herbs, salt, pepper, peas and apples, and mix well with water. Put into a piedish and cover with the rolled out pastry. Bake for 30 minutes at 200°C. Serves 4.

Tongue and Vegetable Pie

6 sheep tongues
2-3 slices lemon
1 onion
2-3 large potatoes, peeled and sliced
2 onions, sliced
1 cup green peas, drained
60g soft breadcrumbs
3 tablespoons chopped parsley
salt
pepper
1 cup milk

Boil the tongues with lemon slices and onion for 3 hours. Cool, skin and slice the tongues. Line a buttered casserole with the potato and onion slices. Arrange the tongue, peas and breadcrumbs in layers over the potato and onion. Sprinkle each layer with parsley, salt and pepper, pour over the milk, and cover with more potato slices. Cook for 45-60 minutes at 200° and serve with a green salad. Serves 6-8.

Sandwiches

Always use a sharp knife in preparing sandwiches. Use bread a day old, the finer grained the better. Spread with butter soft enough to distribute evenly but never melted. Butter with a broad knife, trim crusts and wrap the sandwiches in a damp cloth or greaseproof paper ready to serve.

Sweet Fillings

Date and honey. Fig, raisins or sultanas may be used.
Banana and honey or jam. Sprinkle with lemon juice.
Cream cheese and chopped walnuts.
Peanut butter and honey.
Minced dried fruits with lemon juice.
Grated raw apple, lemon juice and honey or sugar.
Mash 1 banana with 3 cooked dried apricots and add a little orange juice and sweeten to taste with icing sugar or honey.

Savoury Fillings

Chopped hard–boiled egg with Marmite, parsley, salad dressing, chives or anchovy sauce.
Lettuce with Marmite, peanut butter or cream cheese.
Chopped celery, apple and nuts bound with mayonnaise.
Egg, French mustard and grated cheese.
Chopped pickled walnut and grated cheese and sufficient mayonnaise to blend.
Grated carrot mixed with mayonnaise to moisten.
Finely-chopped raw vegetables (carrots, lettuce, celery), mixed with sufficient mayonnaise to blend.
Minced ham and chutney.
Sardines seasoned with lemon juice and chopped parsley.
Cream cheese with anchovy, beetroot, or chutney.
Olive and Cucumber: Mix chopped olives and cucumbers with cream cheese, Spread between crisp lettuce leaves and buttered white bread.
Ham and Celery: Put ham through meat mincer and add finely-chopped celery. Mix with salad dressing. A finely-chopped green pepper can also be used with this.
Cheese and Olive: Press cheese through a strainer. Chop olives and then combine the two with salad dressing to make it into paste. A combination of white and brown bread, having 3 layers of bread, is a nice change.
Peanut: Mash peanuts in a mortar or chop as fine as possible and mix with Worcestershire sauce. Spread on thin slices of buttered bread.

BEVERAGES

Orangeade

rind 6 oranges
2kg sugar
60g tartaric acid
5*l* boiling water

Mix all the ingredients and leave to stand
overnight. Boil up, strain and bottle. To serve put
a little into a glass and fill with iced water.

Banana Cup

6 bananas, mashed
juice 6 oranges
juice 1 lemon
1 cup pineapple juice
8 passionfruit, or 1½ cups pulp
250g sugar
2 small bottles soda
2 small bottles gingerale

To the bananas add the orange, lemon and
pineapple juice, the passionfruit pulp and cover
with the sugar. Leave for 2 hours then sieve. For
serving add the soda and gingerale and serve over
ice. Serves 8-10.

Coffee Punch

3¾ cups ice-cream, vanilla or part chocolate
4 cups hot coffee
¼ teaspoon grated nutmeg

Pour the coffee over the ice-cream and beat lightly
until ice-cream is partially melted. Pour into
individual glasses and sprinkle with nutmeg.
Serves 8.

Passionfruit Syrup

pulp 24 passionfruit
3 teaspoons tartaric acid
650g sugar
3 cups water

Put the pulp into a large jug. Add the acid. Boil
the sugar and water for 20 minutes and pour over
the pulp. When cold strain and bottle. Allow ½
cup to 1 glass of water.

Iced Coffee

1¼ cups strong, cold coffee
½ cup cream
½ cup milk
¼ cup sugar syrup

Mix all the ingredients and chill. Serve topped with
sweetened, whipped cream. Serves 4.

Christmas Punch

5 cups cider
2 small bottles gingerale
3 cups rum
6 cloves
125g sugar
30g chopped, preserved ginger
juice 2 oranges
juice 2 lemons
2 apples, peeled, cored and sliced
2½ cups boiling water

Warm the cider, gingerale and rum. Add the
remaining ingredients stirred into the boiling
water. Serve very hot. Serves 10-12.

Cordial

30g citric acid
1½ cups water
1kg fruit, raspberries, loganberries or
    strawberries
875g sugar

Mix the acid and water and pour over the prepared fruit. Leave for 24 hours, then strain. Add the sugar and dissolve over heat. Do not boil or the flavour will be destroyed. Cool and bottle

Fruit Punch

5 cups water
440g sugar
1 x 350g tin crushed pineapple
½ cup lemon juice
1 cup orange juice
2 small bottles gingerale

Boil the water, sugar and pineapple for 20 minutes, then add the fruit juices. Cool, strain and dilute with iced water and gingerale. Serves 8-10

Ginger Punch

250g ginger root, chopped
5 cups cold water
220g sugar
½ cup lemon juice
½ cup orange juice

Boil the ginger, water and sugar for 15 minutes. Add the juices, cool, strain and dilute with cracked ice. Serves 6.

Gingerale

5l water
1.5kg sugar
3 egg whites, beaten
60g ground ginger
juice 4 large lemons
15g compressed yeast

Dissolve the sugar in the water, then add the egg whites and ginger dissolved in a little water. Bring to the boil, skim and cool. Add the juice and yeast and stir until dissolved. Leave for 10 minutes, then strain through cheesecloth. Bottle and cork well and keep in a cool place for 3 days.

Grape Juice

1.5kg grapes, stemmed
3l water
125g sugar per 5 cups liquid

Boil the grapes in the water for 5 minutes. Strain and add sugar. Boil for 20 minutes. Heat bottles and bottle while liquid is boiling hot.

Gingerade

juice 2 lemons
juice 1 orange
1 cup strained sugar syrup
2 cloves
rind 1 orange
rind 1 lemon
thinly-sliced, preserved ginger
gingerale

Add the lemon and orange juice to the syrup to which the cloves and rinds have been added during cooking. Pour 2-3 tablespoons over crushed ice in each glass, add 1 tablespoon of ginger and fill with gingerale.

Ginger Beer

Method 1
500g sugar
1 level tablespoon ground ginger
1 teaspoon tartaric acid
1 teaspoon cream of tartar
5l cold water

Mix all the ingredients and add to the cold water, stirring until everything is dissolved. Keep in an earthenware container until used.

Method 2
155g preserved ginger
9l water
2.5kg sugar
1¼ cups lemon juice
125g honey
1 egg white, well-beaten
1 teaspoon lemon esence

Boil the ginger in 12 cups of the water for 30 minutes. Add the sugar, lemon juice, honey and remainder of the water. Strain and when cold add the egg white and essence. Leave for 4 days then bottle, and allow to stand for 3 days before serving.

Lager Beer Punch

peel 1 lemon
1 cup water
½ cup sherry
juice 2 lemons
pinch grated nutmeg
1 tablespoon castor sugar
few leaves mint
1 bottle lager beer

Put the peel into a jug with the water, sherry, lemon juice, nutmeg, castor sugar and mint. Cover and leave for 20 minutes. Strain and add the beer. Serve over ice.

Lemonade

2 fresh lemons, sliced
1kg sugar
5*l* boiling water
60g cream of tartar

Place all the ingredients in a stone crock and leave for 24 hours, then bottle and leave for a week before serving.

Lemon Fizz

¼ cup lemon essence
6 pieces loaf sugar
250g baking soda
125g tartaric acid
1kg castor sugar

Pour the essence on to the loaf sugar. When absorbed and dry, roll out to a fine powder. Mix with the soda, acid and sugar and store in an airtight jar. Add 1 heaped teaspoon to each glass of water and serve with ice.

Lemon Syrup

2*l* boiling water
2kg sugar
grated rind and juice 6 lemons
30g citric acid
60g tartaric acid
60g epsom salts

Add the boiling water to the sugar and lemon juice and rind, stir until sugar has dissolved, then add the acids and salts. Stir until all have dissolved, cool, strain and bottle. Use 1-2 tablespoons in a glass of water.

Mint Cup

juice 1 lemon
juice 1 orange
2-4 mint leaves, chopped
grated nuts
strawberries

Put some ice chips into a shaker until half full, add the lemon and orange juice and the mint. Shake well, strain and serve topped with nuts and strawberries.

Mint Julep

juice 10 lemons, strained
2 bunches mint leaves, bruised
600g sugar
1 cup water
4*l* gingerale

To the lemon juice add the mint leaves, sugar and water, and bring to the boil. Cover and leave for 30 minutes, then strain and add the gingerale. Stir and chill. Garnish with mint leaves.

Orangine

5*l* frozen orange water ice
gingerale, as required

Place the orange ice in a punch bowl and over this pour sufficient gingerale to cover. Freshly made cold tea may replace the gingerale.

COCKTAILS

THE time to serve cocktails is just before dinner. All the equipment required is a shaker, a measure, crushed ice and, of course, the necessary ingredients. Anything will serve as a measure, the size depending on the number of people drinking. Just before serving, the drink must be strained to remove any ice or pips. Some well known recipes are:

A Simple Vermouth Cocktail:

One-third French dry vermouth, ⅓ Italian sweet vermouth, ⅓ gin. Add a dash curacao or maraschino.

Bronx:

Half gin, ¼ each dry vermouth and sweet vermouth, 1 teaspoon orange juice.

Dry Martini:

Half each dry vermouth and gin, squeeze of orange skin. Serve with an olive.

Sweet Martini:

Two-thirds gin, ⅓ sweet vermouth, dash orange bitters. Serve with a cherry.

Manhattan:

Large dash angostura bitters, 2 dashes curacao, ½ whisky, ½ sweet vermouth. A squeeze of lemon peel.

White Lady:

Quarter lemon juice, ¼ curacao triple sec, ½ gin.

Rum Cocktail:

Half rum, ¼ orange or lemon juice, ¼ sweet vermouth, 1 teaspoon tip of cinnamon.

R. N. Cocktail:

Two-thirds rum, ⅓ lime juice. Sweeten with a little powdered sugar.

Sidecar:

One-third each curacao triple sec, lemon juice, brandy. Shake well but do not ice.

Planters' Special:

Half teaspoon lemon juice, ⅛ cup orange juice, ⅛ cup rum. Ice and shake well.

South Seas:

Quarter brandy, ½ cider, ¼ pineapple juice.

Caterpillar Club:

Quarter dry gin. ¾ cider, 2 dashes angostura bitters.

Moulin Rouge:

Three dashes curacao, juice ¼ orange, ¼ dry vermouth, ¼ sweet vermouth, ½ dry gin.

Green Dragon:

One-sixth each lemon juice, kummel, creme de menthe, ½ gin.

Pineapple Slice:

One third dry vermouth, ⅔ gin, 4 dashes maraschino, 1 slice pineapple.

Will Rogers:

Quarter orange juice, ¼ dry vermouth, ½ Plymouth gin, 4 dashes curacao.

Old Fashioned:

One lump loaf sugar, 1 teaspoon orange bitters, 1 teaspoon angostura bitters, ⅛ cup benedictine, 1 dash lemon juice, 1½ tablespoons water. Serve iced.

Hurricane:

Quarter each whisky, gin, creme de menthe, lemon juice.

Blue Lagoon:

One teaspoon blue curacao, ⅛ cup gin. Fill up with lemonade and garnish with 2 cherries.

Cider Cocktail

1 lump loaf sugar per person
1 teaspoon orange juice per person
iced cider

Put the sugar in a glass, pour over the juice, leave to melt then fill with cider.

Fruit Juice Cocktail

3 cups orange juice
1½ cups grapefruit juice
½ cup lemon juice
3 cups gingerale

Strain the fruit juices, mix well and chill. Just before serving, add the chilled gingerale. Serves 20-25.

Grapefruit Cocktail

1 grapefruit per person
2 teaspoons castor sugar per person
white wine, as required
¼ teaspoon ground ginger per glass

Squeeze the juice from the grapefruit and pour into a shaker with plenty of ice chips. Shake well and add sugar. Half fill wine glasses then fill with white wine. Stir in the ginger and serve.

Tomato Cup

1kg ripe tomatoes
1 onion, grated
1 tablespoon salt
3¾ cups boiling water
¼ teaspoon pepper
1 tablespoon sugar
pinch celery salt
juice 1 lemon
few drops almond essence
soda

Put the tomatoes in a large bowl with the onion. Sprinkle with salt and pour over the boiling water. Leave for 2 hours, pass through a sieve, then add the remaining ingredients. Bottle and keep cool. Serve with crushed ice and fill glasses with soda.

Tomato Juice Cocktail

3½ cups tomato juice
juice 1 lemon
1 tablespoon tomato sauce
2 teaspoons sugar
pinch salt
dash cayenne pepper
1 teaspoon Worcestershire sauce

Combine all the ingredients, mix well, chill and serve in cocktail glasses. Serves 6.

HOMEMADE WINE AND CIDER ETC.

Apricot Wine

6kg firm apricots, stoned and chopped
500g sugar
15*l* water
1 teaspoon compressed yeast
2½ cups white wine

Put the apricots in a large pot with the water, sugar and half the kernels. Simmer for 1 hour. Turn into an earthenware vessel, cool then stir in the yeast. Cover with a cloth and leave for 3 days. Strain into a clean, dry cask, add the white wine and bung tightly. After 6 months draw off the wine into bottles, cork tightly and store in a cool place for 12 months.

Apple Cider

Method I:
apples
boiling water
brown sugar

Cover any quantity of apple skins, cores and flesh with boiling water and stand in a warm place for 3 days when it will start frothing. A little brown sugar added improves the flavour. Strain through a cheesecloth. Leave for another 3 days, strain again and bottle in strong bottles. Tie corks down and leave for 2 days when it will be ready.

Method II:
1.5kg apples, chopped
2.5*l* boiling water
125g sugar
155g sultanas

Cover the apples with the water and leave for 3 days. Strain and add the sugar and sultanas. Stand for 24 hours, stir once or twice, then strain and bottle. Ready in 3 days.

Passionfruit Cider

100 passionfruit
10*l* water
4kg sugar

Scoop out the passionfruit pulp and put in an earthenware bowl with the water. Leave for 3 days then strain and add the sugar. Skim and stir every day. When fermentation ceases, bottle. After 2-3 months it will open up like champagne.

Grape Wine

1.5kg black grapes
5*l* cold water
1.5kg sugar

Put the grapes in a bowl and crush. Cover with water, let stand for 5 days, stirring several times daily, then strain. Add the sugar, stir until dissolved, then set in a warm place to ferment. Leave for 10 days, then strain and bottle.

Parsnip Wine

2kg parsnips, quartered
30g hops
1.5kg sugar
1 tablespoon yeast
slice toast

Boil the parsnips and the hops tied in a muslin bag, uncovered until tender enough to lift out on a sieve without breaking. Strain and add sugar. Let the wine cool to lukewarm, then add the toast spread with the yeast and allow to stand in a tub or wooden vessel for 36 hours to ferment. Cask the wine as soon as the hissing sound stops, when it will be sufficiently fermented. Bottle and store lying down. Wine is ready after 1 month, and improves with age.

Rhubarb Wine

5kg rhubarb pulp
10*l* water
3kg sugar per 5*l* liquid
25g gelatin per 5*l* liquid
2 lemons per 5*l* liquid

To the rhubarb add the water and let stand for 36 hours, stirring often. Strain and add the sugar, dissolved gelatin and lemon rind. Stir well and allow to ferment for 1 week until fermentation subsides. Strain off into a cask. If it ferments again, strain once more. Bung loosely and tighten after 1-2 weeks. Can be bottled, and improves with age.

Beetroot Wine

2kg beetroot
5*l* water
2kg sugar
juice 3 lemons
8 cloves

Wash the beetroot, cut it up quickly into the water, boil for 20 minutes, then strain. Add the sugar and lemon juice while hot and stir until the sugar has dissolved. Add the cloves and leave to ferment for 3 weeks. Skim, strain and bottle.

Blackberry Wine

15kg blackberries
4kg sugar per 10*l* blackberry juice

Stand the berries in a bowl for 3-4 weeks, then strain into a barrel and add the sugar. Leave for another 12 days, then cork down and leave in the barrel for 9 months. Bottle and tie down the corks. The wine is better the longer it is kept, and good as a port wine.

Hop Beer

125g hops, secured in an oatmeal bag
3kg sugar
1 tablespoon compressed yeast

Boil the bag of hops in a large pot of water for 1 hour. Dissolve the sugar in 5*l* of water and boil for 15 minutes. Drain in the hops and fill with the boiling water. Set aside, cool, then add the yeast. When specks of froth come to the top, bottle and cork well. This beer is made stronger by boiling a handful of wheat or barley with the hops. More hops makes it bitter.

Homemade Stout

1.5kg black malt, in a muslin bag
20*l* water
125g hops, tied in a muslin bag
2kg brown sugar
2 tablespoons treacle
2 tablespoons salt
30g compressed yeast
1 egg white, beaten

Place the malt bag in the water, bring to the boil and boil for 45 minutes. Add the bagged hops and boil for another 15 minutes. Remove the bags from the water and add more hot water to make up the initial quantity. Allow to cool to 100°C, add the sugar, treacle and salt and stir well until dissolved. Strain into a wooden vat or container and let stand until it reaches blood heat – or nearly cold, then dissolve the yeast in 1 cup of the brew and pour back. Add the egg white and stir the brew well. Leave for 12 hours, skim and stir again. Skim frequently every day until the working stops and no scum appears on the surface, approximately 7-8 days in summer, 14 in winter. Syphon into bottles and add 1 teaspoon of sugar into each bottle. Leave 5cm at the top for air. Bottles must be dry. Soak the seals in warm water before use. The brew will be ready in 3 weeks.

JAMS, JELLIES AND PRESERVES

In addition to the fruit pulp or fruit juice needed in jam or jelly making, three other factors must be present. These are:

1. **Sugar:** This is usually added in the proportion of 500g per 500g of fruit used. Sugar is added after the fruit is cooked and should be warmed. In this way it dissolves better and saves time. Once the sugar is added, boil the jam rapidly and test frequently.

2. **Acid:** Present in most fruits and especially in apples, currants, gooseberries and rhubarb. Strawberries contain none and must have added acid (tartaric acid is suitable) or be combined with an acid fruit when used in jam making.

3. **Pectin:** Usually abundant in under-ripe fruits but present in minute quantities only in ripe fruits. Apples contain pectin both when ripe and under-ripe. Home-made pectin may be made from apples.

To get the jam to gel it is necessary to boil it until the right amount of steam is evaporated. Frequent tests must be made, the common one being to drop a little of the jam on to a cold saucer. If the jam is done it will soon form a skin which will wrinkle when touched with the finger.

Pot the jam or jelly into warm sterilised jars and seal; either immediately or when the jam is thoroughly cold. If possible store in a dark cupboard.

Home-made Pectin

1.5kg tart green apples, chopped
2½ cups water

Put the chopped apple, skin and core included, into a saucepan with the water and cook until a pulp. Strain through a jelly bag, retaining the juice. Add water to the pulp to thin and simmer for 1½ hours. Combine the two liquids and pour into jars. As no sugar is used these must be well sealed and sterilised. Add to the jam before adding sugar.

Apple Jelly

1.5kg apples, chopped
water
1 lemon, sliced, or lemon essence
1 cup sugar per 1 cup juice

Reduce the chopped apple, core and peel included, to a soft pulp. Add half their measure of water and boil slowly after adding the lemon. Drain through muslin, add the sugar and boil for 20 minutes, or until it gels.

Apple Marmalade

6 lemons, sliced
3.5l boiling water
3kg Cox's orange apples, peeled and chopped
4kg sugar

Soak the lemons overnight in the water and next day boil until the rind is tender. Add the chopped apples and cook quickly until soft, then add the sugar and cook for 30-45 minutes.

Carrot and Orange Marmalade

2 carrots, shredded
2 lemons, shredded
2 oranges, shredded
1 teaspoon salt
5 cups boiling water
1 cup sugar per 1 cup fruit pulp

Place the carrots, fruit and salt in boiling water. Stand overnight, then boil for 20 minutes. Measure the pulp and add the sugar. Boil until it gels.

Crab Apple Jelly

crab apples, topped and tailed
cold water
1 cup sugar per 1 cup juice
50g whole, bruised ginger tied in a muslin bag, or juice 2-3 lemons, or 1 x 300g tin pineapple juice

Put the fruit in a pan, cover with cold water and boil until soft. Pour into a clean muslin bag, hang up and allow to drip overnight. Measure the pulp and add the appropriate quantity of sugar. Add the desired flavouring and boil for 1 hour, skimming often. While hot pour into jars, and seal when cold.

Blackberry and Apple Spread

1.5kg blackberries, cleaned
1.5kg tart apples, chopped but not peeled
1 cup sugar per 1 cup fruit
juice 2 lemons
knob butter

Partly cover the berries with water in a saucepan and mash as they boil. Add the apple and boil until soft, then rub through a sieve. Measure the amount and add the appropriate quantity of sugar. Bring to the boil and cook briskly for 5 minutes. Add the lemon juice and boil until it gels. To settle the scum add a knob of butter before bottling.

Blackcurrant Jam

1kg blackcurrants
1l water
1.5kg sugar

Boil together the fruit and water for 45 minutes. Add the sugar and boil a further 20-30 minutes, or until it gels. Place in warm jars and cover when cold.

Apricot and Pineapple Marmalade

500g dried apricots, soaked overnight in 2.5l
  water
1 x 450g tin crushed pineapple
1.5kg sugar
½ teaspoon salt

To the soaked apricots add the pineapple and cook until apricots are tender. Stir in the sugar and salt until dissolved, then boil until it sets, stirring continuously to avoid burning. Bottle and seal while hot.

Apricot Marmalade

1.5kg apricots
juice 2 oranges
juice 2 lemons
grated rind 2 lemons
1 x 350g tin crushed pineapple
2.5kg sugar, warmed

Put all the fruit, juices and rind in a saucepan and boil for 5 minutes, then add the sugar and boil for 20 minutes, or until it gels. Stir frequently to avoid sticking. Bottle and seal while hot.

Blackcurrant Jelly

1kg sugar
300ml water
1kg blackcurrants

Boil together the water and sugar for 10 minutes, then add the prepared fruit, stalks and a few leaves and boil for 5 minutes. Strain and bottle.

Cape Gooseberry Jam

1.5kg cape gooseberries
750g apples, peeled and sliced
750g tomatoes
2¾kg sugar
6 bananas, peeled and sliced

Put the gooseberries, apples, tomatoes and sugar in a preserving pan. Boil for 15 minutes, then add the bananas and boil for 5 minutes more. Bottle and seal once cooled.

Cucumber Jam

4½kg long cucumbers, diced
3¾kg sugar
100g whole ginger
4 oranges, shredded
4 lemons, shredded
5 cups water

Leave the diced cucumber overnight in the sugar. Put the ginger in a muslin bag and add to the cucumber with the other ingredients. Boil for 2½ hours, or until it sets on a saucer. Stir as little as possible. Bottle while hot.

Green Gooseberry Jam

1.5kg gooseberries
5 cups water
3kg sugar

Boil the fruit in water for 20 minutes, then add the sugar and boil for 5 minutes, no longer or it will turn red. Put through a sieve to remove the skins and bottle.

Gooseberry Jelly

gooseberries
¾ cup sugar per 1 cup juice
1 teaspoon butter

Put the prepared fruit in a pan and just cover with water. Stew until pulp, then strain through a jelly bag. Strain overnight to obtain all the juice. Measure the juice and add the appropriate quantity of sugar, and the butter. Boil rapidly for 5 minutes, when it should gel.

Spiced Fig Jam

375g dried figs, chopped
1 teaspoon lemon rind, chopped
2 cups water
1¼kg sugar
50g chopped walnuts
1 teaspoon cinnamon
1½ teaspoons ground cloves

Soak the figs and lemon in water overnight. Next day add the sugar, walnuts and spices and bring to the boil, stirring constantly. Boil for 5 minutes. Bottle while hot.

Fruit Salad Jam

Method I
1kg apricots, stoned and chopped
1 x 300g tin crushed pineapple
1kg peaches, stoned and chopped
5 bananas, peeled and sliced
pulp 3 passionfruit
juice 2 oranges
juice 1 lemon
2¼kg sugar

Boil together all the ingredients for 30 minutes and bottle while hot.

Fruit Salad Jam

Method II
1kg dried peaches
2l water
1 x 300g tin crushed pineapple
juice 2 lemons
juice 1 orange
3¾kg sugar, warmed
8 bananas, peeled and chopped

Soak the peaches in water for 24 hours. Put into a preserving pan with the pineapple and juices. Boil for 1 hour then add the sugar and bananas. Boil slowly for 30 minutes, stirring frequently. Bottle while hot.

Ginger Marmalade

1.5kg tart apples, chopped
700g preserved ginger, chopped
5 cups water
1 cup sugar per 1 cup juice

Put the chopped apples, peels and cores included, into a preserving pan with the ginger and water and cook to a pulp. Strain through a jelly bag. Measure the juice and add the appropriate quantity of sugar. Bring to the boil and cook rapidly for 8-10 minutes. Bottle and seal while hot.

Golden Jam

4 sweet oranges
125g dried apricots
1¾l water
1 x 400g tin crushed pineapple
2¼kg sugar

Mince together the oranges and apricots. Soak in the water overnight, then boil for 1 hour. Add the pineapple and sugar and boil until it sets. Bottle while hot.

Grape Jam

2kg grapes
1 cup water
1½kg sugar

Place the grapes in a preserving pan with water to prevent burning. Boil for 1 hour, add the sugar and simmer. Skim constantly to remove pips. Boil until it gels, about 1 hour, then bottle and seal.

Green Tomato and Ginger Jam

3kg green tomatoes, quartered
grated rind and juice 2 lemons
1.5kg sugar
75g whole, bruised ginger
1¾kg sugar, warmed

Put the tomatoes in a preserving pan with the rind and juice, sprinkle with the first portion of sugar and leave overnight. Simmer with the ginger for 30 minutes then add the warmed sugar. Stir until dissolved and boil rapidly until it gels. Remove the ginger and bottle while hot. When cold, seal.

Green Tomato and Pineapple Jam

2kg green tomatoes, sliced
250g sugar
1 pineapple, shredded, or 1 x 850g tin crushed
  pineapple
100g preserved ginger, chopped
1 teaspoon salt
juice 3 lemons
grated rind 1 lemon
1.5kg sugar, warmed

Sprinkle the tomatoes with sugar and leave overnight. Add the pineapple, ginger, salt, juice, rind and boil until tender, then stir in the warmed sugar. Boil until it gels and bottle while hot. Seal when cold.

Lemon Honey

100g butter
350g sugar
rind and juice 3 lemons
4 whole eggs or 8 egg yolks, beaten

Put the butter, sugar, finely grated lemon rind and lemon juice in the top half of a double boiler and heat over hot water. Stir until butter has melted and the sugar dissolved. Stir in the beaten eggs. Continue stirring until the curd thickens. Pour into clean jars, cover and seal while hot.

Orange Honey

1 cup sugar
grated rind and juice 1 orange
grated rind and juice 1 lemon
2 eggs, well beaten
50g butter

Into a saucepan place the sugar, rinds and juices, the eggs and butter. Stand over a gentle heat and stir until thick, but do not allow to boil. Bottle while hot.

Melon Five-in-One Jam

1 x 5.5kg melon
1kg sugar per 1kg fruit
grated rind and juice 3 lemons
pulp 6 passionfruit
500g dried apricots, soaked overnight and
    quartered
1 cup cape gooseberries, chopped
400g preserved ginger, chopped

Remove the rind and pips from the melon, cut up and mince, then weigh. Add the appropriate quantity of sugar and leave for 24 hours. Stir thoroughly and divide into 5 vessels. To the first add the lemon rind and juice. To the second add the passionfruit pulp. To the third the apricots. To the fourth the gooseberries and to the fifth the ginger. Boil until melon is clear, approximately 1½ hours. Put into jars while hot and seal when cold.

Nectarine Jelly

nectarines, washed and stemmed
water
1 cup sugar per 1 cup juice

Put the nectarines in a saucepan with water to cover. Boil until juice is extracted, then place in a jelly bag and allow to drip. Add the appropriate quantity of sugar and boil for 20 minutes. Bottle while hot and seal when cold.

Pear Ginger

pears, quartered
¾kg sugar per 1kg fruit
75g preserved ginger per 1kg fruit

Sprinkle half the sugar over the pears and leave overnight. Next day add the remaining sugar and chopped ginger and boil for 2 hours, or until clear. Bottle while hot and seal when cold.

Pear Marmalade

3kg pears, minced
4 sweet oranges, minced
4 lemons, minced
2½ cups water
3kg sugar

In a large pan put all the fruit, sprinkle with the sugar, cover with the water and leave overnight. Boil for 3½ hours. If fruit is juicy 2 cups of water is sufficient.

Persimmon Jam

500g rhubarb, chopped
½ cup water
1.5kg sugar, heated
1kg persimmon pulp

Cook the rhubarb gently in the water and when tender add the pulp and sugar. Boil until it sets. Bottle and seal while hot.

Plum Jam

1.5kg plums
1.5kg sugar
½l water

Boil together all the ingredients until a rich colour and sets. Bottle and seal while hot.

Plum and Honey Butter

plums
1.5kg honey per 2.5l purée

Cook the fruit slowly in just enough water to prevent burning. When quite soft press through a sieve. Heat the purée to boiling point and add the honey. Cook until thick, then bottle and seal while hot.

Plum – Raspberry Conserve

1.5kg plums
1 cup water
1.5kg raspberries
2.5kg sugar

Boil the plums in water until soft and red. Remove the stones by putting through a sieve, then boil for 30 minutes. Add the raspberries and sugar and boil for 15 minutes. Bottle and seal while hot.

Redcurrant Jelly

500g redcurrants
125g raspberries
¾ cup sugar per 1 cup juice

Heat the prepared fruit in a preserving pan but do not boil. Strain thoroughly. Measure the juice, add the appropriate quantity of sugar and boil for 15 minutes. Bottle and seal while hot.

Rhubarb Marmalade

3 sweet oranges, peeled
1kg rhubarb, cut in 2.5cm lengths
2kg sugar

Shred the orange skins as for marmalade. Place the peel and orange pulp into a preserving pan with the rhubarb. Add the sugar, stir until dissolved and boil quickly for 30 minutes, or until it sets. Bottle and seal while hot.

Rhubarb Jelly

1.5kg rhubarb, chopped in 2cm lengths
juice, grated rind and chopped pith of
  3 lemons
750g green apples, chopped
1¾l water
1 cup sugar per 1 cup juice

Gently cook the fruit in a preserving pan with the water, mashing frequently until fruit turns to a pulp. Strain overnight through a jelly bag, measure the juice, add the appropriate quantity of sugar and boil until it sets. Bottle and seal while hot.

Strawberry Jam

3kg strawberries, hulled and rinsed
2¾kg sugar
juice 2 lemons

Boil together the ingredients until the mixture gels, stirring constantly to prevent burning.

Raspberry Jelly

raspberries
¾ cup sugar per 1 cup juice

Put the fresh raspberries into a jar, place in a pan of boiling water, boil until juice flows freely, then strain through a muslin cloth. Measure the juice, add the appropriate quantity of sugar and boil quickly, removing the scum. When it gels pour into pots and seal.

Quince Honey

3 quinces, peeled and minced
1.5kg sugar
5 cups water
6 cloves
1 teaspoon salt
juice and grated rind 1 lemon, optional

Sprinkle the fruit with 500g of the sugar and leave overnight. Boil the skins with the water, cloves and salt. Strain and pour over the fruit the following day. Add the remaining sugar and the lemon juice and rind, and boil until a honey consistency. Bottle and seal while hot.

Quince Jam

3kg quinces
2¼l water
4kg sugar

Boil the quinces whole in water until soft, then strain and make a syrup with the water and half the sugar. Boil for 30 minutes. Peel the quinces, cut up into small pieces and boil for 30 minutes in the syrup. Add the remaining sugar and boil until bright red. Bottle and seal while hot.

Raspberry Jam

1.5kg raspberries
1.5kg sugar, warmed

Cook the fruit over gentle heat with a little water to prevent burning. Mash to extract the juice. Simmer until soft and then stir in the sugar, stirring until completely dissolved. Boil rapidly for 10 minutes. Bottle and seal while hot.

Tamarillo Jam

2.5kg tamarillos
water
2kg sugar

Cover the fruit with water and boil until tender. Add the sugar and boil rapidly for 30 minutes. Bottle and seal while hot.

Tomato and Quince Jam

1kg ripe quinces, peeled, cored and minced
1.5kg tomatoes, skinned and chopped
2.5kg sugar
juice 2 lemons

Boil together all the ingredients for 2 hours, or until the mixture sets. Bottle and seal while hot.

FOOD PRESERVATION

Food decomposes by the action of micro-organisms which require the presence of warmth, moisture and air. Therefore, when preserving food, it is necessary to eliminate some or all of these conditions. This may be done by any of the following methods:
1. **Freezing and cold storage:** This is becoming increasingly popular and is the best way to preserve vegetables and many fruits. The initial cost of a freezer is high and consequently this method is not universally used. Instructions accompany the unit purchased, so the method will not be dealt with in this book.
2. **Canning and bottling:** The most popular method for the housewife. The micro-organisms are destroyed by heat and the food is sealed in an airtight container, thus preventing the entry of fresh bacteria.
3. **Dehydration:** All moisture is removed by slow drying. Suitable for herbs, mushrooms, and many fruits and vegetables.
4. **By excluding air:** Preserving eggs in waterglass or a special preparation is using this method of food preservation. The same applies to root vegetables, which may be kept some time if completely submerged in clean sand.
5. **By the addition of preservatives,** such as sugar, salt, spices and vinegar.

Bottled Spaghetti

5.5kg ripe tomatoes
4 medium onions, peeled
1½ cups sugar
2 tablespoons salt
1 teaspoon pepper
4 tablespoons flour
250g melted butter
500g vermicelli, cooked

Boil together the tomatoes, onions, sugar, salt and pepper until tender, then strain. Return to the boil and thicken with the flour mixed to a paste with the butter. Add the vermicelli and bottle while hot.

Candied Peel

skin of 1 large grapefruit, or 3 large oranges,
**   or 4 large lemons**
½ cup cold water
1½ cups sugar
green or red food colouring, optional

Cover the skins with water, bring to the boil and cook until tender, pouring off the water and adding fresh cold water several times. Drain the peel and cut into 6mm strips. Make a syrup by boiling 1 cup of the sugar and ½ cup of water until it spins a thread (120°C on a candy thermometer.) Add the colouring and the peel and cook over a low heat until syrup is absorbed. Remove the peel and roll in the remaining sugar. Cool, then pack in airtight containers.

Christmas Mincemeat

1kg beef suet, chopped
1kg raisins, minced
1.5kg currants, minced
1 tablespoon cinnamon
1kg castor sugar
1 teaspoon salt
juice and grated rind 4 lemons
500g mixed peel, chopped
1 cup brandy
1 cup port wine

Mix together all the ingredients and stand overnight. Store in jars and leave for 2 weeks before using. Keeps well.

Dried Apples

apples, peeled, quartered and cored

Slice the apples finely, place on a tray covered with clean greaseproof paper and put in the sunshine. Allow them to stand in the sun 3 or 4 days following the sun around during the day.
When well dried and brown, pack into thoroughly-dried and airtight bottles. Screw down lids and store in a cool dry spot. See that apples and bottles are well dried before storing. These apples make delightful apple pies and tarts when apples are not so plentiful.

Potted Blackberries

blackberries
100g sugar per 1kg fruit

Strip the berries with a fork, weigh and measure out the appropriate quantity of sugar. Put into jars and sprinkle the sugar on to the fruit. When full put the jars in a slow oven, 120°C, cover and cook until juice is completely drawn, approximately 45-60 minutes. Fill jars one from another. Seal and test the following day.

Dried Mushrooms

Gather mushrooms fresh and dry out gently, either in a warm oven or in the sun. Have them standing on a rack and turn them frequently until they are quite free of any moisture. Thread them on a piece of string and hang in a dry place (such as your hot-water cupboard) for a few days. Then put them in paper bags until required.

Soak them in boiling water when they are wanted and they are then ready for a stew or even for grilling. An alternative method is to crush and lightly flour them prior to drying. The resultant crumble can be kept in dry sterilised jars and used for soups, gravies, or as a filling for pancakes or omelettes.

Dried Parsley, Celery and Mint

Surplus parsley, mint and celery leaves should be well washed, then dried slowly in the oven. When quite dry the leaves should be rubbed fine and bottled for winter use.

Green Tomato Mincemeat

2kg brown sugar
1¾l water
4kg green tomatoes, chopped and drained
  before weighing
750g raisins
½ cup mixed peel
1 cup vinegar
3 tablespoons cinnamon
1 tablespoon ground cloves
1 tablespoon salt
1 teaspoon black pepper

Make a syrup with the sugar and water and when hot, add the other ingredients and cook for 1½ hours. Add butter when using for pies.

Preserved Tomato Soup

5.5kg ripe tomatoes
1l water
2 tablespoons sugar
4 teaspoons salt
pepper to taste
2 large onions
2 teaspoons celery salt
3 tablespoons cornflour

Boil together the tomatoes, water, sugar, salt, pepper, onions and celery salt. Cook to a pulp, then rub through a sieve. Bring to the boil in a preserving pan and thicken with the cornflour mixed to a smooth paste with a little water. Boil for 10 minutes. Pour into sterilised jars and seal while hot. When needed, heat the desired quantity and add one cup milk and a knob of butter to each 1l of soup.

Rose Hip Syrup

1kg red rose hips, grated finely
1.5l boiling water
500g sugar

Put the rose hips into boiling water and bring to the boil. Stand for 10 minutes then strain through a jelly bag. Add ¾l boiling water and re-boil. Stand aside and drain as before. Combine both lots of juices and boil together until reduced to ¾l. Add the sugar and stir well. Pour into sterilised jars to within 4-5cm of the top and stand in a water bath. Bring slowly to the boil and simmer for 20 minutes. Remove and seal with sterilised corks or jar covers. Seal corks by dipping in melted wax. It is best to use small jars as only a small quantity should be opened at one time.

FRUIT BOTTLING

Fruit for bottling should be firm, only just ripe, and free from blemishes. Apples and pears, which quickly discolour, are dropped into a weak brine once they are peeled, then rinsed, wiped and packed into the jars when needed. An alternative is to include a small slice of lemon in each jar, this acts as a bleach. Fruit may be bottled whole, halved, quartered or pulped as desired. Any of the following methods may be used:

1. **The hot pack:** The prepared fruit is dropped into boiling syrup and cooked until tender but not broken. It is then packed into hot sterilised jars, covered with syrup until overflowing and sealed at once with a sterilised cover. Jars are sterilised by boiling in water 20 minutes. This is an economical method, as much more may be packed into each jar, but the fruit loses much of its flavour, vitamin content and appearance when cooked this way.

2. **The cold pack:** The prepared fruit is packed into clean dry bottles and filled up to the neck of the bottle with syrup. The fruit may be blanched first, i.e. plunged into boiling water, boiled 1-2 minutes and then run under cold water. It is then peeled and packed into the jars. Place the lids on top and partially seal; screw-tops lids are turned until they catch, then loosened half a turn. The fruit is then sterilised, jar and all, either in a water bath, pressure cooker or oven. Protect the jars by standing on a folded tea towel, a wooden rack or, in the oven, on folded newspaper; the jars mustn't touch each other or the container.

The water bath is brought slowly to the boil, taking about 1 hour, and is then kept simmering for 15 minutes for most fruits; 30 minutes for pears, quinces and tomatoes. Remove one at a time, seal tightly and stand to cool; do not test for 24 hours. Then remove rings, test the seal and store in a cool dark place. Do not retighten rings. When using the oven, the syrup in the jars should take 1 hour to reach simmering point and is then cooked the same time as in the water bath. Remove the jars and seal in the same way. The ideal oven temperature for preserving is 140°C. A special pressure cooker is required for fruit bottling and instructions will accompany each individual make. General household pressure cookers are not suitable for bottling fruit.

3. **Fruit pulp:** Peel and stew the fruit in very little water until quite soft. If it is to be sweetened, allow 50g to every 500g fruit. Pour into hot jars, cover with seals and place in a water bath or oven. Cook as for bottled fruit, allowing 15 minutes for sterilisation. Tomato juice and purée may be done this way.

Syrups

These will vary according to personal tastes but the following guide may be helpful. Boil in covered pan for 5 minutes. Strain and cool for cold packing.

Thin syrup: Boil 1 cup sugar to 3 cups water. Use for apples, pears, pineapple.

Medium syrup: 1 cup sugar to 2 cups water. Use for strawberries, raspberries, peaches, apricots, cherries.

Thick syrup: 1 cup sugar to 1 cup water. Use for plums, gooseberries, rhubarb and all sour fruit.

Preserved Fruit Salad (I)

1kg bananas, peeled and sliced
juice 2 lemons
pulp 6 passionfruit
1kg sugar
2.5*l* water
3 oranges, peeled and chopped
500g peaches, chopped
500g pears, chopped
1 x 350g tin pineapple pieces

Pour the lemon juice and passionfruit pulp over the sliced bananas. Make a syrup from the sugar and water, bring to the boil then add the chopped peaches, pears and oranges and boil for 15 minutes. Add the pineapple and bananas and just bring to boiling point again. Bottle in sterilised jars and seal immediately.

Preserved Fruit Salad (II)

pulp 12 passionfruit
1 cup sugar
3*l* water
1.5kg sugar
2kg peaches, chopped
1kg pears, chopped
1kg bananas, peeled and chopped
juice 1 lemon
1 teaspoon salt

Boil the pulp with the cup of sugar for 20 minutes. Prepare a syrup with the water and second portion of sugar, add the fruit, juice and salt, bring to the boil, and simmer for 20 minutes, then add the passionfruit pulp. Bottle in sterilised jars and seal immediately.

VEGETABLES

Although people do bottle vegetables successfully, it is not to be recommended unless done with a special pressure cooker. The temperature reached by home-bottling methods is not sufficient to kill the factors which may cause the food to be tainted. Food poisoning which may arise from inadequately sterilised vegetables is very serious and is often difficult to detect, and it is advisable to preserve vegetables by other methods. Freezing is recommended, and in some cases, salting and drying. Tomatoes, however, may be successfully bottled, either whole, pulped or puréed.

Bottled Tomatoes

**small, firm tomatoes, blanched and peeled
1 teaspoon salt for each jar
1 teaspoon sugar for each jar
fresh tomato juice, or water**

Pack the tomatoes into sterilised jars. Add the salt and sugar and fill up to the neck with tomato juice or water. Partly seal and sterilise by standing jars in a large pan of boiling water. Simmer for 30 minutes once simmering point is reached. Seal and test in the usual way.

Tomato Pulp

**large tomatoes, skinned or unskinned
salt**

Cut up the tomatoes, pack into jars and sprinkle with salt at intervals. Press down and fill jars tightly. Partly seal and sterilise in the usual way.

Tomato Purée

**2kg tomatoes, chopped
2 teaspoons salt
1½ teaspoons pepper
bouquet garni
1 large onion
1 stick celery
½ cup water**

Put the tomatoes in a pan with the salt, pepper, bouquet garni, onion and celery. Add the water and stir over a low heat until simmering. Cook until tender then rub through a sieve. Pour into hot jars and sterilise in the usual way for 30 minutes.

Salted Beans

500g non-iodised salt
1.5kg string beans, washed, dried and sliced

Put a layer of salt in a glass or earthenware container and then a layer of prepared beans. Continue layering until container is filled, finishing with a layer of salt. More beans may be added after a few days as the level would have gone down. Cover and store in a cool dry place. When required the beans must be soaked 1-2 hours and well washed in running water to remove some of the salt. Cook until tender in boiling unsalted water.

CHUTNEYS, PICKLES AND SAUCES

Apple Chutney

1 tablespoon peppercorns
6-8 cloves
3kg apples
1.5kg onions
1.5kg sugar
375g dates, chopped
375g seedless raisins
1 tablespoon allspice
125g mixed peel
salt, to taste
vinegar, as required

Place peppercorns and cloves in a muslin bag. Put with all the other ingredients in a preserving pan, cover with vinegar and boil for 1 hour. Bottle while hot and seal when cold. Will keep indefinitely.

Banana and Walnut Chutney

1kg bananas, peeled and minced
500g pitted dates, minced
500g apples, minced
50g chopped walnuts, minced
50g ginger, thinly sliced
2 onions, chopped
500g light brown sugar
2 tablespoons salt
pinch cayenne pepper
pinch ground nutmeg
2½ cups vinegar

Put all the ingredients in a preserving pan and boil for 1 hour. Bottle while hot and seal when cool. Leave for a week before using.

Green Gooseberry Chutney

1.5kg gooseberries, chopped
500g brown sugar
500g onions, peeled and chopped
1 tablespoon salt
1 tablespoon pickling spice, tied in a muslin bag
1l malt vinegar
250g sultanas
250g seedless raisins

Cook all the ingredients in a preserving pan for 2 hours. Bottle and seal as usual.

Plum Chutney

2kg ripe plums, skinned and stoned
500g apples, peeled and cored
750g brown sugar
750g sultanas
1 onion, chopped
1 tablespoon chillies, chopped
2 tablespoons ground ginger

Boil together the plums, apples and sugar for 15 minutes, then add the remaining ingredients and boil for 3 hours. Strain before bottling and seal while hot.

Rhubarb Chutney

1kg rhubarb, chopped in small pieces
1kg sugar
375g sultanas, minced
4 onions, minced
1½ tablespoons salt
1 teaspoon ground cloves
¼ teaspoon cayenne pepper
2½ cups vinegar

Boil together all the ingredients for 1 hour. Bottle and seal while hot.

Tomato Chutney

3kg ripe tomatoes
1kg apples, peeled, cored and chopped
1kg onions, peeled and chopped
500g sultanas
1kg tin golden syrup
250g brown sugar
125g salt
1 tablespoon allspice
1 teaspoon cayenne pepper
1l vinegar

Boil together all the ingredients for 2 hours. Bottle and seal while hot.

Tamarillo Chutney

36 tamarillos
boiling water
6 apples, peeled, cored and sliced
6 onions, peeled
12 prunes, pitted
3 cups brown sugar
1*l* vinegar
25g pickling spices, tied in a muslin bag
2 tablespoons salt
½ teaspoon pepper
½ teaspoon dry mustard

Put the tamarillos in a large saucepan, cover with boiling water, cover and leave for 10 minutes, then skin. Place the tamarillos and the other ingredients in a buttered preserving pan and boil for 2½ hours, stirring occasionally. Strain half the quantity and bottle as a sauce. Thicken the remainder with 1 tablespoon of flour dissolved in a little vinegar and bottle. This makes 6 bottles of sauce and 3kg of chutney.

Tropical Fruit Salad Chutney

2 apples, peeled, cored and chopped
2 onions, peeled and chopped
500g bananas, peeled and chopped
500g dates, pitted and chopped
1 lemon, chopped
1 tablespoon curry powder
50g chopped walnuts
250g brown sugar
50g salt
½ teaspoon ground nutmeg
¼ teaspoon pepper
50g shredded, preserved ginger
2½ cups vinegar

Boil together all the ingredients for 1½ hours. Bottle and seal while hot. Keep for 3 weeks before using.

Pickled Onions

salt
water
pickling onions, peeled
2*l* vinegar
50g peppercorns
24 cloves
1 tablespoon salt
1 tablespoon brown sugar

Make a brine using 2 tablespoons of salt to each litre of water. Pour over the onions and leave overnight. Boil together the remaining ingredients for 15 minutes and allow to get cold. Drain the onions, put into sterilised jars and cover with the vinegar mixture. Store for a few weeks before using.

Pickled Carrots

4kg small carrots
250g sugar
1 cup water
2 cups vinegar
3-4 cloves
1 teaspoon salt

Cook the carrots in a little water until tender. Drain. Make a syrup by boiling together for 5 minutes the sugar, water, vinegar, cloves and salt. Add the carrots and cook gently for 10 minutes. Remove the carrots and pack upright in sterilised jars. Pour the hot syrup over them, covering the carrots completely, and seal immediately.

Pickled Eggs

12 eggs, hard-boiled
vinegar, as required
1 bay leaf
20 peppercorns
blade mace
1 heaped teaspoon salt

Cool and shell the eggs and pack in a wide-mouthed, sterilised jar. Boil sufficient vinegar, approximately 2½ cups, to cover the eggs. Add the remaining ingredients and pour warm over the eggs. Tie down when cool and store for 2 months before using.

Uncooked Chutney

500g ripe tomatoes, minced
500g sour apples, peeled, cored and minced
3 onions, peeled and minced
250g sultanas, minced
3 cups vinegar
2 teaspoons salt
3 tablespoons dry mustard
1kg sugar

Combine all the fruit. Boil together the vinegar, salt, mustard and sugar, cool, then add to the fruit. Mix thoroughly, bottle and leave for 10 days before using. Keeps well.

Pickled Peaches

1kg brown sugar
1 tablespoon ground cloves
2 cups vinegar
2 tablespoons cinnamon
2kg peaches, peeled

Boil together the sugar, cloves, vinegar and cinnamon for 20 minutes, until syrupy. Place the peaches, a few at a time, in the boiling syrup and cook until tender. Pack in sterilised jars, pour over the syrup and seal.

Pickled Green Tomatoes

2kg small, green tomatoes
salt
2½ cups vinegar
1½ cups sugar
10 cloves
10 peppercorns
1 heaped teaspoon mixed spice
¼ teaspoon cayenne pepper

Prick the tomatoes with a fork, cover with salt and leave overnight. Next day drain. Tie cloves and peppercorns in a muslin bag. Prepare brine made by boiling together the vinegar, sugar, cloves, peppercorns, spice and pepper for 10 minutes. Add the strained tomatoes and boil for 3-4 minutes, so that tomatoes remain whole. Put the tomatoes into sterilised jars, bring the brine to the boil and carefully pour over the tomatoes. Seal well. Store for 3 months before using.

Pickled Walnuts

100 walnuts, shelled and pricked
175g salt
2l cold water
50g black pepper
75g ground ginger
75g ground cloves
50g mustard seeds
2 blades mace
2l vinegar

Place the walnuts in a brine of salt and water. Change the brine every 3 days for 9 days and keep stirring. Remove the walnuts, drain and expose to the sun until black. Boil together the remaining ingredients for 10 minutes, strain and pour over the walnuts in sterilised jars. Seal immediately.

Pickled Watermelon Rind

rind 1 watermelon
1 teaspoon salt
6 cups water
2 cups white vinegar
1 cup sugar
4 sticks cinnamon, or 2 teaspoons ground cinnamon

Trim the green from the rind, retaining the thick white rind. Cut into cubes and soak overnight in a brine made with the salt and 5 cups of water. Next day drain, rinse and boil in fresh water until tender but not broken. Make a syrup from the vinegar, remaining water, sugar and cinnamon, boiling for 5 minutes. Add the rind and boil long enough for the rind to absorb the flavour but not break up. Place in warm, sterilised jars and seal as for bottled fruit.

Apple Sauce

6 large onions, peeled and chopped
3kg apples, peeled and cored
2 tablespoons allspice
4 tablespoons salt
1kg brown sugar
2 tablespoons ground cloves
2 tablespoons peppercorns
2l vinegar

Put the onion and apples in a saucepan, cover with water and boil until soft. Strain through a colander, add the remaining ingredients and boil for 1 hour. Keeps well.

Tomato Relish

3kg tomatoes, skinned and quartered
1kg onions, sliced
½ cup salt
vinegar, as required
750g sugar
2 tablespoons curry powder
2 level tablespoons dry mustard
3 tablespoons cornflour
1 teaspoon mace
1 teaspoon pepper
1 teaspoon ground cloves
1 teaspoon cinnamon
1 teaspoon ground nutmeg
1 teaspoon ground ginger

Cover the tomatoes, onions and salt with water and leave overnight. Next day drain, almost cover with vinegar, bring to the boil and add the sugar. Stir well. Mix to a smooth paste with a little cold vinegar, the curry powder, mustard and cornflour, and stir into the mixture until it thickens. Boil for 30-60 minutes. Add the remaining spices, stir well and bottle. Keeps indefinitely.

Mustard Pickle

1 cabbage, chopped
4 onions, chopped
1 cauliflower, chopped
1 head celery, chopped
1.5kg green tomatoes, chopped
500g green peppers, chopped
1 cup salt
water
2.5l vinegar
2 tablespoons dry mustard
1 tablespoon cornflour
450g sugar
1 teaspoon turmeric

Cover the vegetables with the salt and water and leave overnight. Next day drain and squeeze dry the vegetables. Make a sauce from the vinegar thickened with the mustard, cornflour, sugar and turmeric. Pour over the vegetables and simmer until tender, approximately 30 minutes. Bottle and seal while hot.

Horseradish Sauce

horseradish, scrubbed, peeled and grated
vinegar

Pack the horseradish into a jar a layer at a time pouring vinegar over each layer. Press down, add more vinegar and continue layering until the jar is full.

Pepper Sauce

12 green peppers, chopped finely
12 red peppers, chopped finely
14 large onions, chopped finely
boiling water
3 tablespoons salt
450g sugar
5 cups vinegar
bunch pickling spice, tied in a muslin bag

Cover the peppers and onions with boiling water and stand for 5 minutes. Pour off the water and add the remaining ingredients. Boil for 20 minutes, remove the spice, bottle and seal. Suitable as a sandwich spread.

Green Tomato and Pineapple Relish

2kg green tomatoes, chopped
1 x 350g tin crushed pineapple
2 large onions
2-4 cloves
250g pitted dates
½ cup golden syrup
1 teaspoon dry mustard
1 tablespoon salt
pinch cayenne pepper
2½ cups vinegar

Cook together all the ingredients for 1 hour. Bottle and seal while hot. Leave for 2 weeks before using.

Apple Relish

3kg apples, peeled, cored and quartered
3 large onions, finely sliced
250g sugar
2 tablespoons ground cloves
spiced vinegar, as required

Place the apples, onions, sugar and cloves in a saucepan, cover with water and cook slowly until apples heat through, but do not allow the apples to break up. Drain, pack into jars and fill with the spiced vinegar and seal.

Plum Sauce

3kg red plums
1.5kg sugar
1½ tablespoons salt
1 teaspoon cayenne pepper
2l vinegar
2 tablespoons ground cloves
1 tablespoon ground ginger

Boil together all the ingredients until thin, approximately 2 hours, strain and bottle while hot.

Tomato Sauce

4kg tomatoes
175g salt
5 cups vinegar
50g whole pepper
1kg onions, sliced
8g chillies
2 tablespoons ground cloves
500g brown sugar
125g whole pimento

Boil together all the ingredients for 3 hours, stirring frequently. Strain, bottle and cork securely.

Worcestershire Sauce

5l vinegar
1.5kg apples, cored and chopped
1kg dark brown sugar
juice and finely grated peel 1 orange
½ tablespoon anchovy sauce
50g garlic
4 tablespoons ground cloves
4 tablespoons salt
1 level tablespoon cayenne pepper

Simmer together all the ingredients for 2 hours, then strain, bottle and seal while hot. Do not boil too rapidly as the sauce will evaporate.

Sweet Chow-Chow

1 cauliflower, chopped finely
3 onions, chopped finely
8 green tomatoes, chopped finely
1 tablespoon salt
½ teaspoon curry powder
¼ teaspoon cayenne pepper
250g brown sugar
1½ cups golden syrup
vinegar, as required
2 tablespoons flour
½ teaspoon turmeric

Cover all the ingredients with vinegar in a saucepan and boil for 20 minutes. Thicken with 2 tablespoons of flour and ½ teaspoon turmeric mixed with a little vinegar. Bottle and seal while hot.

Pineapple and Cucumber Pickle

1 pineapple, peeled and shredded, or 500g tin
  sliced pineapple
2 cucumbers, sliced thinly
2 onions
1¼ cups white vinegar
250g sugar
1 tablespoon salt
1 tablespoon curry powder
juice 1 lemon

Cook together all the ingredients until clear, like
marmalade, approximately 40-60 minutes.

Sweet Cucumber Pickle

6 large cucumbers
1kg brown sugar
5 cups vinegar
2 teaspoons mixed spice
3 lemons, chopped finely
500g seedless raisins, chopped

Soak the cucumbers in salt water for 3 days after
scraping out the seeds. Rinse in cold water and
chop up. Boil together for 10 minutes the
remaining ingredients and pour over the cucumber.
Leave for 5 days, then strain off the liquid, boil it
again and pour over the cucumber. Bottle and seal
while hot. Keeps indefinitely.

CONTINENTAL COOKING

Although some expensive and special-occasion
Continental dishes have been included in this
section, many are simple enough for everyday use.
Some have been adapted where necessary. With
ingredients such as spices, which play such an
important part in foreign cooking, quantities
depend to a certain extent on personal taste.
Most national dishes – French Onion Soup or
Hungarian Goulash, for example – vary from
district to district in the country to which they
belong. Where possible, the best or most common
variation is given here.

Minestrone – Italy

1 onion, chopped finely
4 potatoes, chopped finely
1 carrot, chopped finely
500g cabbage, chopped finely
1 stick celery, chopped finely
few sprigs parsley, chopped
2 tablespoons olive oil
1 teaspoon butter
2.5l beef stock, or water
1 clove garlic, crushed
½ teaspoon beef extract
salt, to taste
pepper, to taste
250g macaroni, chopped
grated Parmesan cheese

Toss the chopped onion in a saucepan with the oil
and butter for 2 minutes. Add the other
vegetables and cook for 5 minutes. Add the stock,
garlic, meat extract and seasoning and simmer for 1
hour, then add the macaroni and cook for 20
minutes. Serve sprinkled with Parmesan cheese.
Serves 6-8.

Spanish Rice

2 tablespoons olive oil
3 small cloves garlic
1 onion, chopped
185g rice, soaked in water for 6 hours
few sprigs parsley, chopped
salt, to taste
pepper, to taste

Heat the oil in a pan, and lightly fry the garlic and
onion. Drain the rice and add to the pan. When the
fat is absorbed, barely cover with water and put on
a low heat. Cover generously with parsley, season,
cover and cook until each rice grain is separate and
dry. Serve with bananas deep-fried in olive oil, or
with fresh avocado pear halves, or with fried eggs.
Serves 4.

Variation:
Red Rice: Follow the above recipe substituting for
the water fresh tomato pulp diluted with a little
water. Peas, carrots or hard-boiled egg pieces may
also be added to the rice.

Gazpacho – Spain

250g tomatoes, chopped
¼ cup olive oil
3 cups water
1 small clove garlic
¼ cup vinegar
salt, to taste
60g croutons
60g tomatoes, diced
60g green pimento, diced
60g cucumber, diced

Blend together the chopped tomatoes, oil, and half the water until creamy. Sieve the mixture into a bowl rubbed with garlic, then add the remaining water, vinegar and salt. The croutons and diced vegetables may be added to the soup or served separately. Serves 4-6.

Borsch-Russian

500g beetroot, or cabbage, or spinach
5 cups boiling, salted water
2 tablespoons sugar
2 teaspoons lemon juice
1 teaspoon salt
1 egg

Peel the beetroot and cook whole in boiling water until soft. Remove from the water, mince and return to the water. Add the sugar, lemon juice and salt to give a sweet-sour taste. Break the egg into a deep bowl and gradually beat the soup into it. Return to the heat and continue beating until it just boils, being careful to avoid curdling. Serve hot or cold. Serves 4-6.

Caldo Verde, Green Broth – Portugal

2 tablespoons olive oil
salt, to taste
pepper, to taste
1-2 potatoes, sliced
kale cabbage leaves, rolled and shredded finely

Half-fill a saucepan with water and when boiling add the oil, salt, pepper and potato. Cook until soft, then mash. Add the shredded cabbage and boil quickly for 2-3 minutes. Serve immediately. Serves 4.

Pasteis De Bacalhau – Portugal

500g dry, salt cod, soaked overnight
500g potatoes, boiled
2 eggs, separated
salt, to taste
pepper, to taste
fat, for frying

Cook the cod and shred finely. Rub the boiled potatoes through a sieve and add to the cod with the egg yolks. Stiffly beat the egg whites and add to the mixture with seasoning. Blend well and deep fry heaped tablespoons of the mixture until golden brown. Serve with black olives and fresh, green salad. Serves 4-6.

Spanish Fish

1½ tablespoons olive oil
1 onion, sliced finely
1 clove garlic, chopped
salt, to taste
pepper, to taste
500g tomatoes, skinned
4 olives, chopped
1 teaspoon capers
1 bay leaf
1.25kg fillet firm, white fish

Fry the onions, garlic and seasoning in the olive oil until the onion is transparent. Add the tomatoes, olives, capers and bay leaf, cover and simmer for 20 minutes, then add the fillets and simmer for a further 20 minutes, covered, until the sauce is thick. Serves 4-6.

✳ Gulyas – Hungary

1kg shoulder of beef, cut into 5cm cubes
4 onions, chopped
2 tablespoons vegetable fat
2 heaped tablespoons paprika
2 tomatoes, sliced
2 green peppers, chopped
8cm slice salt pork
salt
flour, as required

Slightly brown the meat and onions in the hot fat. Remove from heat and stir in the paprika, return to the heat and add the tomatoes and green peppers. Reduce heat, add the salt pork and cover. Shake pot frequently for the first 30 minutes until the vegetable juices rise. Cook for 1½ hours more or until meat is tender, stirring gently every 10 minutes. Season and thicken with flour if necessary. Serve with boiled new potatoes. Serves 4-6.

Hungarian Veal

500g veal, diced
cornflour
2 tablespoons butter
1 large onion, chopped
2 cloves garlic, chopped
1¼ cups milk, soured with ½ teaspoon lemon
  juice
2 thin slices lemon
1 Oxo cube, or 1 teaspoon Marmite, or
  1 tablespoon soy sauce
1 teaspoon caraway seeds
1 heaped teaspoon paprika
salt,
pepper

Lightly roll the meat in cornflour and fry gently in
butter. Add the onion, and garlic and when all are
golden browned cover with the milk. Add the
lemon slices and simmer for 5 minutes, then add
the Oxo cube. Add the caraway seeds, paprika, salt
and pepper to taste. Transfer to a casserole and
cook gently for 1½-2 hours at 180°C, adding more
milk if the mixture becomes too dry. Serves 4-6.

Roast Beef in White Wine Sauce

8 slices cooked beef
1 onion, finely-chopped
1 clove garlic
2 tablespoons olive oil
2 tablespoons chopped parsley
250g tomatoes, sliced
salt, to taste
pepper, to taste
2 tablespoons chopped olives
1 tablespoon chopped raisins
½ cup dry white wine
1 tablespoon ground almonds

Place the beef slices in an ovenproof dish. Fry the
onion and garlic in oil for 10 minutes, add the
parsley, tomatoes, salt and pepper and cook gently
for 5 minutes. Add the olives, raisins, wine and
almonds and simmer for 10 minutes. Pour over the
beef and heat for 15 minutes at 180°C. Serves 4.

Onion Soup – France

2 large onions, sliced thinly
2 tablespoons butter
4 cups chicken broth, or beef stock
salt, to taste
black pepper, freshly-ground
1 teaspoon French mustard
½ teaspoon thyme
2cm thick slices dried bread
Gruyere cheese, freshly-grated

Gently fry the onions in melted butter until
transparent. Add the broth, seasoned with salt,
pepper, mustard and thyme and simmer for 20
minutes. Pour over the bread that has been
sprinkled with cheese, and brown under a grill.
Serves 4.

Paella – Spain

½ small chicken, cut into small pieces
cooking oil
3 cups water
1 onion, chopped
1 clove garlic, crushed
2 medium tomatoes, sliced
155g rice
8 mussels, cooked
4 prawns, cooked
1 small lobster, cooked and cut up
2-3 artichokes, cut up
250g green peas
3 cups chicken broth
salt, to taste
¼ teaspoon powdered saffron
1 green pepper, sliced in rings

Fry the chicken pieces in hot oil until golden
brown, then boil it in the water for 20 minutes.
Gently fry the onion in the same frying pan, add
the garlic and tomatoes and fry until cooked. Add
the rice and mix well with the fat, without frying.
Arrange the mussels, prawns, lobster, chicken,
artichokes and peas on top of the rice and add 2
cups of chicken broth. When the rice boils, add salt
and saffron. Decorate with green pepper rings and
continue cooking until rice is done, approximately
15-20 minutes, adding remaining broth if
necessary. Serves 4-6.

Spaghetti à la Bolognese – Italy

2 tablespoons olive oil
30g butter
1 onion, chopped finely
1 carrot, chopped finely
1 stick celery, chopped finely
1 clove garlic, chopped finely
1 bay leaf
125g raw, minced, beef
1 cup dry red or white wine
8 tomatoes, skinned
2 tablespoons tomato paste
½ teaspoon meat extract
salt, to taste
pepper, to taste
375g spaghetti
grated Parmesan cheese

Heat the oil and butter in a saucepan and fry the
onion, carrot, celery, garlic and bay leaf for 5
minutes. Add the meat, wine, tomatoes, paste,
extract and seasoning and cook slowly for 30
minutes. Cook the spaghetti in plenty of salted,
boiling water for 20 minutes. Drain, put on a hot
serving dish, cover with the sauce and serve with
grated cheese. Serves 4-6.

Macaronia Tou Fournou – Greece

2 large onions, thinly sliced
1 clove garlic, finely chopped
3 tablespoons olive oil
500g mincemeat
1 tablespoon tomato sauce
½ teaspoon mixed herbs
2 tablespoons sultanas
4-6 dates, pitted and chopped
2 tomatoes, chopped
1 apple, diced
salt, to taste
pepper, to taste
250g macaroni, or vermicelli
2½ cups white sauce
250g cheese, grated

Fry the onions and garlic in oil until transparent.
Add the meat and brown. Stir in the sauce, herbs,
sultanas, dates, tomatoes, apple and seasoning.
Cook for 2-3 minutes. Boil the macaroni in salted,
boiling water with a cut garlic clove until almost
cooked. Strain and put a layer in a deep buttered
casserole, cover with a layer of meat mixture and
continue layering finishing with the macaroni. Pour
over the white sauce mixed with half the quantity
of grated cheese. Cover the top with the remaining
cheese and cook for 15 minutes at 200°C. Longer
cooking improves the flavour. Brown under a grill
before serving. Serves 4-6.

Rice Pilaf

155g rice, uncooked
1 teaspoon paprika
2 tablespoons butter
1 onion, chopped
2 cups beef stock
salt, to taste
pinch cayenne pepper

Brown the rice and paprika in 1 tablespoon of
butter. Separately fry the onion in the remaining
butter until transparent. Add to the rice, cover
with stock, season and bring to the boil. Cover and
cook for 20 minutes at 220°C. Stir gently with a
fork to loosen grains, add a little butter and return
to the oven for 5 minutes. Serves 4.

Cannelloni – Italy

250g minced meat, or poultry
125g spinach, cooked, and sieved, or tomato
    puree
1 teaspoon mixed herbs
salt, to taste
pepper, to taste
thin pancakes
2½ cups thick, white sauce flavoured with
    Parmesan cheese
grated Parmesan cheese
sliced tomatoes, for garnish

Combine the meat, spinach, herbs and seasoning.
Pile the pancakes on a dish with a layer of meat
mixture between each. Pour over the sauce,
sprinkle with cheese and brown under a grill.
Garnish with tomatoes. Pancakes may be cooked in
advance and wrapped in greaseproof paper to
prevent drying. Serves 4-6.

Cheese Fondue – Switzerland

1 clove garlic
500g Gruyere cheese, finely-grated
15g butter
¼ cup white wine, or cider
1 tablespoon kirsch, or cherry brandy, optional
salt, to taste
pinch cayenne pepper
pinch nutmeg

Rub the inside of a heavy saucepan with garlic. Put
on top of a pot of boiling water, add the cheese
and stir over a gentle heat until melted. Stir in the
butter, wine, kirsch and seasonings. Serve with
pieces of French bread. The mixture can also be
poured over toast or fried bread and browned
under the grill. Serves 4-6.

Quiche Lorraine – France

250g flaky, or short pastry
1 tablespoon flour
4 tablespoons finely-grated Gruyere cheese
1¼ cups cream
salt, to taste
pinch nutmeg
pinch sugar
45g butter
4 egg whites, stiffly beaten

Roll out the pastry, line a buttered 23cm piedish
and bake blind. Put the flour and cheese in a
saucepan mixed with a little cream. Add
seasonings, butter and remaining cream and cook
over a low heat until all is melted. Cool, then fold
in the egg whites. Turn into the prepared pastry
shell and bake for 15 minutes at 220°C. Serves 4-6.

Chicken Paprikasch – Hungary

3 large onions, finely-chopped
1 tablespoon lard
1 tablespoon paprika
1 young chicken, cut into serving pieces
2 green peppers, chopped
salt, to taste
1 teaspoon flour
2 tablespoons cream

Gently fry the onion in a heavy pan with the lard for 40 minutes until almost a jelly. Add the paprika and simmer a further 10 minutes. Add the chicken pieces, cover the pan and stew for 30 minutes, then add the peppers, and salt and stew for 30 minutes. Mix in the flour blended with the cream and remove as soon as it boils. Serve with rice. Serves 4.

Beef Stroganoff

500g fillet steak, cut in 1.2cm x 5cm strips
salt
pepper
paprika
2 tablespoons butter
250g mushrooms, sliced
1½ cups sour cream
3 tablespoons dry sherry

Season the beef with salt, pepper and paprika and brown quickly in hot butter. Add the mushrooms and cook quickly for 3 minutes. Add the cream, reduce the heat, cover and simmer for 10 minutes. Stir in the sherry, season to taste and serve with rice. Serves 4.

Wiener Schnitzel – Austria

500g veal cutlet, boneless and thinly sliced into
    4 equal portions
1 egg, beaten with 4 teaspoons cold water, salt
    and pepper
1 cup breadcrumbs
3 tablespoons butter
gherkin, sliced
2 slices pickled beetroot,   ⎫
slices lemon   ⎬ for garnish
2 anchovy fillets   ⎭
pickled capers

Dip each steak in crumbs, egg and crumbs again, and fry in hot butter until golden brown on both sides, until tender, approximately 20 minutes, covering for the last 10 minutes. Remove the steaks to a hot dish, sprinkle 2 tablespoons of water into the pan and stir with the meat juices until boiling. Pour over the schnitzels. Garnish and serve with potato salad, or noodles and lettuce. Serves 4.

Shish Kebab – Turkey

leg of lamb, cut in 4cm cubes
250g mushrooms
2 onions, cut in squares
3-4 tomatoes, quartered
2 green, or red peppers, cut in squares
bay leaves

Alternately skewer one portion of each ingredient and grill or cook over an open fire for 15-20 minutes, turning occasionally. Serve with rice pilaf. Serves 4-6.

Potato Salad – Germany

4 large potatoes, boiled whole until almost
    tender
1 onion, thinly-sliced
1 cup chopped celery
3 tablespoons chopped parsley
1 teaspoon salt
3 tablespoons flour
60g sugar
1 teaspoon dry mustard
1 teaspoon salt
1 egg, beaten
⅔ cup vinegar
⅓ cup water
4 rashers bacon, chopped and fried crisp
1 tablespoon butter
chopped chives, optional
chopped garlic, optional

Dice the potatoes and blend gently with the onion, celery, parsley and salt. Mix the flour, sugar, mustard and salt. Stir in the egg, vinegar and water, and bring to the boil over a low heat, stirring constantly. Add the bacon and butter and stir until blended. Pour this mixture over the hot potatoes. Serve hot or cold. Serves 6-8.

Salsa Verde – Italy

1 onion, finely-chopped
1 clove garlic, finely-chopped
4 capers, finely-chopped
1 egg, hard-boiled and chopped
1 cup chopped parsley
1 anchovy fillet, chopped
salt
pepper
4 tablespoons olive oil
1 tablespoon vinegar

Blend together the onion, garlic, capers, egg, parsley and anchovy, and season to taste. Beat together with a fork the olive oil and vinegar, and mix into the other ingredients. Serve with cold lamb, mutton or chicken. Serves 4.

Apple Cake – Denmark

2.25kg cooking apples, peeled and sliced
125g sugar
½ cup butter
1 cup coarse breadcrumbs
jam, or marmalade
1 teaspoon cinnamon
½ cup cream, whipped

Stew the apples in a little water with half the sugar. Melt the butter and mix in the breadcrumbs and the remaining sugar until golden brown. In a greased 23cm tin place alternate layers of crumbs, apple, jam and cinnamon, finishing with crumbs. Press down firmly and cook for 30 minutes at 180°C. Turn out and decorate with whipped cream and jam. Serve hot. Serves 4-6.

Pesche Ripene – Italy

sponge cake, chocolate-flavoured, if possible
raspberry jam, heated and sieved
100 chopped, blanched almonds
4 peach halves
50 ground almonds
¼ cup castor sugar
1 egg yolk
liqueur, to taste, Benedictine, Cointreau,
   Cherry Brandy, or Curacao
30g blanched almonds

Cut 4 rounds of cake 1.2cm thick, spread with jam, roll in chopped almonds and place 1 peach half on each. Mix the ground almonds, sugar, egg yolk and liqueur and fill the centre of each peach. Place an almond on top and bake for 10 minutes at 200°C. Pour over a sauce made with sieved jam diluted with a little peach syrup and liqueur. Serves 4.

Stuffed Baked Apples – Germany

5 apples, peeled and cored
2 tablespoons raspberry jam
3 eggs, separated
1-2 tablespoons boiling water
½ cup sugar
100 grated, blanched almonds
6 tablespoons flour

Fill the apple centres with jam. Whip the egg yolks, water and sugar for 10 minutes, then carefully blend in the almonds and flour. Fold in the stiffly-beaten egg whites, pile around the apples in a buttered baking dish and bake for 30-45 minutes at 200°C. Serves 5.

Linzertorte – Austria

220g butter
125g flour, sifted
250g unblanched almonds
125g sugar
⅛ teaspoon ground cloves
⅛ teaspoon cinnamon
2 egg yolks
⅓ cup raspberry jam
¼ egg white, slightly beaten
1 tablespoon icing sugar
slivered almonds, optional

Heat the oven to 160°C. Crumble or chop the butter into the flour. Add the almonds, sugar, spices and egg yolks. Knead to a smooth dough. Press two-thirds over the bottom and sides of a 23cm tin lined with greaseproof paper, and spread with the jam. Roll egg-size balls of the remaining dough between the palms to make long rolls, 1.2cm in diameter and 20cm long. Chill until firm on a baking sheet. Using a spatula, lift the rolls and arrange in a lattice over the jam and press to the dough around the edges. Brush with egg white and bake on the lower shelf of the oven for 1¼ hours. Before serving sprinkle with icing sugar and decorate with almonds if desired.

Sachertorte – Chocolate Cake – Austria

100g butter
6 tablespoons sugar
100g cooking chocolate, melted
4 eggs, separated
1 tablespoon sifted flour

Heat the oven to 160°C. Grease and lightly flour a deep 20cm cake tin. Cream together the butter and sugar until fluffy. Add the chocolate and mix thoroughly. Add the egg yolks one at a time, mixing well after each addition. Stir in the flour, then fold in the stiffly-beaten egg whites. Turn into the prepared tin and bake on the lower shelf for 1¼ hours until the cake shrinks from the side of the tin and rebounds when pressed lightly in the centre. Leave for 10 minutes before turning out. When cool, stand the rack and cake on waxed paper, spread the top with jam and cover with chocolate icing.

Chocolate Icing
125g sugar
⅓ cup water
100g cooking chocolate

Simmer together for 2 minutes the sugar and water, stirring until dissolved. Remove from the heat and stir in the chocolate until it has melted and the mixture is smooth. Bring again to the boil while stirring. Remove from the heat, stir for a moment until thick and pour immediately over the cake.

CONFECTIONERY

Acid Drops

1.5kg sugar
2½ cups water
1½ tablespoons tartaric acid

Bring to the boil the sugar and water, stirring constantly. When mixture boils stop stirring and test frequently until a little, when dropped into cold water, first cracks then rolls into a hard ball when pressed in the fingers. Pour on to a board, or a marble slab, and work in the acid. Form drops while the mixture is hot.

Almond Rock

500g brown sugar
1 cup water
125g butter
few drops almond essence
2 tablespoons blanched, ground almonds

Boil together for 15 minutes the sugar, water, butter and essence, until a little, when dropped into cold water, is crisp. Blend in the almonds, pour the mixture into a buttered tin and leave to set.

Glacé Apricots

1 x 850g tin apricots, drained
250g granulated sugar

Boil together the sugar and drained syrup which should measure 1¼ cups. The syrup is ready when a little, dropped in cold water, becomes brittle. Rub the apricots through a sieve, add the juice to the syrup when it reaches the brittle stage, then stir over a gentle heat until a thick paste leaves the side of the pan, taking care it does not burn. Spread in a shallow, buttered tin and cut when cold. Sprinkle with icing sugar.

Barley Sugar

1 kg sugar
pinch cream of tartar
2½ cups water
1 teaspoon lemon juice

Boil together the sugar, cream of tartar and water until a little of the syrup can be rolled into a ball when dropped into cold water. Add the lemon juice and boil slowly until a little cracks in cold water. Pour into a buttered tin and cut when cold. Leave until nearly cold, then twist.

Candied Fruit Bars

rind 1 orange, finely grated
½ cup water
1½ cups sugar
2 halves candied orange or lemon peel, finely shredded
2 halves glacé apricots, finely shredded
75g mixed peel, shredded
150g glacé cherries
125g pitted dates, chopped
150g figs, chopped
125g walnuts, chopped
4 slices candied pineapple, shredded

Boil together the orange rind, water and sugar until it forms a thread. Pour over the combined remaining ingredients, mix well and pack into a buttered 23cm tin and leave to cool. Cut into bars and wrap each in cellophane or greaseproof paper.

Chocolate Fudge

¾ cup brown sugar
1 cup white sugar
1½ tablespoons golden syrup
1 tablespoon butter
½ cup milk
1 teaspoon vanilla essence
2 teaspoons cocoa

Boil together for 2½ minutes the sugars, golden syrup, butter, milk and vanilla. Add the cocoa and boil for 7 minutes. Cool and beat until creamy. Turn into a buttered tin and when set, cut into squares. Leave to set firmly before removing.

Maple Cream

As for Chocolate Fudge, omitting the cocoa and using all brown sugar. Add maple essence, and chopped nuts if desired.

Chocolate Truffles

100g dark chocolate
2 tablespoons cream
1 tablespoon brandy or rum
250g icing sugar, sieved
chocolate hail

Melt the chocolate in a basin over hot water. Stir until melted then remove from heat. Stir in the cream and brandy, or rum, and blend until smooth. Gradually stir in the icing sugar adding sufficient to make a smooth, fairly stiff consistency. Roll teaspoons of the mixture into small balls and then roll in chocolate hail. Leave in a cool place until firm. Makes 24.

Chocolate Clusters

400g milk chocolate
2 tablespoons desiccated coconut
100g mixed fruit
50g chopped, mixed nuts

Melt the chocolate in the top of a double boiler over gentle heat. Remove from heat and stir in the other ingredients. Mix well and when beginning to set place teaspoon lots on greaseproof paper. Leave until quite firm.

Coconut Ice

450g sugar
150ml water
1 teaspoon vanilla essence
100g coconut
1 tablespoon cream
pink colouring

Dissolve the sugar in water in a saucepan over a low heat. Cook rapidly until a little of the boiling syrup forms a soft ball when dropped into cold water. Remove from the heat and stir in the vanilla, coconut and cream. Stir gently until the mixture thickens and goes cloudy. Pour half the mixture into a buttered, 18cm square tin. Quickly colour the remainder of the mixture with a drop of pink colouring and pour on top. Leave until quite cold and firm then cut into pieces. Makes 700g.

Honey Fudge

2 cups sugar
2 tablespoons cocoa
1 cup unsweetened condensed milk
¼ cup liquid honey
1 teaspoon butter
pinch salt
1 cup mixed nuts, chopped

Boil together for 5 minutes the sugar, cocoa and milk. Add the honey and cook until slightly firm, stirring as little as possible. Add the nuts, salt and butter, cool and beat until creamy. Spread in greased tins to set.

Marshmallows

2 cups sugar
2 tablespoons glucose
1 heaped tablespoon gelatine
1½ cups boiling water
toasted coconut

Dissolve sugar and glucose in one half of the boiling water and the gelatine in the other half. Cool both mixtures. Mix together beating well, until the mixture creams and thickens. Pour into 28cm x 18cm tin. When set, cut into squares and roll in toasted coconut. Makes 36.

Chocolate Caramels

¾ cup brown sugar
1 cup treacle
1 cup milk
1 tablespoon glycerine
400g grated chocolate

Boil together for 5 minutes the sugar, treacle, milk and glycerine. Add the chocolate and test for a soft ball in cold water. Pour into a buttered tin and cut into squares.

Chocolate Walnut Fudge

½ tin sweetened condensed milk
2 tablespoons lemon juice
1 tablespoon melted butter
1 teaspoon vanilla essence
2 tablespoons cocoa
500g icing sugar, sifted
250g chopped walnuts

Gradually stir into the milk the lemon juice, butter and essence. Mix well and add the cocoa, icing sugar and the walnuts. Mix thoroughly and turn on to a flat, greased dish, spreading to a 2.5cm thickness. Leave to set for 2-3 hours, cut and store in airtight containers.

Chocolate-coated Orange Peel

½ block easy to melt chocolate
orange peel, cut in strips

Melt the chocolate in the top of a double boiler over a gentle heat. Dip the peel strips in the chocolate and place on greaseproof paper to set.

Turkish Delight

2 tablespoons gelatine
½ cup cold water
2 cups castor sugar
½ cup boiling water
flavouring, as desired
colouring, as desired
50g chopped, mixed nuts
juice and grated rind 1 orange
juice 1 lemon

Soak the gelatine in cold water for 5 minutes. Put the sugar and boiling water in a saucepan and bring to the boil. Add the gelatine and boil for 20 minutes. Add the flavouring and colouring, then the nuts, juices and rind, blend well and turn into a cold pan. When set, lay on an icing sugared board and cut into cubes. Roll in the sugar.

Marzipan

250g sugar
¼ cup water
250g ground almonds
1 egg white
flavouring, as desired
colouring, optional

Boil together for 10 minutes the sugar and water. Stir in the almonds and cook for 5 minutes. Remove from heat and when cool, stir in the egg white. Return to heat and cook until the mixture thickens and can be stirred cleanly away from the side of the pan. Knead on a cold, buttered slab or floured board until cool. Flavour and colour as desired. Makes 500g.

Sweet Nuts

1 cup sweetened condensed milk
1 cup dry breadcrumbs
1 cup chopped walnuts
2 teaspoons cinnamon

Mix together thoroughly all the ingredients and place teaspoon lots on a buttered tray and bake for 10 minutes at 180°C.

Toffee Apples

8 clean eating apples
450g sugar
3 good tablespoons golden syrup
150ml water
8 wooden skewers

Insert a skewer into the stalk end of each apple. Measure the sugar, golden syrup and water into a saucepan and stir over low heat, until the sugar is dissolved. Bring the mixture to the boil and cook rapidly, without stirring, until beginning to caramelise. Draw the pan off the heat and dip the apples immediately. Tilt the pan so that each apple can be evenly coated with syrup. Drain and stand the dipped apples on a buttered baking tray to harden. Keep in a dry place.

After-Dinner Sweets

Apricot Balls

¾ cup dried apricots, minced
1 cup desiccated coconut
¼ cup sweetened condensed milk

Mix all ingredients together blending well to get a firm mixture. Shape into small balls and roll in castor sugar or coconut. Leave in a cool place until firm. Makes 24.

Chocolate Fruit Dominoes

125g walnuts, finely chopped
60g figs, finely chopped
90g dates, pitted and finely chopped
grated rind 1 orange
1 tablespoon orange juice
60g cooking chocolate, melted

Combine all the ingredients, mix well and turn on to a board sprinkled with icing sugar. Roll out to a 1cm thickness and cut. Coat thinly with melted chocolate and decorate with small pieces of blanched almonds.

Coffee Cream

250g butter
1 x 397g tin condensed milk
1 packet gingernut biscuits, crushed
1 packet wine biscuits, crushed
1 cup walnuts, minced
1 cup coconut
2 tablespoons coffee essence

Melt butter and condensed milk together and bring to boil slowly. Add other ingredients and mix well. Press into a 23cm x 35cm sponge roll tin. Ice with coffee icing.

Icing
125g butter, melted
2 cups icing sugar, sieved
1½ tablespoons coffee essence
2 teaspoons vanilla essence

Add melted butter to other ingredients and mix well. Spread over base and leave to cool. Cut into squares. Makes 36.

Ginger Fudge

125g butter
1 cup sugar
1 tablespoon golden syrup
½ cup condensed milk
1 packet gingernut biscuits, crushed
½ teaspoon vanilla essence

Boil together butter, sugar, golden syrup and condensed milk, for 10 minutes. Add biscuit crumbs and vanilla. Beat a few minutes. Pour into a buttered 23cm square tin. Mark into squares and put in fridge to set. Makes 36.

 # Jane's Fudge

125g butter
½ tin condensed milk
2 tablespoons cocoa
10 cereal biscuits, crushed
½ cup coconut
1 cup dried fruit

Melt together the butter, condensed milk and cocoa. Add crushed biscuits, coconut and dried fruit. Spread into buttered, 23cm square pan. Sprinkle little extra coconut over surface. Leave in fridge to set and cut in squares. Makes 36.

Marzipan Balls

100g ground almonds
50g icing sugar, sifted
50g castor sugar
½ teaspoon almond essence
1 egg yolk
10 glacé cherries, halved

Place almonds and both sugars into a bowl. Add essence and yolk and work well to a stiff paste. Knead until smooth then roll into 20 small balls. Toss in a little extra castor sugar and press a half cherry into each. Leave overnight to harden. Makes 20.

Rumbles

125g butter
1 cup icing sugar, sieved
½ cup cocoa
1 cup coconut
1 cup moist dried fruit and glacé fruit, mixed
2 tablespoons rum

Cream butter and icing sugar until light and fluffy. Add remaining ingredients and mix well. Shape into balls and roll in a little extra coconut. Makes 36.

Sugar Balls

100g plain chocolate
3 tablespoons cream
50g castor sugar
1½ cups dry sponge crumbs
2 tablespoons sweet sherry or rum or brandy
castor sugar for coating

Break the chocolate in pieces and melt over hot water, stirring until smooth. Remove basin from hot water and stir in remaining ingredients. Mix well. Place in cool place to stiffen up. Shape into small balls and roll in castor sugar. Makes 24.

Snowballs

125g butter
2 tablespoons golden syrup
½ tin condensed milk
1 teaspoon vanilla essence
250g packet malt biscuits, crushed
1 cup dried fruit

Melt together the butter, syrup, condensed milk. Add the vanilla and remaining ingredients and mix well. Shape into balls and roll in a little extra coconut. Makes 36.

SPECIAL DIETS

Obesity is extremely bad for the health, often precipitating such diseases as diabetes, high blood pressure, arthritis and arterial and heart degeneration. Grossly overweight people should make a very earnest attempt to keep their weight within normal limits.

Dieting is the only sensible and effective way to lose weight. This should always be done intelligently, and if a lot of weight needs to be lost, it is advisable to do so under regular medical supervision.

Reduction diets, like all good specialised diets, are based fundamentally on a balanced diet. This means that the body still receives its necessary allotment of health-giving foods, while the ones tending to put on weight are partially eliminated. Weight must be lost gradually and consistently at the rate of 1-1.5kg per week and once the desired weight is achieved the diet may be increased slightly, keeping a careful eye on the scales to ensure that the indicator doesn't start to rise.

Diet fads and special preparations should be avoided. They are often effective, but it is unwise to lose weight suddenly and from a cosmetic point of view the results are not good.

Foods which must be avoided when reducing include all fat meats and bacon, thickened soups, gravies and sauces, cereal foods like macaroni, sago, rice and tapioca; all fried foods; cakes, sweets, cream, biscuits, jams, ice-cream and alcoholic beverages.

Some foods have low calorie values and are permitted in almost unlimited quantities. This is because the water content is relatively high. Dissolved in this water are most of the valuable minerals and vitamins our bodies require so you needn't feel that you are filling up on a lot of useless watery food. Included here are leafy green vegetables, most fruits, raw or cooked with no added sugar, clear soups, tea, coffee (unsweetened), skimmed milk, lean meat, eggs, fish and cheese. Foods allowed in limited quantities are bread (preferably wholemeal), unsweetened porridge, potatoes, root vegetables, and specially prepared sweets containing no sugar (see special section of low-calorie sweets.)

Suggested Day's Menu

Breakfast:

fruit, raw or cooked, unsweetened
1-2 eggs, not fried, or steamed fish
1½ slices thin bread, or toast with a scraping of butter
tea, or coffee, unsweetened

Mid-Morning:

tea, coffee, fruit juice or clear soup

Lunch:

fish, egg or lean meat with fresh vegetable salad, flavoured with vinegar or lemon juice
1½ slices wholemeal bread with scraping of butter and Marmite
tea, coffee or skimmed milk

Afternoon Tea:

unsweetened tea
thin slice wholemeal bread

Dinner:

clear, vegetable soup
100-125g lean meat, roasted, grilled, or boiled, but not fried
1 medium potato
1 medium serving carrot, parsnip, swede, peas, beans or pumpkin
1 generous serving green leaf vegetable
raw fruit, or low calorie sweet

Supper:

tea, coffee or skimmed milk

Essentials:

– 1½ cups milk daily, with cream removed
– no alcoholic drinks
– a weekly weight check, in order to modify the diet if weight loss is over 1.5kg per week
– regular medical consultation for the grossly overweight.

Low Calorie Dishes for Diabetic and Reduction Diets

This section is included in this publication for the use of diabetic persons, but the recipes would be ideally suited to anyone wishing to lose weight. The total calories are given along with each recipe.

Asparagus Au Gratin

½ cup unsweetened, condensed milk
30g cheese, grated
6-8 asparagus spears, cooked

Heat the milk in the top of a double boiler, add the cheese and stir until dissolved. Pour over the hot asparagus and garnish with parsley. 160 calories. Serves 1.

Cabbage Roll

90g lean beef, minced
1 slice onion, chopped
1 teaspoon diced green pepper
salt
pepper
1 large cabbage leaf

Brown the meat in a heavy frying pan and stir in the onion, pepper and seasoning. Roll up this mixture in the cabbage leaf and fasten with toothpicks if necessary. Bake in a covered casserole with a little water until the cabbage is tender and beginning to brown. 220 calories, serves 1.

Dutch Spinach

1 lean rasher bacon, diced
125g spinach, cooked
1 tablespoon vinegar
1 teaspoon bacon fat

Crisp the bacon in a hot frying pan. Add the vinegar to the spinach and stir, with the bacon fat, into the bacon. Mix well and serve hot. 90 calories. Serves 1.

Stuffed Tomato

1 medium tomato
1 rasher bacon, fried
½ slice wholemeal bread, toasted and cubed
salt
pepper

Wash the tomato, cut off the top, scoop out the seeds and to the pulp add the cubed toast. Season to taste and return to the tomato case. Bake for 20 minutes at 200°C and serve with bacon. 80 calories. Serves 1.

Low Calorie Sweets

Apple Charlotte

¼ cup breacrumbs
350g stewed apple
1 egg
½ teaspoon cinnamon

Line a buttered piedish with half the breadcrumbs. Over this place the apple mixed with egg. Flavour the remaining crumbs with cinnamon and scatter over the top. Bake for 30 minutes at 200°C. 200 calories. Serves 2.

Baked Date Custard

1 egg
1 cup milk
30g dates, chopped

Beat together the egg and milk and pour over the dates in a piedish. Stand the dish in a pan of hot water and bake for 30 minutes at 150°C. 200 calories. Serves 2.

Banana Cream

1 cup milk
1 egg
1 teaspoon liquid sweetener
125g mashed banana
2 level tablespoons powdered gelatine, dissolved in 2 teaspoons water

Make a boiled custard with the milk and egg. Add the sweetener and banana and cool to body temperature. Add the dissolved gelatine, whisk and leave to set. 200 calories. Serves 2.

Bread and Butter Custard

30g wholemeal bread, diced
2 tablespoons raisins
1 egg
⅔ cup milk
pinch nutmeg

Put the bread and raisins in a piedish. Beat together the egg and milk and pour over the bread, leaving to soak for 30 minutes. Flavour with nutmeg and bake at 150°C until brown. 200 calories. Serves 2.

Cereal Puddings

10g rice, sago, tapioca or semolina
½ cup milk
1 tablespoon water
pinch salt
pinch nutmeg

Boil the cereal in milk and water, add salt and flavour with nutmeg. 100 calories. Serves 1.

Custards, Junket and Milk Jellies

1 cup milk
1 egg, or ½ teaspoon rennet, or 2 teaspoons powdered gelatine
1 teaspoon liquid sweetener
flavouring, as desired

Make a boiled custard thickening the milk with egg, sweetening and flavouring as desired. 120 calories. Serves 2. A serving of stewed fruit completes the dish.

Ice-Cream

2½ cups milk
3 eggs, separated
2 teaspoons powdered gelatine, dissolved in a little hot water
⅓ cup cream, whipped
¼ teaspoon vanilla essence
½ teaspoon liquid sweetener

Make a custard with the milk and beaten egg yolks. Cool, then add the dissolved gelatine. Fold in the stiffly-beaten egg whites and whipped cream. Lastly add the vanilla and sweetener. Freeze. Serves 6. 100 calories per serving.

Spanish Cream

1 cup milk
1 egg, separated
2 level teaspoons powdered gelatine
1 teaspoon vanilla essence
stewed fruit, optional

Make as for normal spanish cream and flavour with vanilla. 120 calories. Serves 2. May be served with stewed fruit.

Sugarless Jam and Marmalade

Because no sugar is used in these recipes they do not keep well, especially once opened. The jars used should therefore be small so that a small quantity at a time is exposed. Sterilise the jars before pouring in the hot jam and seal carefully. If possible keep the opened jam in a refrigerator.

Diabetic Raspberry Jam

500g raspberries, or other berries
3 tablespoons water
8 teaspoons sweetener, dissolved in 1 teaspoon hot water
1 tablespoon gelatine per 1¼ cups pulp

Gently stew the berries with water until reduced to ⅔ of the original quantity. Add the dissolved sweetener and add to the berries. Dissolve the appropriate quantity of gelatine in a little boiling water and add to the berries while both are hot. Pour into small, heated jars and seal with paraffin wax.

Diabetic Marmalade

3 oranges
2½ cups water
8 teaspoons sweetener, dissolved in 3 teaspoons hot water
2 teaspoons lemon juice, optional
1 tablespoon powdered gelatine per 1¼ cups pulp

Cut the rind from the orange, removing all the pith. Cut up the oranges and put in a preserving pan with the rind and water. Simmer for 30 minutes, then add the sweetener. Add the lemon juice and cook until the pulp and rind are tender. Stir in the gelatine and pour into small, heated jars. Seal immediately with hot paraffin wax.

HOUSEHOLD HINTS

How to Launder:

1. Sort the clothes out into piles to be washed together.
2. Remove all stains and organic material before putting the clothes into soap and water. Soap will set a stain. Hot water will cook any organic substance, such as egg, blood or milk, and make it difficult to remove. Rinse these in cold water first.
3. Soak very dirty things first, using cold or lukewarm water. Soak soiled handkerchiefs in salt and water before boiling.
4. Use only slightly-warm water for coloureds which may fade or run. The addition of salt or Epsom salts to this and the rinsing water will minimise this danger.
5. The sun is a wonderful bleaching agent so spread white cottons and linens out to get as much sun as possible. This does not apply to white woollies.
6. Fold clothes as you take them in from the line, making ironing easier.

Cottons:

Soak in cold water if very dirty. White cottons may be boiled 10-15 minutes, rinsed 3 times, blued and dried in the sun. Coloureds are hand or machine washed, rinsed, starched, if necessary, and dried, inside out, and preferably in the shade. If the colours tend to run, wash individually. Dampen cottons to iron and iron on the right side. Denim is ironed on the wrong side with a hot iron. Use a warm iron on glazed cotton and raffle cloth and iron on wrong side.

Linens:

White linen may be laundered as cotton, but needs no starching. A fine lustre is obtained if it is ironed while very damp.

Flannelette:

Wash in hot soap suds (do not boil), rinse well and dry in the wind. Do not iron.

Woollies:

Hot water will shrink woollen fibre; rubbing and cold soaking will mat it; and strong soap will discolour and damage it. Woollens should be washed in lukewarm water, using a mild soap. Gentle squeezing removes the dirt; use a second lot of suds if necessary. Rinse 2 or 3 times; also in lukewarm water. Squeeze dry but never use a wringer as this will twist and tear the fibre. Dry out of doors when possible, preferably on a windy day and in the shade. The sun will fade coloureds and yellow the white garments. Cardigans and sweaters are best threaded on old nylon stockings; these are put through the one sleeve, twisted around the line, and then put through the other sleeve. pegs are attached to the stockings rather than the clothes.
Buttons and zip fasteners should be done up and the garments gently pulled into shape. If necessary, press with a warm iron and damp cloth.

Broderie Anglais and Embroidered Linens:

Iron very damp and on the wrong side. Place over a thick towel or piece of blanket.

Nylon:

Hand wash all nylons with a gentle soap solution. Dry over a towel or, if put on a line, thread the garments on old nylon stockings. This avoids any possibility of pegs damaging the fabric. Use only a cool iron. Nylon undies need no ironing at all and garments need gentle ironing at the seams only. Dry shirts and frocks on a coathanger.

Shantungs:

Wash in a mild soap and dry carefully. Iron dry on the wrong side with hot iron.

Silks:

Pure silk is an animal fibre and, like wool, needs careful handling. Wash in mild soap. Do not use strong acids or alkalis as the material will yellow. Iron while slightly damp, on the wrong side, using a warm iron.

Rayon:

Wash as for silk, never boil, and iron damp with a cool iron on the wrong side.

Corduroy:

Wash in lukewarm water and a white soap solution (or a Lux solution). Do not wring, but hang it inside out so that when drying should any warm water rings appear they will show on the wrong side. After the garment is thoroughly dry, put it on the ironing board but do not iron it. Instead, with a very stiff whisk-broom, brush both with and against the nap. A circular motion gives excellent results. This brushing restores the corduroy to its original velvety appearance and successfully disguises the fact that it has been washed.

Babies' Napkins:

As soon as wet or soiled, place in a covered bucket containing cold water. Rinse soiled napkins under cold water and wash with a little soap. Boil rinsed napkins daily, using soap. Rinse very well and dry in the fresh air and sun whenever possible. Never use strong soaps, bleaches, soda or blue.

SOFTENING HARD WATER

Water containing some mineral salts will require special treatment, especially on washday, otherwise the soap will form small curds and its cleansing action be destroyed unless large quantities are used. Common water softeners include:
Washing Soda: Effective and economical and an excellent bleach. Not suitable for coloured things. Dissolve 1 kg crystals in 1*l* boiling water. Use 2-4 tablespoons to 5*l* water. Always use dissolved crystals.
Borax: A mild alkali suitable for use on fine fabrics. Use one tablespoon to 5*l* water.
Ammonia: Also a mild alkali. Use in liquid rather than powdered form.

SOME BLEACHING TIPS

The whitening-properties of many commercial soap powders are partly due to the bleaching agents the powders contain. If bar soaps or detergents are used the washing may appear yellow after a time, even though the actual clothes are just as clean as those washed with a soap powder. It is sometimes advisable to include a bleaching agent in the washing machine or copper. If using detergent, allow two tablespoons and add one tablespoon perborate of soda as a bleach.

To Whiten Cottons and Linens:

Use washing soda or a chlorinated bleach (see recipe for javelle water).

To Whiten Yellowed Woollies:

Wash and rinse carefully in lukewarm water. Prepare a solution of perborate of soda, allowing 30g per 5*l* water. Place the wet garments in this and soak, stirring frequently during the first hour. Rinse well and dry. Never use strong bleaches on woollen fabrics. Peroxide may be substituted for the perborate.

To Whiten Yellowed Nylon Materials:

Nylon cannot be bleached by ordinary bleaching agents. Whiteness is restored by the use of a white dye. When making the purchase make sure the dye is one that can be used on nylon or other synthetic materials. All synthetics, including orlon, terylene, rayon and dacron, are treated this way.

RECIPES FOR WASH DAY

Starch

1 tablespoon laundry starch
½ teaspoon borax
5 cups boiling water
½ teaspoon cooking oil

Mix the starch and borax with a little cold water. Add the boiling water, stirring constantly. Stir in the oil and boil for 5 minutes. Use while hot, diluting if necessary.

Javelle Water

250g washing soda
2½ cups boiling water
125g chloride of lime
5 cups cold water

Dissolve the soda in boiling water and cool. Dissolve the chloride of lime in cold water and when settled, pour off the clear liquid and add to the cold soda solution. Bottle, cork and label, and store in a dark place. Exposure to light will weaken the solution. Use as a bleach for linens, cottons, enamelware and porcelain. This solution will rot fabrics if left for too long and requires thorough rinsing.

Soap Jelly for Babies' Woollens

250g mild soap, shredded
60g borax
5 cups water

Boil all together until the soap dissolves. Cool until it forms a jelly. Add to warm water when washing woollens or flannel.

SOAP-MAKING

Soap is made from fat and caustic with the possible addition of a softening agent, such as borax. All old household dripping should be saved for a time and excellent laundry soap can be the result of a little rather interesting work. Caustic soda must be carefully handled and not allowed to touch the bare skin. The fat must be clarified before being used; this is done by boiling it in water and then cooling. The clean fat is then lifted off and is ready to be made into soap.

Household Soap

Method I
4kg dripping
750g caustic soda
750g resin
250g borax
250g soap flakes
12l water

Boil together for 1 hour the dripping, caustic soda and resin. Just before it goes off the boil add the borax and soap flakes. Leave until the following day.

Method II
500g caustic soda
2l water
1 cup soap powder
3.5kg clarified fat

Dissolve the soda in water. Add the soap powder and stir well. Melt the fat and when both mixtures are just warm, add the caustic to the fat. Stir vigorously for 2 minutes, or until the consistency of thick honey. Pour into wet, calico-lined boxes and leave to set for 12 hours. Cut into bars.

Toilet Soap

2kg clarified fat
375g caustic soda
4l water
5cm wax candle

2 cups coconut oil
1 tablespoon glycerine
1 tablespoon citronella

Boil together for 30 minutes, or until soap is stringy, the fat, soda, water and candle wax. When nearly ready add the oil, glycerine and citronella. Pour into a washtub and leave to set.

Soft Soap

1 large bar soap, cut up
500g borax

Put the soap in a large pot half filled with water. Add the borax, stir well and put over heat until all is dissolved. Remove from the heat and leave to cool.

Cleanser

1 tablet coarse sandsoap, crushed finely
2 packets soap powder
3 cups boiling water

Mix to a paste the sandsoap and soap powder with boiling water. Use for removing grease etc. from hands.

TO REMOVE STAINS

Blood and Meat Juice

Soak in cold water, then wash with warm soap and water. Never put into hot water until after cold soaking. A paste of raw starch and water applied to bloodstains on flannel, heavy woollens and blankets will help to remove them; repeat 2 or 3 times if necessary.

Blue

Boil; use vinegar if a bleach is needed.

Cream, Fat and Clear Oils

Sponge first with cold water, then wash with hot water and soap. Sponge unwashable materials with carbon-tetrachloride or petrol. Sponge from the outside to the centre of the stain.

Cocoa

Sponge with warm solution of borax 15g to 1¼ cups and rinse; or, treat as cream stain.

Coffee and Tea

As for cocoa, or hold stain over a basin and pour boiling water over the stain.

Creosote

Rub with a cloth soaked in benzol.

Egg

Sponge first with cold water, then wash in hot soap suds. Treat as a cream stain.

Fruit Juice

Treat with boiling water as for tea or coffee. Peach stains are more stubborn. If boiling water does not remove them, bleach with javelle water or oxalic acid.

Grass

Rub with methylated spirits.

Iodine

Soak area in diluted ammonia.

Iron Rust

Use salt, lemon juice and sunlight.

Ink

Rub with lemon and soak in milk. Rinse in cold water, then wash.

Indelible and Ball-Point Ink

Use methylated spirits. Test fabric first by applying a little on a seam.

Nail Varnish

Use acetone or the remover, then methylated spirits. Test fabric, as it cannot be used on synthetics.

Mildew

Scrape off any deposit, then bleach with hydrogen peroxide. Use a very weak solution on coloured materials.

Paint and Varnish

Sponge with white spirit, turpentine or carbon-tetrachloride. Then wash with soap and water.

Scorch

Rub with dry borax and wash with soap and water. If the scorch is severe nothing can be done.

Tar and Black Grease

Scrape off any surplus, then sponge with oil of eucalyptus. Once all the grease is removed the stain will come out with soap and water.

Perspiration

Use warm water, soap and ammonia. If possible, dry in the sun.

USE AND CARE OF KITCHENWARE

Aluminium

Light, durable, easily cleaned, rustproof and a good heat conductor. Ideal for saucepans, kettles, pressure cookers, etc. Wash, preferably while hot, in hot soap and water, burnish with the occasional use of a fine steel wool and avoid contact with washing soda and alkaline substances which will stain it. Unaffected by acids.

Cast Iron

Durable, retains heat, but will rust and discolour acid foods. Used for frying-pans and some heavy kettles. Wash in hot soapy water and scour with powders and pot mitts. Dry well and oil slightly to prevent rusting. Sometimes cast iron is covered with an enamelled preparation and rusting is avoided. This is cleaned and scoured the same way.

Glassware

Wash with hot soap or detergent; have a teatowel in the sink to avoid casualties. Rinse with clear warm water, drain, and dry while hot. Polish with clean teatowel. Use a soft brush for cut crystal. A touch of blue in the rinse will make it sparkle.

Oven Glass

Used for casserole dishes, etc. Clean as for ordinary glass, using a fine steel wool if necessary. N.B. Glass will stand heat, even boiling temperature, if brought to the boil slowly, but sudden changes of heat and cold will crack it.

Kettles

If lined with fur due to the use of hard water, remove the fur by boiling potatoes in the kettle.

Chromium

Wash in soap and water, dry and polish with methylated spirits. Used extensively for fittings, teapots, coffee percolators. Durability will depend on its thickness and the material over which it is applied.

Enamelware

Not used extensively now as it chips. Used for mixing bowls, jugs and saucepans. Is not very durable but some brands are better than others. Wash with soap and water and clean with fine scouring powders only. Avoid quick changes of temperature as it may crack.

Plastic

Widely used as it is attractive, light and inexpensive. Will not stand high temperatures but can be scalded. Ideal for mixing bowls, measuring cups, picnic ware, refrigerator containers and many small kitchen appliances. Wash with warm soap and water, rinse and dry.

GLOSSARY

Aspic: savoury meat jelly.

Baste: to spoon a liquid over a cooking food, done at intervals during cooking.

Braise: method of meat cookery. Brown in hot fat, then add water and gently simmer.

Broil: to grill.

Broth: soup made of stock, meat, chopped vegetables and thickened with a grain such as barley or rice.

Bouillon: a clear soup.

Bouquet Garni: bunch of herbs tied with muslin, used to flavour soup or stew (bay leaf, thyme, sage, parsley)

Choux Pastry: that used in cream puffs.

Coleslaw: raw cabbage salad.

Compote: fruit prepared and served without any additional substances. Usually served whole.

Cornstarch: cornflour.

Crackers: water biscuits.

Devilled: cooked and highly seasoned, usually with onions and gravy or sauce.

Fillet: without bone.

Flan: an open tart with a jellied fruit filling.

Fondant: creamy filling used in chocolates.

Fricassee: food prepared in white sauce.

Galantine: a cooked pressed meat loaf of veal or poultry served cold.

Giblets: the internal edible parts of poultry.

Glace: glossy sugared surface as in icing or fruit.

Marinate: to steep and soak in a brine or oil.

Mocha: a combination of coffee and chocolate.

Mornay: using cheese.

Mousse: a rich frozen sweet using eggs and cream.

Panade: a paste of flour plus water or fat.

Parkin: a moist spicy loaf.

Pectin: a substance in apples or green fruit which causes jams and jellies to set.

Prove: to set aside yeast breads to rise to the desired size.

Purée: material which has been sieved.

Quickbreads: those made with baking powder or soda.

Ragout: rich highly-seasoned stew.

Roux: melted fat and flour used for thickening sauces, etc.

Raspings: dried breadcrumbs.

Saute: to fry in shallow fat.

Sear: to cook meat at high heat to seal outside.

Shortening: fats (butter, lard, dripping, etc.).

Souffle: a fluffy baked egg dish, sweet or savoury.

Soubise: using onions, e.g. soubise sauce.

Tuber: thickened underground stem of a plant, e.g. potato or kumara.

Vol-au-Vent: a rich pastry case with a lid; may be filled with a sweet or savoury preparation.

METRIC CONVERSION COOKERY GUIDE

The tables below enable conversion between the imperial and the metric standard cooking measures of the Standards Association of Australia. The old standard 8 fl oz cup was replaced by the standard metric cup with a capacity of 250 ml. The Standard tablespoon and teaspoon remain unchanged at 20 and 5 millilitres respectively. Recipes in this book have been tested using New Zealand standard metric measuring spoons and cups. All cup and spoon measurements are level. The standard N.Z. tablespoon measures 15 millilitres, therefore Australian readers must substitute 3 teaspoons. Metric equivalents of imperial weights and measures have been rounded off to the closest convenient figure. Although the yield is slightly greater (10%) the proportions remain the same.

For successful cooking use EITHER metric weights and measures OR imperial weights and measures – DON'T USE A MIXTURE OF THE TWO.

LIQUID AND DRY MEASURES (volume)

Taking 1 imperial cup as equivalent to 1 metric cup this table provides a guide to convert volume measure in recipes.

IMPERIAL		METRIC	
LIQUID (fl oz) = IMPERIAL CUP		METRIC CUP = LIQUID	
1 oz			30 ml
2 oz	¼ cup	¼ cup	
	⅓ cup	⅓ cup	
3 oz			100 ml
4 oz	½ cup	½ cup	
5 oz (¼ pint)			150 ml
	⅔ cup	⅔ cup	
6 oz	¾ cup	¾ cup	
8 oz	1 cup	1 cup	
10 oz (½ pint)	1¼ cups	1¼ cups	
12 oz	1½ cups	1½ cups	
15 oz (¾ pint)			475 ml
16 oz	2 cups	2 cups	
20 oz (1 pint)	2½ cups	2½ cups	

ABBREVIATIONS

Kilogram	centimetre
Kg	cm
gram	millimetre
g	mm
millilitre	degree Celsius
ml	°C

Everyday Equivalents

Butter

1 cup	250 g
2 cups	500 g
1 tablespoon	15 g
1 dessertspoon	10 g

Sugar

1 cup	250 g
2 cups	500 g
1 tablespoon	15 g
1 dessertspoon	10 g

Flour

2 cups (sifted)	250 g
4 cups (sifted)	500 g
2 tablespoons	15 g
2 dessertspoons	10 g

WEIGHTS

When metric scales are not available, use these approximate conversions, as recommended by Metric Advisory Boards.

IMPERIAL TO METRIC – AUSTRALIA

Ounces	Grams	Ounces	Grams
½ oz	15 g	11 oz	345 g
1 oz	30 g	12 oz (¾ lb)	375 g
2 oz	60 g	13 oz	410 g
3 oz	90 g	14 oz	440 g
4 oz (¼ lb)	125 g	15 oz	470 g
5 oz	155 g	16 oz (1 lb)	500 g (0.5 kg)
6 oz	185 g	24 oz (1½ lb)	750 g
7 oz	220 g	32 oz (2 lb)	1000 g (1 kg)
8 oz (½ lb)	250 g	(3 lb)	1500 g (1.5 kg)
9 oz	280 g	4 lb	2000 g (2 kg)
10 oz	315 g		

NEW ZEALAND

Ounces	Grams	Ounces	Grams
1 oz	25 g	11 oz	325 g
2 oz	50 g	12 oz	350 g
3 oz	75 g	13 oz	375 g
3.5 oz	100 g	14 oz	400 g
4 oz	125 g	15 oz	425 g
5 oz	150 g	16 oz	450 g
6 oz	175 g	1 lb 2 oz	500 g
7 oz	200 g	2 lb 4 oz	1000 g (1 kg)
8 oz	225 g		
9 oz	250 g		
10 oz	275 g		
10.5 oz	300 g		

OVEN TEMPERATURE GUIDE

THERMOSTAT SETTING

DESCRIPTION OF OVEN	ELECTRIC °F	°C	GAS °F	°C
Cool	200	110	200	100
Very Slow	250	120	250	120
Slow	300	150	300	150
Moderately slow	350	180	325	160
Moderate	400	200	350	180
Moderately hot	425	220	375	190
Hot	450	230	400	200
Very hot	475	250	450	230

25 cm	10 in
23 cm	9 in
20 cm	8 in
18 cm	7 in
15 cm	6 in
13 cm	5 in
10 cm	4 in
8 cm	3 in
6 cm	2½ in
5 cm	2 in
4 cm 40 mm	1½ in
2.5 cm 25 mm	1 in
2.0 cm 20 mm	¾ in
1.2 cm 12 mm	½ in
6 mm	¼ in
3mm	⅛ in

INDEX